P9-AQJ-058

And You Welcomed Me

And You Welcomed Me

Migration and Catholic Social Teaching

Edited by
Donald Kerwin
and
Jill Marie Gerschutz

LEXINGTON BOOKS
A division of
ROWMAN & LITTLEFIELD PUBLISHERS, INC.
Lanham • Boulder • New York • Toronto • Plymouth, UK

Published by Lexington Books
A division of Rowman & Littlefield Publishers, Inc.
A wholly owned subsidiary of The Rowman & Littlefield Publishing Group, Inc.
4501 Forbes Boulevard, Suite 200, Lanham, Maryland 20706
http://www.lexingtonbooks.com

Estover Road, Plymouth PL6 7PY, United Kingdom

Copyright © 2009 by Lexington Books

All rights reserved. No part of this book may be reproduced in any form or by any
electronic or mechanical means, including information storage and retrieval systems,
without written permission from the publisher, except by a reviewer who may quote
passages in a review.

British Library Cataloguing in Publication Information Available

Library of Congress Cataloging-in-Publication Data

And you welcomed me : migration and Catholic social teaching / edited by
Donald Kerwin and Jill Marie Gerschutz.
     p. cm.
  Includes index.
  ISBN 978-0-7391-4099-4 (cloth : alk. paper) — ISBN 978-0-7391-4100-7
(pbk. : alk. paper) — ISBN 978-0-7391-4101-4 (electronic)
  1. Emigration and immigration—Religious aspects—Catholic Church. 2. Christian
sociology—Catholic Church. 3. Catholic Church—Doctrines. I. Kerwin, Donald,
1961– II. Gerschutz, Jill Marie, 1980–
  BX1795.E44A53 2009
  282.086'912—dc22   2009024853

∞™ The paper used in this publication meets the minimum requirements of American
National Standard for Information Sciences—Permanence of Paper for Printed Library
Materials, ANSI/NISO Z39.48-1992.

Printed in the United States of America

Contents

Acknowledgments

This book is a product of the Theology of Migration Project at Woodstock Theological Center in Washington, D.C. Many thanks to the Rev. Gasper F. Lo Biondo, S.J., executive director of the Woodstock Theological Center, for his steadfast support for this project, for sponsoring two gatherings of Catholic leaders on migration issues which helped shape the book, and for recognizing the need to educate Catholics on what their faith tradition teaches about migrants and newcomers.

Many thanks as well to the book's authors who include some of the very finest academics, service providers, and activists in the migration field. We also wish to thank the members of Woodstock's Theology of Migration Project advisory board who guided this project. They are Kim Bobo, executive director, Inter-faith Committee for Worker Justice; Joseph Chamie, executive director, Center for Migration Studies, and former director, United Nations' Population Division; Mary DeLorey, strategic issues advisor, Global Relations Department, Catholic Relief Services; Most Rev. Nicholas DiMarzio, Diocese of Brooklyn; Mark Franken, former executive director, United States Conference of Catholic Bishops (USCCB), Migration and Refugee Services; Jill Marie Gerschutz, migration policy director, Jesuit Conference USA; Rev. Daniel Groody, C.S.C., director of Latino Ecclesial and Pastoral Concerns, Institute for Latino Studies, Notre Dame University; Timothy Kelly, social and international ministries, Maryland Province, Society of Jesus; Donald Kerwin, vice president for programs, Migration Policy Institute; Rev. John Langan, S.J., Joseph Cardinal Bernardin professor of Catholic social thought at the Kennedy Institute of Ethics, Georgetown University; Rev. Gasper F. Lo Biondo, S.J., Cecile Motus, director, USCCB Secretariat of Cultural Diversity in the Church, assistant director of Asian Pacific Affairs; Rev. William Rickle,

S.J., director, Institute on Migration, Culture, and Ministry, Loyola College of Maryland; Rev. Richard Ryscavage, S.J., director, Center for Faith and Public Life, Fairfield University; Most Rev. Jaime Soto, Diocese of Sacramento; Mirna Torres, director of the Center for Citizenship and Immigrant Communities, Catholic Legal Immigration Network, Inc.

We also wish to acknowledge the important input and contributions provided by J. Kevin Appleby, director of policy, Migration and Refugee Services; Elzbieta Gozdziak, director of research, Institute for the Study of International Migration, Georgetown University; and the Rev. David Hollenbach, S.J., the Margaret O'Brien Flatley Chair in Catholic Theology at Boston College.

Special thanks to the Catholic Legal Immigration Network, Inc., the Jesuit Conference USA, and Migration Policy Institute for supporting the co-editors throughout the course of this project; to Rev. Richard Ryscavage, S.J. and the Center for Faith and Public Life at Fairfield University for co-hosting (with Woodstock) one of the two migration gatherings that led to the book; and to Fernando Garcia, director of the Border Network of Human Rights in El Paso, for contributing migrant narratives. We also wish to thank Sheryl Modlin for her editorial support and Marley Moynahan for her energy and support. Finally, we are grateful to the staff at Rowman & Littlefield for shepherding us through the publication process.

Above all, we would like to acknowledge the courageous and selfless migrants who have inspired this book, and the people whose faith has inspired them to devote their lives to welcoming the stranger and to gathering into one God's scattered children.

Introduction

Gasper Lo Biondo and Richard Ryscavage

Human beings leave their homelands for many reasons and they are called by many names: illegal aliens, strangers, asylum-seekers, displaced persons, economic migrants, lawful permanent residents, refugees, temporary workers. Some are forced to flee because of violence, persecution, or natural disasters. Many others choose to emigrate in search of work and a better life. The movement of people from one place to another has remained a constant feature of human history. Of course, immigration has strongly shaped U.S. economic, political, and cultural development. Because immigration plays so central a role in our national story, one might expect U.S. citizens, even if they have lost touch with their own immigrant roots, to share a basic empathy for newcomers. For over 200 years, however, Americans have been arguing about immigration. Periodic cycles of vigorous, sometimes violent, anti-immigration movements have swept through the nation. Religion has always played a significant part in these debates. Because so many U.S. immigrants have been Catholic, the Catholic Church has often found itself at the center of public policy discussions. Today as we complete the first decade of the twenty-first century, the number of foreign-born residents has again reached record levels and once again the Church is involved in a national debate over immigration law and policy.

This book emerged from a multidisciplinary reflection on migration carried out over several years by the Woodstock Theological Center located at Georgetown University in Washington, D.C. Donald Kerwin, former executive director of the Catholic Legal Immigration Network, Inc. (CLINIC) and current vice president for Programs at the Migration Policy Institute, and Gasper LoBiondo, S.J., executive director of the Woodstock Theological Center, coordinated the project. It represents the fruit of a collaboration by

Catholic theologians, lawyers, social scientists, and a variety of experts in the field of migration. Given the coarse tenor of the national immigration debate, the contributors felt the need to engage U.S. Catholics in a deeper, more sophisticated discussion of migration and faith. The book does not seek to "bring religion" into the study of migration but to demonstrate how Catholicism as a faith, with one of the world's richest intellectual and spiritual traditions, can frame the issues of migration in a vibrant and challenging way. Hence it is an instance of "faith seeking understanding," of theological reflection from the perspective of practical commitment to the global common good.

The common good—an old concept with deep roots in Catholic social thinking—suggests that we need to provide the social conditions that allow for the participation and full development of human beings (including newcomers) in our society. The global common good, in turn, argues for improved social conditions in migrant countries of origin. The question of how to serve the common good in our community, nation, and at the international level drives all the contributions to this book.

Immigration is an immensely complex issue. Catholics often disagree on specific legislation and courses of action. This book affords an introduction to the many dimensions of immigration by persons with expertise in these areas. More importantly, the book tries to weave and integrate into the many legal and social science perspectives the distinctive Catholic way of looking at migration, with special consideration for the lived experience of immigrants themselves and their host communities. Faith seeking understanding must join secular disciplines in order to grasp the issues more accurately and from the perspective of safeguarding human dignity. Faith must also seek understanding by entering into the concrete reality of the human family where, since the beginning of time, migration has played such an enormous role.

While law, labor economics, and sociology are important lenses for viewing immigration, the Catholic Church views immigration primarily through the much richer prism of a global history, spirituality, theology, Catholic social teaching, and its concrete pastoral experience with migrants. While recognized by the Church, the standard categories for classifying migrants—such as economic migrants, unauthorized (undocumented) workers, asylum seekers, and refugees—are not the primary way that the Church approaches the immigrant. She does not ask first whether a person is legal or illegal but rather looks at the migrant as a human person in a human family.

Perhaps the main reason why the Church's political reflection on migration seems exceptional lies in its spiritual origin. The faith that guides our view of migration has deep biblical roots beginning with God's call to Abraham, our father in faith, to abandon his homeland and migrate. Migration was central to the Jewish experience of God. Christianity built on this tradition through its notion of "mission," incorporating the idea of encountering God in the outward movement of the Church into the world and facing the paradox of bringing Christ to the stranger while recognizing that Christ *is* the stranger (Mt. 25:35). Migration became part of the Christian identity. Even at the level of individual spirituality, St. Augustine, among many other Christian teachers, emphasized how we should view ourselves as resident aliens in this life, "pilgrims" on a journey home to the City of God.

Above all, the Christian point of view is anchored in Christ's statement in Matthew 25: "if you welcome the stranger, you welcome me." A Christian is expected to see Christ in the stranger. The foundation principle of Catholic social thought involves respecting the dignity of the human person; every human being has God-given worth.

OUTLINE OF CHAPTERS

Ultimately the human phenomenon of migration can help to clarify our understanding of God. How a Christian thinks about God shapes her perspective on migration, and migration shapes the spirituality of those who experience it. Chapter 1 by Father Daniel Groody, C.S.C. focuses on the theological foundations of migration and its implications for Christian life.

The Church has always stressed the importance of labor but today labor needs to be understood in a much more globalized frame. In chapter 2, Mary DeLorey, strategic issues advisor of Catholic Relief Services, places migration in a global context by considering how free trade agreements impact migration. She reviews academic theories on why people migrate, illustrating the complexity of the decision and the agency of the migrant. Finally, she highlights the vulnerabilities of migrants as governments fail to protect them.

The Catholic Church—as a global entity—views migration from a transnational perspective. Most of the people entering the United States without authorization identify themselves as Catholics. Allowing for cultural differences, the Church in the United States is organically part of the Church in Mexico. The Church sees the problems of migration from both sides of the border. The Church's transnational identity as a faith community demands that its pastoral care of people transcend borders. In chapter 3, John J. Hoeffner and Michele R. Pistone, professors of law at Villanova University, discuss business, labor, and economic migration in the evolving context of globalization and development and apply John Paul II's concept of "authentic development." Moreover, they call for a reevaluation of the Church's thinking on "brain drain" policies in light of modern technology.

In chapter 4, Donald Kerwin surveys how Catholic social thinking informs the issue of immigrants' human rights and the responsibilities of a sovereign state. He explains how the Catholic social vision has as its centerpiece the human person and service to the common good. Distinct from secular human rights advocates, the Church considers human rights to be inherent in the nature of the human being. The sovereign responsibility of a government to control its borders must be understood in the context of the human rights of the migrant and a core purpose of sovereign states, which is to safeguard rights, asserts Kerwin.

The Church understands that of all the needs of the human spirit, the need for roots is exceptionally important. The concept of home is never as truly appreciated as when one leaves home and feels the uprootedness of not being in a place of one's own. Migrating is never a casual decision. Emigration can represent a family's longing for happier life in a better place where its members can develop their full potential as human beings. But it is a longing that can turn a family's life upside down. Something is always lost in the process of migration; sometimes even faith in God is lost. But it is also not unusual for a person to discover God in the process of migration. The act of uprooting tends to concentrate the mind on the true priorities in life, including our dependence on God. Because migration is such a difficult experience, the Church places great emphasis on welcoming the stranger, social integration, and helping the immigrant lay down a new set of roots. In chapter 5, Jill Marie Gerschutz, migration policy director of the Jesuit Conference, with Lois Ann Lorentzen, professor of social ethics of the University of San Francisco, explores the challenges facing the Church when it tries to help immigrants adjust to a new land. They also compare the Church's vision for integration to secular descriptions.

The God of Jesus Christ is a God who loves all creation and is personally present to the world in myriad ways. This way of envisioning God challenges people of faith to discern where and how the divine presence is at work and to take responsibility for freely cooperating with God. It is this spirituality that has inspired the work reflected in the pages of this book and that informs our way of "reading the signs of the times." The book ends with a reflection by Rev. William O'Neill, S.J., professor of social ethics of the Jesuit School of Theology at Berkeley, on Christian hospitality and solidarity with strangers, sojourners, and other neighbors in need.

A note on vocabulary is necessary. The term "migrant" is used in this text to refer to individuals in the act of moving from one country to another, but also more broadly to cover those who have arrived in their new homes. "Emigrants" describes individuals who have left their countries of origin, while "immigrants" refers to the newcomers in a country who intend to live there either temporarily or permanently. In secular language, migrants or immigrants differ from "refugees" who enjoy the protection of international law. Some migrants may apply for refugee status. A refugee is defined by the 1951 Convention relating to the Status of Refugees as a person who:

> owing to well-founded fear of being persecuted for reasons of race, religion, nationality, membership of a particular social group or political opinion, is outside the country of his nationality and is unable, or owing to such fear, is unwilling to avail himself of the protection of that country; or who, not having a nationality and being outside the country of his former habitual residence as a result of such events, is unable or, owing to such fear, is unwilling to return to it.[1]

Asylum-seekers are those who seek protection under the same legal standard within the United States. Much of the modern migration debate surrounds migrants who are out of status; that is, individuals living in a country without or with outdated or false documents. While such migrants are often referred to as "illegal aliens," the Church rejects this dehumanizing language, teaching that human beings cannot be illegal. Such migrants are referred to often as "undocumented," "unauthorized," or "irregular," which, although nuanced terms, are used interchangeably in this book. Given their precarious situation, undocumented immigrants receive special concern and attention by the Church.

THEMES AND USE OF THE BOOK

The question of migration raises fundamental human issues. Against the vast canvas of the Church's reflections on the social order, Catholics can differ on what constitutes the best public policy and law. But the book shows that the foundations of human dignity and the common good can offer Catholics and others a guiding, integrated vision that runs through the many intricate legal, sociological, economic, ethical, and theological dimensions of the immigrant reality.

Taken together, these chapters provide a foundation and framework not only for seeing and detecting important data, but also for judging and acting according to the values of our faith tradition. They remind us that migration, which formed both the Catholic Church and the United States, often enables people to become the people they were created to be. By highlighting the agency of migrants, the book highlights the value of freedom. In emphasizing the true meaning of the rule of law, it argues that protection of all peoples promotes the common good and human rights. In asserting that authentic development means more than economic development, it reminds us of the human beings at the heart of this phenomenon. In acknowledging the cultural diversity of today's newcomers, it recalls the melting pot of U.S. history and calls for a response to migrants and newcomers that is consistent with the biblical virtue of hospitality. Each of these themes pervades the book, calling Catholics to a higher ideal of their faith and their heritage. The various disciplines constantly invite introspection regarding who we are as Catholics and good citizens.

Seeing Christ in the stranger and supporting the dignity of the human person must begin at the interpersonal level. To respect the dignity of each person, whether she or he is a migrant or a host citizen, offers another opportunity to live out the virtue of hospitality. Catholics and others who take the time to see the migrant experience through the eyes of faith and community can transform the rough, polarizing national debate into an intelligent and specific discourse about what God wants for the human family and how best to foster the common good.

NOTE

1. Office of the High Commissioner for Human Rights, *United Nations Convention relating to the Status of Refugees* (1951), article 1(2), http://www.unhchr.ch/html/menu3/b/o_c_ref.htm.

Chapter One

Crossing the Divide: Foundations of a Theology of Migration and Refugees

Daniel G. Groody

Migration has been part of human history since its origins.[1] But today, due to widespread changes precipitated by globalization, more people are migrating than ever before—twice as many now as twenty-five years ago.[2] Nearly 200 million people, or one out of every thirty-five people around the world, are living away from their homelands. This is roughly the equivalent of the population of Brazil, the fifth-largest country on the planet.[3] Many of these migrants are forcibly uprooted: approximately 30 to 40 million are undocumented, 24 million are internally displaced, and almost 10 million are refugees.[4]

These flows of people precipitate conflict and controversy; they affect not only migrants but receiving communities as well, making migration an increasingly volatile and contentious political issue.[5] The clash of cultures, identities, and religions, along with debates over economics, resources, and rights, has polarized public discourse, making the migration debate convoluted and confused. Not only does rhetoric about immigration conflate, if not manipulate, multiple issues like national security and human insecurity, sovereign rights and human rights, civil law and natural law, but the disciplines governing the debate have not given us the concepts necessary to move beyond unfruitful, polemical discourse and reach the core issues.

Categories such as legality and illegality, the documented and the undocumented, and citizen and alien, not only fail to come to terms with a new global reality, but they also leave gaping areas of injustice in their wake. Some argue that tougher enforcement will resolve the problem of migration and refugees (as evidenced by the United States, Israel, "fortress Europe," and other parts of the world), but this massive movement of peoples, regardless of the policies of nation-states, will continue, transforming the contours of communities around the globe. Affecting all areas of human life, migration is arguably one of the most complex issues in the world, and it will become more significant in the future.[6] Because migration is one of its defining issues, the twenty-first century has been referred to by some scholars as "the age of migration."[7]

CROSSING OVER: BRIDGING THE MIGRATION-THEOLOGY DIVIDE

Migration issues are so complex and far-reaching that understanding them demands a broad range of interdisciplinary research.[8] Economics, politics, geography, demography, sociology, psychology, law, history, anthropology, and environmental studies are foremost among the disciplines that shape the emerging field of migration studies and migration theory. Theology, however, is almost never mentioned in major works or at centers of migration studies. Some research has been done on migration and religion from a sociological perspective, but there is virtually nothing on the topic from a theological perspective.[9] Theology seems to enter the academic territory from the outside, as if it were a "disciplinary refugee" with no official recognition in the overall discourse about migration.[10]

Even among theologians the topic of migration is largely undocumented.[11] The Vatican and various episcopal conferences have notable writings about the pastoral care of immigrants,[12] but currently little has been written about migration as a theological reality. The current climate points to the need to move the migration debate to an even broader intellectual terrain, one in which theology not only has something to learn but something to offer. My aim in this chapter is to reflect critically on the mystery of God in an age of migration, which is a way of thinking about the gospel message in light of the signs of the times.[13]

Since Vatican II, theology has been recast in various ways in response to the challenges of the modern world, such as those presented by liberation movements, feminism, religious pluralism, postmodernity, cultural diversity, and esthetics. The longstanding but now accelerating reality of global migration presents another opportunity to ground theological analysis in a specific social location that emerges from "the joys and hopes, the griefs and anxieties" of many marginal people today.[14] Our understanding of God and of migration can mutually shape and enrich each other and help bridge theology and migration studies, tradition, and one of the most vexing social issues of the modern world. I hope not only to highlight the moral demands related to displaced peoples but also to explore new ways in which we might examine the theological territory of migration and even challenge some of the underlying philosophical, if not ideological, presuppositions behind the debate about migrants and refugees.

This study focuses on four foundations of such a theology as indicated by the following subtitles: (1) *Imago Dei*: Crossing the Problem-Person Divide; (2) *Verbum Dei*: Crossing the Divine-Human Divide; (3) *Missio Dei*: Crossing the Human-Human Divide; and (4) *Visio Dei*: Crossing the Country-Kingdom Divide. Each offers a way of thinking about theology and migration as a call to cross borders and overcome barriers. Migration is not only a social reality with profound implications but also a way of thinking about God and what it means to be human in the world, which can become an important impetus in the ministry of reconciliation and a compelling force in understanding and responding to migrants and refugees.

IMAGO DEI: CROSSING THE PROBLEM-PERSON DIVIDE

One of the initial challenges in the immigration debate deals with language. A great divide exists between the problem of migration and migrating people, between those who are labeled and their labelers, between the political and social identities of migrants and refugees and their human and spiritual identities.

Scholars have recently attended to the categorization of the forcibly displaced.[15] Terms like *refugee, migrant, forced migrant, immigrant, undocumented, internally displaced person*, and *alien* are some of the most common.[16] The literature on this subject is coming to terms with the inherent limitations of such terminology. The problem is that these labels are largely political, legal, and social constructions. As Roger Zetter notes, "Far from clarifying an identity, the label conveys, instead, an extremely complex set of values, and judgments which are more than just definitional."[17] Although labeling may be an inescapable part of policy-making and its language, the difficulty arises when migrants, immigrants, refugees, and asylum seekers are identified principally and primarily in terms of their political status rather than their human identity. The implications involve more than semantics.

Labels often generate asymmetrical relationships, leaving migrants and refugees vulnerable to control, manipulation, and exploitation. Identifying immigrants in terms of political descriptors can unintentionally create new forms of psychological colonization. Referring to the problem of cultural labels, Virgilio Elizondo notes:

> The most injurious crime of the conquest of Latin America, and there were many horrible things about it, was that the white European conquistadores imposed a

deep sense of shame of being an indio, mestizo, mulatto. . . . Many today still experience shame regarding their skin color, their way of life, their way of being, their way of dress, their way of speaking, and their ways of worship. Such rejection brands the soul, in a way worse and more permanent than a branding of the master's mark with a hot iron on the face.[18]

Part of the task of a theology of migration is to bridge the gap created by these labels, challenge the dehumanizing stereotypes created by these labels, and build up (in the words of Paul VI and John Paul II) "a civilization of love" and "a culture of life."[19] The task entails helping those on the move discover an inner identity that fosters their own agency rather than an imposed external identity that increases their vulnerability and subjugation.

As valuable as social science contributions have been in understanding migration, its own disciplinary limitations prevent its making an explicit theological affirmation about migrants and refugees. Theology takes the discourse to a deeper level. "The Judeo-Christian tradition," as the U.S. Catholic bishops have noted, "is steeped in images of migration," from the migration of Adam and Eve out of the garden of Eden (Gen 3:23–24), to the vision of the New Jerusalem in the final pages of the New Testament (Rev 21:1–4).[20]

In the book of Genesis we are introduced to a central truth that human beings are created in the image and likeness of God (Gen 1:26–27; 5:1–3; 9:6; 1 Cor 11:7; Jas 3:9). This is not just another label but a way of speaking profoundly about human nature. Defining all human beings in terms of *imago Dei* provides a very different starting point for the discourse on migration and creates a very different trajectory for the discussion. *Imago Dei* names the personal and relational nature of human existence and the mystery that human life cannot be understood apart from the mystery of God.[21] Lisa Sowle Cahill notes that the image of God is "the primary Christian category or symbol of interpretation of personal value."[22] "[This] symbol," Mary Catherine Hilkert adds, "grounds further claims to human rights" and "gives rise to justice."[23] One reason why it is better to speak in terms of irregular migration rather than "illegal aliens" is that the word *alien* is dehumanizing and obfuscates the *imago Dei* in those who are forcibly uprooted.

On the surface it may seem basic to ground a theology of migration on *imago Dei*, but the term is often ignored in public discourse. Defining the migrant and refugee first and foremost in terms of *imago Dei* roots such persons in the world very differently than if they are principally defined as social and political problems or as illegal aliens; the theological terms include a set of moral demands as well. Without adequate consideration of the humanity of the migrant, it is impossible to construct just policies ordered to the common good and to the benefit of society's weakest members. The fact that in our current global economy it is easier for a coffee bean to cross borders than those who cultivate it raises serious questions about how our economy is structured and ordered.

In its efforts to safeguard the dignity of all people, Catholic social teaching has consistently argued that the moral health of an economy is measured not in terms of financial metrics like the gross national product or stock prices but in terms of how the economy affects the quality of life in the community as a whole.[24] Catholic social teaching states that an ordered economy must be shaped by three questions: What does the economy do *for* people? What does it do *to* people? and, How do people participate in it?[25] It puts strongest emphasis on what impact the economy has on the poor. It stresses that the economy is made for human beings, not human beings for the economy. In the immigration debate this means that the primary costs have to do first with human costs; Catholic social teaching asks to what extent the economy of a country enhances the dignity of every human being, especially of those who are vulnerable and deemed insignificant.

As noted in *Gaudium et spes (Joy and Hope)*, *imago Dei* also means that people, by implication, ought to have available "everything necessary for leading a life truly human, such as food, clothing, and shelter; the right to choose a state of life freely and to found a family, the right to education, to employment, to a good reputation, to respect, to appropriate information, to activity in accord with the upright norm of one's own conscience, to protection of privacy and rightful freedom, even in matters religious."[26] Preferably, people can meet such needs in their homeland, but when these conditions are not met, as John XXIII noted, people have a right to emigrate in order to "more fittingly provide a future" for themselves and their family.[27]

For many forced migrants, moving across borders is connected to finding a job. Writing against the backdrop of the exploitation of migrant workers and much global unemployment, John Paul II in *Laborem exercens (On Human Work)* addressed the connection between human dignity, social justice, and work.[28] He notes that "the person working away from his native land, whether as a permanent emigrant or a seasonal worker, should not be placed at a disadvantage in comparison with the other workers in that society in the matter of working rights. Emigration in search of work should in no way become an opportunity for financial or social exploitation."[29]

Catholic social teaching recognizes the right, and even the responsibility, of a state to control its borders, but it also argues that, when a state cannot provide the conditions necessary for human dignity, people have a right to migrate to foreign lands, even without proper legal documentation.[30] The bishops of the United States have added that "any limitation on international migration must be undertaken only after careful consideration of the demands of international solidarity. These considerations include development, trade and investment programs, education and training, and even distribution policies designed to narrow the wide gaps between the rich and the poor."[31]

The notion of *imago Dei* and human dignity is rooted in Christian theology, but its implications are universal in scope, with corollaries in other religious, philosophical, and humanitarian traditions. Human dignity, rooted in theological premises, also has close affinities with human rights language, particularly as it is expressed in the 1948 Universal Declaration of Human Rights,[32] and the 1951 United Nations Convention relating to the Status of Refugees,[33] which remains the charter document for refugee rights and protections. Human dignity and human rights language underscore the inherent value and worth of every person, regardless of their political, economic, social, or geographical status.

Imago Dei is integrally related to the Trinity, which means it is not primarily an individualistic notion but a relational one. Most migrants leave their homes to realize a greater dignity not only for themselves but also for their families. Statistics on global remittances offer one indicator of the connection between migration and relationships. In 2006, migrants sent home to their families, often in small amounts of $100 to $300 at a time, more than $300 billion. Meanwhile, the total Overseas Development Aid from donor nations to poorer countries was $106 billion. This means that migrants living on meager means spent three times as much money helping alleviate global poverty as the wealthiest countries of the world.[34] Contrary to popular perceptions, such statistics further elucidate the *imago Dei* in the poor, especially in its generative and sacrificial dimensions.

Imago Dei is a two-edged sword that positively functions as an affirmation of the value and worth of every person and evaluates and challenges any tendencies to dominate or oppress the poor and needy, or degrade them through various manifestations of racism, nativism, and xenophobia.[35] The expulsion from Eden of Adam and Eve, the original *imagines Dei*, and their border-crossing into the land beyond, names the human propensity to move toward a state of sin and disorder (Gen 3:1–13). Sin disfigures the *imago Dei*, resulting in a fallen world that creates discord in relationships. The territory into which the Prodigal Son migrates and squanders all his worldly wealth (Lk 15:11–32) symbolizes this barren terrain; it is a place that moves people away from the original creative design into a place of estrangement from God, others, and themselves.[36]

VERBUM DEI: CROSSING THE DIVINE-HUMAN DIVIDE

The notion of *imago Dei* put forth in the Old Testament is realized in the New Testament through the *imago Christi*. Christ is the perfect embodiment of *imago Dei* and the one who helps people migrate back to God by restoring in them what was lost by sin.[37] In ways that resonate with Thomas Aquinas's notion of *exit et reditus*,[38] Karl Barth writes about the incarnation in terms of "the way of the Son of God into the far country."[39] He does not explicitly use the term "migration," but his reflections are a way of speaking of God's crossing over into the dark territory of a sinful, broken humanity. What distinguishes the Christian God from other, false gods, Barth notes, is that they are not ready for this downward mobility, "this act of extravagance, this far journey."[40] Through the *Verbum Dei*, Jesus' *kenosis* and death on the cross, God overcomes the barriers caused by sin, redraws the borders created by people who have withdrawn from God, and enters into the most remote and abandoned places of the human condition.

No aspect of a theology of migration is more fundamental, nor more challenging in its implications, than the incarnation. Through Jesus, God enters into the broken and sinful territory of the human condition in order to help men and women, lost in their earthly sojourn, find their way back home to God. As noted in the gospel of John, migration shapes Jesus' own self-understanding: "Having loved his own who were in the world, he loved them to the end. . . . Jesus knew that the Father had given everything into his hands, that he had come from God, and that he was going back to God" (Jn 13:1, 3). The *Verbum Dei* from this perspective is the great migration of human history: God's movement in love to humanity makes possible humanity's movement to God. Hans urs von Balthasar adds, "If the Prodigal Son had not already believed in his father's love, he would never have set out on his homeward journey."[41]

The sojourn of the *Verbum Dei* into this world is riddled with political and religious controversies, many of which are connected to narratives about migration. In Luke's Gospel, Jesus enters the world amidst a drama involving documentation (Lk 2:1–5). In Matthew's account, Jesus and his family must flee a threat that endangers their lives, making them political refugees (Mt 2:13–17, a parallel to a foundational migration in biblical history, Exodus 1). In John's Gospel, many have trouble believing in Jesus precisely because of the place from which he emigrates (Jn 7:41–43, 52). In a fallen world, human beings find many compelling political, legal, social, and religious reasons to exclude—and reject—the migrant Son of God.[42]

In migrating to the human race God enters into a place of "otherness," the very migration that human beings fear and find so difficult to make. This movement of divinity to humanity is predicated not on laws, institutions, or any form of human merit but, above all, on God's gratuity. In crossing borders of every kind for the good of others, the *Verbum Dei* reveals the mystery of God's *a priori*, self-giving love. As Barth observes:

The incarnation of the Word . . . His way into the far country, His existence in the *forma servi*, is something which we can understand . . . by supposing that in

it we have . . . a *novum mysterium* . . . with what is noetically and logically an
absolute paradox, with what is ontically the fact of a cleft or rift or gulf in God
Himself, between His being and essence in Himself and His activity and work
as the reconciler of the world created by Him.[43]

The *Verbum Dei* means that for God there are no borders that cannot be
crossed, neither within himself nor in the created world. According to Barth,
"the mystery reveals to us that for God it is just as natural to be lowly as it is
to be high, to be near as it is to be far, to be little as it is to be great, to be abroad
as it is to be at home."[44] The *Verbum Dei* manifests that, even as human beings
erect barriers of every sort, God walls off no one from the divine embrace.

Another paradoxical dimension of the mystery of the incarnation is that,
while human migration tends toward an upward mobility and the greater re-
alization of human dignity, divine migration tends toward a downward mobility that is even willing to undergo the worst human indignities (Phil
2:5–11). Scripture depicts the movement of a people toward a promised land,
but God's movement is just the opposite: it is an immersion into those territories of human life that are deprived of life and prosperity. God migrates into
a world that is poor and divided, not because God finds something good about
poverty and estrangement, but because it is precisely in history's darkest
place that the God can reveal hope to all who experience pain, rejection, and
alienation.

Christ reaches out to all those considered, in Barth's terms, "alien life."[45]
Christ moves not away from alienation, difference, and otherness but toward
it, without ceasing to be who he is: "He went into a strange land, but even
there, and especially there, He never became a stranger to Himself."[46] God's
identification with humanity is so total that in Christ he not only reaches out
to the stranger but becomes the stranger: "He does not merely go into lowli-
ness, into the far country, to be Himself there, as He did in His turning to Israel. But now He Himself becomes lowly. He Himself is the man who is His
Son. He Himself has become a stranger in Him."[47] In the journey into otherness and vulnerability, the *Verbum Dei* enters into total identification with
those who are abandoned and alienated.

The downward way of the *Verbum Dei* leads ultimately to the cross.[48] The
kenosis of Jesus is God's radical risk of movement into the broken territory
of human life, with potentially cataclysmic consequences if it fails. For many
compelling reasons, numerous migrants and refugees reframe their own story
in the light of Jesus' journey. Leaving their homelands, undergoing dangerous
journeys, and taking up residence in a foreign land entails not only emptying
themselves but radically surrendering everything they own, without any assurance that what they lose will come back to them.[49] The cross is the ultimate expression of God's self-giving love, God's solidarity with those who

suffer, and God's power at work amid human struggle and weakness. The notion of the crucified God and the crucified peoples is a topic that requires indepth consideration beyond the scope of this chapter, but this notion is a central dimension of a theology of migration and has tremendous implications for those who are forcibly displaced, especially for addressing the inner wounds that migrants and refugees experience.[50]

Although the incarnation saves, Barth notes that it also "offends." It offends precisely because it brings into question the disordered values of a society that has lost its sense of *imago Dei*. It challenges especially those who exclude on the basis of superficial notions of private property, legal status, and personal or even national rights without any social, moral, or divine reference point, or any regard for the exigencies of distributive, contributive, and restorative justice that flow as a natural consequence from divine gratuity. The incarnation moves people beyond a narrow, self-serving identity into a greater identification with those considered "other" in society, particularly those like migrants and refugees who are poor and regarded as insignificant.

Reflecting on the implications of the parable of the Good Samaritan for human relationships, Augustine writes, "our Lord and God himself wished to be called our neighbor because it is himself that the Lord Jesus Christ is indicating as the one who came to the help of that man lying half dead on the road, beaten up and left there by robbers" (Lk 10:25–37).[51] Following Christ in a way shaped by the gift of self to others becomes a way of speaking about participation in the self-giving love of God. In becoming neighbor to all in the incarnation, that is all who live in the sinful territory of a fallen humanity, God redefines the borders between neighbors and opens up the possibility for new relationships.

The incarnation, as a border-crossing event, is a model of gratuitous self-giving through which God empties himself of everything but love, so that he can more fully identify with others, enter completely into their vulnerable condition, and accompany them in a profound act of divine-human solidarity. This gratuitous nature of the incarnation offers a different framework for evaluating human migration and questions some of the underlying premises of the debate. In crossing the borders that divide human beings from God, the *Verbum Dei* is a profound gift that makes profound demands on those who receive it.[52] Migration becomes a descriptive metaphor for the movement of God toward others in the human response of discipleship.

MISSIO DEI: CROSSING THE HUMAN-HUMAN DIVIDE

The *missio Dei* is to restore the *imago Dei* in every person through the redemptive work of the *Verbum Dei*. The universal message of the gospel is directed to all nations and all peoples, and it is concerned with all aspects of human beings and the full development of every person.[53] The church, through the power of the Spirit, takes up the Great Commission of Jesus by migrating to all nations, proclaiming the Good News of salvation and working against the forces of sin that disfigure the *imago Dei* (Mt 28:16–20). In addition to the foundational ministries of Peter and Paul, tradition holds that such missionary endeavors led James to migrate to Spain, Phillip to Asia, and Thomas to India. "While it transcends all limits of time and confines of race," notes *Lumen gentium (Light of the Nations)*, "the Church is destined to extend to all regions of the earth."[54]

A central dimension of this mission is Jesus' ministry of reconciliation, which deals largely with overcoming human constructions that divide the insider from the outsider, particularly those constructions generated by law in its various forms.[55] The *missio Dei* challenges human tendencies to idolize the state, religion, or a particular ideology and use it as a force that excludes and alienates, even when it does so under the guise of obedience to a greater cause. Jesus' openness to Gentiles, his reaching out to the Syrophoenician or Canaanite woman (Mt 15:21–28; Mk 7:24–30), his response to the Roman centurion (Mt 8:5–13; Lk 7:1–10), and many other encounters illustrate Jesus' willingness to go beyond borders and narrow interpretations of the law in obedience to a greater law of love (Mk 12:28–34).

Jesus' fellowship with sinners (Mt 9:9–13), his concern for those outside the law (Mt 8:1–4), and his praise of the righteous Good Samaritan (Lk 10:25–37) raise important questions about law, its purposes, misuses, and abuses. Jesus recognized the value of the law (Mt 5:17–18), but he also challenged people to see the larger picture of the law and understand its deeper meaning (Lk 13:10–17). In the Gospels there are three parallel accounts of Jesus' disciples picking heads of grain on the Sabbath to assuage their hunger and of Jesus healing a man with a shriveled hand on the Sabbath. When challenged by the religious leaders and crowds about breaking Sabbath laws, Jesus responds that the Sabbath is made for man, not man for the Sabbath, and that the "higher law" is that it is lawful—even required—to do good on the Sabbath and, by extension, on every other day as well (Mt 12:1–14; Mk 2:23–3:6; Lk 6:1–22). By his words and actions, Jesus demonstrates that compassion requires a reading of the law that gives primary consideration to meeting human needs.

No area is more divisive in the immigration debate than the issue of immigration law and public policy.[56] In public discourse, people commonly say they have no problem with immigration, but they do have a problem with people breaking the law. The problem with this perspective is that it makes no distinction between various kinds of law and assumes equal binding force for all law. In Thomistic terms, there is divine law, eternal law, natural law, and civil law.[57] This confusion, resulting in a failure to differentiate, becomes particularly problematic when some, invoking supposedly Pauline theology (Rom 13:1–7), unquestioningly and mistakenly equate the current civil law and public policy with a divinely ordained mandate. The ordinances and regulations related to sovereign rights and civil law must be seen alongside the needs, duties, and responsibilities proper to human rights and natural law.[58] Even if the notion of natural law is a hotly contested topic in theological studies, and even if our understanding of divine and eternal law is incomplete, at the very least, law here must first be understood in light of the protection of human dignity. Catholic social teaching uses this line of reasoning in arguing that people have a right to migrate when their country of origin lacks the necessary means to provide them with the capacity and opportunity to provide for themselves.[59]

The structures of a society must be seriously examined under the entirety of legal reasoning when thousands of immigrants and refugees die each year trying to cross areas like the deserts of the American Southwest or the waters dividing North Africa from Europe. Here many different kinds of law are at work: laws of nations that control borders; laws of human nature that lead people to seek opportunities for more dignified lives; natural law that deals with ethical dimensions of responding to those in need; and divine law that expresses the Creator's will for all people. The fact that so many migrants are dying in their efforts to meet basic human needs raises serious questions about current civil laws and policies and their dissonance with other forms of law. Quoting Aquinas from a Birmingham jail, Martin Luther King Jr. put it this way: "An unjust law is a human law that is not rooted in eternal law and natural law";[60] it is violence against the *imago Dei.*

When people cross borders without proper documentation, most are not simply breaking civil laws but obeying the laws of human nature, such as the need to find work so as to feed their families and attain more dignified lives. Moreover, crossing international borders without papers in most countries is an administrative infraction, not a felony; it is not a violation of divine law or natural law, and in such cases undocumented immigration should in no way be confused with serious criminal activity or threats to national security.[61] Much misunderstanding and injustice occur when immigrants and immigration are perceived primarily as problems in themselves rather than as symptoms of deeper social ills and imbalances, as matters of national security rather than as responses to human insecurity, as social threats rather than as foreign neighbors.

Conventional wisdom that guided much of policy-making throughout history implied that dealing with the problem of undocumented immigrants will keep a country safer. Recent history shows, however, that such a rationale is untenable: the terrorist bombing of the Murrah Federal Building in Oklahoma City was perpetrated by American citizens, not by outsiders, and although the 9/11 attacks were done by people born outside the United States, all 19 terrorists came into the country on legal visas. Rhetorically mixing criminals and terrorists with undocumented immigrants seeking work only inflames and distorts the debate and makes the vulnerable easy targets for a country's unrest and anxiety.

The United Nations' Convention and Protocol relating to the Status of Refugees helps foster some legal protection for refugees, but the situation is bleaker for economic migrants.[62] Neither international law nor particular nation states recognize the category of economic migrants as one that merits legal protection. Amidst contemporary polemics around the legal status of forced migrants, theology and philosophy help expand the intellectual terrain by providing a broader understanding of law.[63] A detailed treatment is not possible here, but the relationship between civil law, natural law, divine law, and eternal law in the ethics of the immigration debate is an area that needs more attention and where theology can be of great value. Theology not only breaks open and judges as inadequate a binary analysis of migration that limits it to categories such as legal/illegal, citizen/alien, and right/wrong; but also theology provides a clearer lens through which to read the complexity of reality and a more adequate framework for responding to the most vulnerable members of society and for building a civilization of love.

Jesus was particularly concerned with the law as it took shape in religious form. His practice of table fellowship gives us a very important window into his understanding of the law in light of the kingdom of God. Luke Bretherton observes that "table fellowship with sinners, and the reconfiguring of Israel's purity boundaries . . . signifies the heart of Jesus' mission."[64] Through table fellowship Jesus fulfills the message of the prophets, invites all people to salvation, and promises his disciples a place "at table" in God's kingdom (Lk 22:30). In sharing a meal with those on the fringes of society in order to create new communities, Jesus frequently crossed borders created by narrow interpretations of the law. He reached out in particular to those who were marginalized racially (Lk 7:1–10), economically (Lk 7:11–17), religiously (Lk 7:24–35), and morally (Lk 7:36–50). His invitation to the table was good news for the poor and others deemed insignificant or rejected by society; others it confused or even scandalized.

Jesus' table fellowship with sinners, in Norman Perrin's words, "must have been most meaningful to his followers and most offensive to his critics."[65] His rejection of social and religious categories of inclusion/exclusion is probably what prompted his critics to want to dispense with him because it affronted their religious vision. As Robert Karris put it, "Jesus got himself crucified by the way he ate."[66] In bringing scribe, tax collector, fisherman, and zealot into one community, Jesus challenged his followers to a new kind of relationship beyond humanly constructed borders, one based not on social status, the rules of a nation, or religious self-righteousness, but on a common hope for the coming of God's reign (Mt 8:11; 11:16–19). For Jesus, God's mercy could not be contained within the walls of limited mindsets (Mt 7:1–5; 13:10–17), and he challenged people to realize a higher law based on God's uncalculating mercy rather than on their restricted notions of worthiness and unworthiness (Lk 6:27–38).

Jesus' practice of table fellowship situates him against the backdrop of covenant theology, which is integrally related to the notion of migration. The promises given to Abraham and Moses both emerge from migration stories, the former from the land of Ur of the Chaldeans to Canaan and the latter from Egypt through Sinai to the Promised Land. Covenant, like migration, was not originally a biblical concept but a sociopolitical one. A covenant (*berit*) was a binding agreement between two parties, which resulted in a new relationship. The covenant helped overcome dividing forces and fostered justice and peace in the community. In describing its relationship with Yahweh, Israel used this sociopolitical concept of covenant as a metaphor that expresses God's unconditional love and the human responsibility to respond to it.

Old Testament scholars have identified two different types of covenant. The first stems from Yahweh's covenant with Abraham (Gen 15:1–18; 17:1–14) with parallels in David (2 Sam 7:1–17); the second flows from the Mosaic covenant (Exod 19–24). The Abrahamic covenant, paralleling royal grant treaties in the ancient Near East, is an unbreakable agreement founded on the gratuity of a greater party to a lesser party. The Mosaic covenant, paralleling the Hittite-Suzerainty treaty, is a conditional agreement founded on a mutual agreement of reciprocal fidelities that can be broken through disobedience. The first covenant stresses God's commitment to Israel; the second emphasizes Israel's responsibility to God.[67] As Raymond Brown notes, "While the covenants of divine commitment gave Israel confidence, the covenants of human responsibility gave Israel a conscience."[68] Through the covenant, God offers Israel a combination of gifts and tasks, promises and responsibilities. The stipulation of the mosaic covenant, later reiterated in Deuteronomy, is that Israel must imitate God's fidelity by reaching out to the most vulnerable of society, most notably the widow, orphan, and immigrant (Exod 22:21–22; 23:9).

The covenant is taken to a new level in the life, death, and resurrection of Jesus. On the cross Jesus accomplishes the *missio Dei* by crossing the border that divides human beings from God and each other, initiating a new creation characterized by right relationships. Paul puts it this way: "For he is our peace, he who made both one and broke down the dividing wall of enmity, through his flesh" (Eph 2:14–15). Although Paul is referring to the hostility between Jews and Gentiles, the implications of his words are more universal in scope. Christ breaks down the wall that separates people and reconciles the world to himself through his death on the cross.

The *missio Dei*, in which the church participates, is not just about helping the poor but about following Christ and discovering that those whom one is called to serve also have something to give. Cathy Ross argues that the heart of the church's mission is about making room and creating space, particularly for "allowing people the space to come to God in their own way."[69] This notion of creating space is foundational to a theology of migration because it sees the *missio Dei* not first as an imposing evangelization but as a ministry of generous hospitality, one that is mutually enriching for those who give and those who receive.

Jesus' obedience to a higher law of love, his practice of table fellowship, his promise of a new covenant, and his breaking down the wall of enmity through his death on the cross are ways in which God opens up a path to freedom in a world of barriers, restrictions, and division. It is this message that, led by the Spirit, compelled Paul, Peter, and the other apostles to witness to Christ and migrate "throughout Judea and Samaria, and to the ends of the earth" (Acts 1:8).

VISIO DEI: CROSSING THE COUNTRY-KINGDOM DIVIDE

The *imago Dei*, *Verbum Dei*, and *missio Dei* are all based on the *visio Dei*. The notion of *visio Dei* is based in large part on the Matthean beatitude, "Blessed are the pure of heart for they shall see God" (Mt 5:8). This blessedness has been debated throughout history, but two classic distinctions emerge in the tradition, namely, what is possible in this life (*in via*) and that of perfect happiness in heaven (*in patria*).[70] Put another way, Christian discipleship, while situated within the citizenship of the *patria* of this world, ultimately is grounded in citizenship of, and movement toward, the *patria* of the next. In addition to pledging allegiance to a particular country, the *visio Dei* brings out that one's ultimate obedience is to God alone, which leads one beyond any national and political boundaries to ultimate fidelity to the kingdom of God. Meister Eckhart adds that the goal of Christian life is not so much to seek the *visio Dei* in heaven as to see things in this life as God sees them.[71] Our focus here is how this vision takes root in human history, how it influences social transformation, and how it transfigures the way we understand migrants and refugees.[72]

A theology of migration seeks to articulate a renewed vision of God and human life as it is lived out between the eschatological horizon of faith and unbelief and a historical horizon of justice and injustice. Augustine believed that love and vision go together in the pursuit of justice.[73] Because Christian orthodoxy and orthopraxis emerge out of an understanding of God and God alone, the *visio Dei* shapes people's ethical dispositions and offers a new way of perceiving the *imago Dei* in those whose dignity is often disfigured by dehumanizing stereotypes and demeaning public rhetoric. In its care for all, especially those most in need, the church not only goes beyond borders but unites itself with those on the other side of them, giving expression to its interconnectedness as the body of Christ. In imitation of its founder, the church serves all people regardless of their religious beliefs, their political status, or their national origins.

The *visio Dei* comes into focus in the person of Jesus Christ and the kingdom he proclaimed. The kingdom of truth and life, holiness and grace, justice, love, and peace brings people into a different kind of social and ethical territory.[74] It is based not on geography or politics but on divine initiative and openness of heart, leading to a different kind of vision of the current world order, where many of the first are last and the last first (Mt 19:30; 20:16; Mk 10:31; Lk 13:29–30). Jesus clearly taught that many of the values and metrics people employ to measure others will be inverted and that the excluded will be given priority in the kingdom. The kingdom calls people into movement, making the church exiles on earth, strangers in this world, and sojourners en route to another place.[75]

The word most frequently used for sojourner in the New Testament is *paroikos*, from which is derived the English word "parish" (Eph 2:19; 1 Pt 2:11). In Philippians 3:20 Paul describes Christians as living in this world but carrying the passport of another world: "But our citizenship is in heaven, and from it we also await a Savior, the Lord Jesus Christ." The author of Hebrews speaks of the journey in hope toward a different place: "here we have no lasting city, but we seek the one that is to come" (Heb 13:14). In the midst of recounting the stories of the major figures of biblical history, the author writes of their faith and hope:

> All these people were still living by faith when they died. They did not receive the things promised; they only saw them and welcomed them from a distance. And they admitted that they were aliens and strangers on earth. People who say such things show that they are looking for a country of their own. If they had been thinking of the country they had left, they would have had opportunity to return. Instead, they were longing for a better country—a heavenly one. Therefore God is not ashamed to be called their God, for he has prepared a city for them. (Heb 11:13–16).

John Henry Newman adds, "Those too who are setting out for a foreign land beg that the Martyrs may be their fellow-travelers and guides of the journey."[76]

Because of the human tendency to make God into our own disordered image and likeness, however, *visio Dei* demands conversion, individually and collectively (*ecclesia semper reformanda*). Exodus 20:2 states, "I, the Lord, am your God, who brought you out of the land of Egypt, that place of slavery." The word Egypt (*mitsrayim*) literally means "double straits," (a reference to upper and lower straits that form the territory of Egypt through which the Nile flows), "narrow places," or "narrow confinement."[77] Beyond the literal reading of the word *mitsrayim*, the subsequent figurative interpretations are striking.

In its story of migration, Israel was delivered not only from a specific national territory but also from a narrow way of thinking. Liberation at Sinai means more than simply taking off the shackles. It involves a cognitive migration, taking on a new mindset, adopting a new way of looking at the world, living out a different vision, and ultimately learning to love as God loves. The migration of Israel after the Exodus was meant to help Israel reenvision how to live in the world, a task that proved more challenging than the geographical migration: it was easier to take Israel out of the *mitsrayim* than to take the *mitsrayim* out of Israel. After coming to power and becoming more prosperous, Israel frequently forgot its history and subsequently those who came to them as strangers and immigrants.

The New Testament also addresses the *visio Dei* by giving the disciples a new imagination about strangers. As Terry Coonan notes,

> there is . . . a discernable shift in the moral paradigm of the New Testament: whereas in the Old Testament, the Jewish people were called to welcome the stranger because they themselves had once been strangers, in the New Testament, the Christian obligation to do so derives from the conviction that, in the face of the stranger, the Christian community encounters the face of Jesus.[78]

Looking into the face of Jesus includes an inescapable dimension of judgment. From the perspective of a theology of migration, no text is more central than Matthew 25:31–46.[79] While scholars continue to debate who are the "least" (*elachistōn*) in this passage, what is significant for my discussion here is that this text describes the social location of many migrants and refugees: hungry in their homelands, thirsty in deserts they attempt to cross, naked after being robbed of their possessions, imprisoned in detention centers, sick in hospitals, and, if they make it to their destination, they are often estranged and marginalized. This text implies that crossing borders makes possible new relationships, and it puts the verdict of judgment, to a great extent, in people's own hands: the extent to which people cross borders in this life determines to what extent they will cross them in the next (Lk 16:19–31). Robert McAfee Brown adds that this text speaks of the judgment of not only individuals but also nations.[80]

The *visio Dei* also challenges people to move beyond an identity based on a narrow sense of national, racial, or psychological territoriality. It holds out instead the possibility of defining life on much more expansive spiritual terrain consistent with the kingdom of God. Corresponding with the positive dimensions of globalization that foster interconnection, it challenges any form of ideological, political, religious, or social provincialism that blinds people from seeing the interrelated nature of reality. The *visio Dei* involves not only passively gazing on God's essence in the next world (*Visio Beatifica*) but also in creating *communio* in this world. Salvation means restoring sight to people who have lost a sense of the *imago Dei*, offering them a new imagination through the work of the *Verbum Dei*, and inviting them to live and move in the world in a different way through the *missio Dei*.

This vision takes shape each November when people gather along the Mexican-American border to celebrate a common liturgy. As with other liturgies, a large crowd gathers to pray and worship together. However, with this liturgy a 16-foot iron fence divides this community, one side in Mexico, the other in the United States. Border Patrol agents in helicopters and trucks keep a strict eye on the crowd to ensure that no one passes over from Mexico to the United States, but those gathered praise God for Christ's "Passover" from death to life. In a global reality that often sets up walls and barriers, this Eucharist bears witness to the primacy of God's universal, undivided, and unrestricted love in the context of political constructions that divide people. It also reminds people that the walls dividing us from God and from one another have already begun to crumble and that this new age of reconciliation has already begun, even as Christians wait for its ultimate fulfillment when Jesus comes again.

CONCLUSION

My primary purpose is not to make a case for or against open borders but to give a new way of conceptualizing a difficult and contentious global issue. This chapter seeks to broaden the intellectual terrain about migration and forge the beginnings of some theological foundations for such a perspective. Viewed as a theological concept, migration offers a rich hermeneutic for some of the most foundational dimensions of human existence and offers a different vantage point for making moral choices; it illuminates the gift and demand of Christian faith in light of the pressing social problems of the modern world, and it opens up a space to bring out what is most human in a debate that often diminishes and dehumanizes those forcibly displaced.

Although some argue that combining theology and migration mixes politics with religion, and others that migration falls more to the domain of social science than theological reflection, migration touches so many aspects of life and society that it cannot be hermetically compartmentalized. Academic reflection requires its own transborder discourse to understand the complex phenomenon of global migration and its multidimensional implications. A theology of migration not only dialogues with other disciplines but integrates their findings into the overall task of faith seeking understanding in the modern world. Moreover, social science and theology need each other in this difficult debate. Social science without theology does not give us a perspective wide enough to account for the deeper relational and spiritual dimensions of human life that shape, define, and sustain human existence—a fact that becomes more evident especially amidst crisis and trial. Theology without social science leaves us less equipped to read the signs of the times, engage contemporary issues, or speak to the pressing questions that affect large portions of the world.

The *imago Dei*, *Verbum Dei*, *missio Dei*, and *visio Dei* are four foundations of a larger theology of migration. Rereading themes such as exodus, exile, diaspora, and the *via crucis* in light of the contemporary experience of migrants and refugees can contribute much to our understanding of God, human life, and the relationship between the two. This work has begun to explore some elements of migration in light of traditional theological themes such as creation, incarnation, mission, and the salvific vision of the kingdom of God. Migrants and refugees bring to the forefront of theological reflection the cry of the poor, and they challenge more sedentary forms of church in social locations of affluence and influence. The migrant reveals the paradoxical truth that the poor are not just passive recipients of charitable giving but bearers of the gospel that cannot be encountered except by moving into places of risk and vulnerability (Mt 25:31–46).

Three focal points in particular begin to bring out some of the implications and ramifications of migration as a theological concept. First, a theology of migration is a way of speaking about the meaning of human life within the economy of creation and redemption.[81] To be human means being on the way to God (*in statu viatoris*), moving forward in hope between the borders of Christ's first and second coming, between the present life and the life to come, between the earthly Jerusalem and the new Jerusalem. "The virtue of hope is the first appropriate virtue of the *status viatoris*," notes Josef Pieper;

"it is the genuine virtue of the 'not yet.'"[82] The migrant gives expression to the transitory nature of existence and to the courage needed to move forward amid the risks, tensions, vulnerabilities, sufferings, and disappointments of life. The closer people move toward union with God and communion with others, the more such union will manifest itself in breaking down walls that divide, exclude, and alienate. The further people move away from integration with the Divine, the more that movement will manifest itself in a fear that creates walls and barriers on every level of human existence.

Second, a theology of migration is a way of speaking about the significance of the incarnation in light of the issues of contemporary society and the injustices of the current global economy. The incarnation has much to say about a God who crosses borders in order to forge new relationships, and the challenge to all human beings to do the same. Even if borders of nation states have some proximate value in constructing identity, protecting values, securing rights, and administering resources, from a Christian perspective, sovereign rights are subject to a larger vision of human rights, the common good, the kingdom of God, and the gratuity of God. A theology of migration underscores that in the final analysis the human and relational costs far outweigh the economic ones. Although many of the specific ethical implications and political ramifications of a theology of migration are beyond the scope of this work, it fosters a systematic framework that safeguards not only "negative" civil-political liberties central to human rights discourse (such as the right not to be tortured or killed), but it also advocates for "positive" economic, social, and cultural rights (such as the right to work, to shelter, to family unity, and even to migrate) that are at the heart of Catholic social teaching and promote correlative duties that flow from human dignity.

Third, a theology of migration is a way of speaking about the mission of the church within the context of a disordered political economy. It seeks to foster human dignity in the poor and vulnerable, to challenge any structures and systems of society that divide and dehumanize, and to uplift all efforts to build a more just and humane world. Reducing people to their legal or political status not only denies dignity to those in need but also dehumanizes those who have the opportunity to help. Aga Khan, a former United Nations High Commissioner for Refugees from 1966–1978, once observed: "The awkward truth about human deprivation is that it demeans those who permit or ignore it more than it does those who are deprived."[83] The question, then, is not whether to allow or restrict migration but whether our moral choices are creating divides that move us toward a globalization of polarity rather than toward a globalization of solidarity. In David Hollenbach's words, "The needs of the poor take priority over the wants of the rich. The freedom of the dominated takes priority over the liberty of the powerful. The participation of marginalized groups takes priority over the preservation of an order which excludes them."[84] Ignoring those in pain and building of walls of separation alienates people not only from each other but also from themselves.

A theology of migration seeks to understand what it means to take on the mind and heart of Christ in light of the plight of today's migrants and refugees. To limit compassion to the borders of one's nationality, one's family, or even one's self is a migration toward disintegration. For those on a trajectory toward disintegration, a theology of migration cannot make sense, since it will always be news from a foreign land. "If I see a person or persons suffer," notes Elie Wiesel, "and the distance between us does not shrink . . . then, my place is not good, not enviable."[85] If the term "alien" is to be used at all, it would be descriptive not of those who lack political documentation but of those who have so disconnected themselves from God and others that they are incapable of seeing in the vulnerable stranger a mirror of themselves, a reflection of Christ, and an invitation to human solidarity.

NOTES

1. This chapter first appeared as an article in *Theological Studies* 70 (September 2009), and I am grateful to the journal for permission to republish it here.

2. Khalid Koser, *International Migration: A Very Short Introduction* (New York: Oxford University, 2007), 5.

3. Some of the most important sources on migration statistics come from the World Bank (http://www.worldbank.org), the International Organization of Migration (IOM, http://www.iom.int/jahia/jsp/index.jsp), the International Labor Organization (ILO, http://www.ilo.org/global/lang—en/index.htm), the United Nations High Commissioner for Refugees (UNHCR, http://www.unhcr.org), the United Nations Department of Economic and Social Affairs (UNDESA; see especially "Trends in Total Migration Stock: The 2005 Revision," http://www.un.org/esa/population/publications/migration/ UN_Migrant_Stock_Documentation_2005.pdf), and the Global Commission for International Migration (GCIM, http://www.gcim.org/en/). See in particular *Migration in an Interconnected World: Report of the Global Commission for International Migration* (Geneva: Global Commission on International Migration), 83–85, http://www .gcim.org/attachements/gcim-complete-report-2005.pdf.

4. For more on these statistics, see http://www.iom.int/jahia/Jahia/pid/254.

5. While often perceived as a problem in itself, forced migration is more often a symptom of deeper issues related to human crises ranging from poverty, persecution, and underdevelopment, to widespread sociopolitical and economic changes such as nation-building and industrial expansion, and to global events like wars and natural disasters. According to the 2005 report of the GCIM, the factors that precipitate migration include: (1) Wage disparities: 45.7 percent of people in Sub-Saharan Africa, 14.4 percent in South Asia, and 10.4 percent in Latin America and the Caribbean earn

less than $1 per day; (2) Unemployment rates: 12.2 percent in the Middle East and North Africa, 10.9 percent in Sub-Saharan Africa, and 6.6 percent in industrialized economies; (3) Differentials in life expectancy: 58 years in low income countries, and 78 years in high income countries; (4) Education gaps: 58 percent women and 68 percent men literate in low income countries, almost full literacy in high income countries; 76 percent primary school enrolment in low income countries, almost full enrolment in high income countries; (5) Demographic gradients: on average 5.4 children born to each woman in Sub-Saharan Africa, compared with 3.8 in the Arab World, 2.5 in Latin America and the Caribbean, and 1.4 in Europe. See *Migration in an Interconnected World: New Directions for Action*, 84, http://www.gcim.org/attachements/gcim-complete-report-2005.pdf.

6. Former UN Secretary General Kofi Annan summarizes the problematic nature of this age of migration in terms of the "issues of human rights and economic opportunity, of labour shortages and unemployment, of brain drain and brain gain, of multiculturalism and integration, of refugee flows and asylum-seekers, of law enforcement and human trafficking, of human security and national security." UNDESA, *World Economic and Social Survey 2004: International Migration* (New York: UN Department of Economic and Social Information and Policy Analysis, 2004), iii.

7. Stephen Castles and Mark J. Miller, *The Age Of Migration: International Population Movements in the Modern World* (London: Guilford, 2003).

8. For a valuable introduction to global migration and refugees, see Philip Marfleet, *Refugees in a Global Era* (New York: Palgrave Macmillan, 2006).

9. Two of the most notable studies on migration and religion are Helen Rose Ebaugh and Janet Saltzman Chafetz, eds., *Religion across Borders: Transnational Immigrant Networks* (Lanham, Md.: Altamira, 2002) and Yvonne Yazbeck Haddad, Jane I. Smith, and John L. Esposito, *Religion and Immigration: Christian, Jewish, and Muslim Experiences in the United States* (Lanham, Md.: Altamira, 2003).

10. For more on the interdisciplinary nature of migration studies and migration theory, see C. B. Brettell and J. F. Hollifield, eds., *Migration Theory: Talking across Disciplines* (New York: Routledge, 2000) and Peter C. Meilaender, *Toward a Theory of Immigration* (New York: Palgrave, 2001).

11. Some of the few studies on migration and theology include Daniel G. Groody and Gioacchino Campese, eds., *A Promised Land, A Perilous Journey: Theological Perspectives on Migration* (Notre Dame, Ind.: University of Notre Dame, 2008); Gioacchino Campese and Pietro Ciallella, *Migration, Religious Experience, and Globalization* (New York: Center for Migration Studies, 2003); William R. O'Neill and William C. Spohn, "Rights of Passage: The Ethics of Immigration and Refugee Policy," *Theological Studies* 59 (1998), 84–106; and Drew Christiansen, "Movement, Asylum, Borders: Christian Perspectives," *International Migration Review* 30 (1996), 7–17.

12. See in particular Pius XII, Apostolic Constitution, *Exsul familia nazarethana (The Émigré Holy Family of Nazareth)* (1952), http://www.papalencyclicals.net/Pius12/p12exsul.htm; Pontifical Council for the Pastoral Care of Migrants and Itinerant People, *Erga Migrantes Caritas Christi (The Love of Christ toward Migrants)* (2004); and Pontifical Council "Cor Unum" and Pontifical Council for the Pastoral Care of

Migrants and Itinerant People, *Refugees: A Challenge to Solidarity* (1992); the joint statement of the United States Conference of Catholic Bishops (USCCB) and the Conferencia del Episcopado Mexicano, *Strangers No Longer: Together on the Journey of Hope* (2003), http://www.usccb.org/mrs/stranger.htm.

13. Pope Paul VI, *Gaudium et spes (Joys and Sorrows)* 4 (1965), http://www.vatican.va/archive/hist_councils/ii_vatican_council/documents/vat-ii_cons_19651207_gaudium-et-spes_en.html. David Tracy notes that "the central theological problem of our day is not the problem of the nonbeliever but the problem of those thought to be nonpersons by the reigning elite" (Tracy, "The Christian Option for the Poor," in *The Option for the Poor in Christian Theology*, ed. Daniel G. Groody [Notre Dame, Ind.: University of Notre Dame, 2007], 119).

14. *GS*, 1.

15. Roger Zetter, "More Labels, Fewer Refugees: Remaking the Refugee Label in an Era of Globalization," *Journal of Refugee Studies* 20 (2007), 172–92.

16. The terms migrant, immigrant, refugee, and internally displaced persons are often used interchangeably, although they carry different nuances. The United Nations uses "migrant" generally to refer to people living outside their homeland for a year or more regardless of their reason or legal status and often includes international business people or diplomats who are on the move but not economically disadvantaged. The IOM's *World Migration Report 2005* defines "undocumented" or "irregular migrants" as "workers or members of their families not authorized to enter, to stay or to engage in employment in a state," http://www.iom.int/jahia/Jahia/cache/offonce/pid/1674?entryId=932. The 1951 United Nations Convention relating to the Status of Refugees defines a "refugee" as one who, "owing to well-founded fear of persecution for reasons of race, religion, nationality, membership of a particular social group or political opinions, is outside the country of his nationality and is unable or, owing to such fear, is unwilling to avail himself of the protection of that country," http://untreaty.un.org/cod/avl/ha/prsr/prsr.html. The United Nations High Commissioner for Refugees (UNHCR), in the document Guiding Principles on Internal Displacement, defines "internally displaced persons" as those "who have been forced or obliged to flee or to leave their homes or places of habitual residence, in particular as a result of or in order to avoid the effects of armed conflict, situations of generalized violence, violations of human rights or natural or human-made disasters, and who have not crossed an internationally recognized State border," http://www.unhchr.ch/html/menu2/7/b/principles.htm. Although these classifications help determine the legal protections available to migrants, many scholars today agree that at some point these categorizations blur. Some people may flee their homelands because of political persecution and fall under the category of forced migrants or refugees, for example, but their motivations may also stem from economic considerations and therefore the same people can be economic migrants as well. Most migrants are motivated by "push" factors that drive them away from their homelands and "pull" factors that draw them to better lives in another place. For my purposes "migration" can be an apt descriptor for the Christian journey, and the term "refugees" highlights some of the most vulnerable people of the migrant population. Among the many reports on migration and refugees, see the appendix of *The World Migration Report 2005*.

17. Roger Zetter, "Labeling Refugees: The Forming and Transforming of a Bureaucratic Identity," *Journal of Refugee Studies* 4 (1991), 39–62, at 40.

18. Virgilio Elizondo, "Culture, the Option for the Poor, and Liberation," in *Option for the Poor in Christian Theology*, ed. Daniel G. Groody (Notre Dame, Ind.: University of Notre Dame, 2007), 164.

19. Paul VI was the first pope to use the expression "a civilization of love": "It is the civilization of love and of peace which Pentecost has inaugurated—and we are all aware how much today the world still needs love and peace!" (Paul VI, Regina Coeli Address, May 17, 1970), http://www.civilizationoflove.net/19700517_Summary.htm. John Paul II also speaks of a civilization or communion of love in several of his encyclicals (*Novo millennio ineunte,* 42; *Redemptor hominis,* 10; *Ecclesia in Europa,* 82–85), as well as "a culture of life" (*Evangelium vitae*, 21, 28, 50, 77, 82, 86, 87, 92, 95, 98, 100).

20. USCCB, *One Family under God: A Statement of the U.S. Bishops' Committee on Migration*, rev. ed. (Washington: USCCB, 1998), 2.

21. Although *imago Dei* is foundational to Christian theology, it has been interpreted in various ways throughout history. Most debates about the term's meaning revolve around the condition of human nature after the Fall, as well as issues related to attributes (such as reason, will, emotions, and creativity), ethical qualities, social characteristics, and divine filiation. Irenaeus distinguished between "image" and "likeness," noting that "image" indicates an ontological participation (methexis) and "likeness" (mimêsis) a moral transformation (Adversus haereses 5.6.1; 5.8.1; 5.16.2). Tertullian believed that the image could never be destroyed, but it could be lost by sin (De baptismo 5, 6.7). Augustine addressed the relational and trinitarian dimensions of *imago Dei*, its threefold structure (memory, intelligence, and will) and the fundamental orientation of human beings to God (Confessions 1.1.1). Aquinas considered three stages of the *imago Dei: imago creationis* (nature), *imago recreationis* (grace), and *similitudinis* (glory) (Summa theologiae [hereafter ST] 1, q. 93, a. 4). He believed that the *imago Dei* enables human beings to participate in the life of God. The classic Reformation traditions tended to stress more the depravity of human nature whereas Catholic and Orthodox positions hold that sin impairs or disfigures the *imago Dei* but does not destroy it. The rise of the Enlightenment and modernity, and movements toward empiricism and rationalism, pushed the notion of *imago Dei* into the background, or eliminated it altogether, replacing it with an anthropology that sees human beings as self-constituting, autonomous subjects. Ludwig Feuerbach, Karl Marx, and Sigmund Freud went further by advancing that God is no more than a projection of the human imagination; thus they open the door to deconstructive interpretations about the human person. After Vatican II, however, the notion of *imago Dei* received renewed attention, and today it grounds much of modern Catholic social teaching. *Imago Dei* provides an important foundation for ecological questions, humanitarian debates, gender issues, eschatological challenges, and social-justice challenges, particularly my treatment of it here in light of the issue of migration and refugees. For a thorough yet concise treatment of *imago Dei*, see International Theological Commission (ITC), *Communion and Stewardship: Human Persons Created in the Image of God*, http://www.vatican.va/roman_curia/congregations/cfaith/cti_documents/rc_con

_cfaith_doc_20040723_communion-stewardship_en.html; Phyllis Trible, *God and the Rhetoric of Sexuality* (Philadelphia: Fortress, 1978), 72–143; David Tracy, "Religion and Human Rights in the Public Realm," *Daedalus* 112 (1983), 237–54; Jürgen Moltmann, *God in Creation* (San Francisco: Harper & Row, 1985); Douglas John Hall, *Imaging God: Dominion as Stewardship* (Grand Rapids, Mich.: Eerdmans, 1986); and Mary Catherine Hilkert, O.P., "Imago Dei," *New Dictionary of Catholic Spirituality*, ed. Michael Downey, Collegeville Catholic Reference Library, version 1, CD-ROM (Collegeville, Minn.: Liturgical, 2000), 535.

22. Lisa Sowle Cahill, "Toward a Christian Theory of Human Rights," *Journal of Religious Ethics* 8 (1980), 279.

23. Mary Catherine Hilkert, "Cry Beloved Image: Rethinking the Image of God," in *In the Embrace of God: Feminist Approaches to Theological Anthropology*, ed. Ann O'Hara Graff (Maryknoll, N.Y.: Orbis, 1995), 190–204.

24. USCCB, *Economic Justice for All*, 14 (1986), http://www.osjspm.org/economic _justice_for_all.aspx.

25. Ibid., 1.

26. *GS*, 26.

27. Pope John XXIII, *Pacem in terris (Peace on Earth)* 106 (1963).

28. Pope John Paul II, *Laborem exercens (On Work)* 1 (1981).

29. Ibid., 23.

30. Sacred Congregation for Bishops, "Instruction on the Pastoral Care of People Who Migrate" (Washington: United States Catholic Conference, August 22, 1969), 7.

31. USCCB, *One Family Under God: A Statement of the U.S. Bishops' Committee on Migration*, rev. ed. (Washington: USCCB, 1998), 6.

32. United Nations, Universal Declaration of Human Rights, http://www.un .org/Overview/rights.html.

33. Office of the High Commissioner for Human Rights, *United Nations Convention relating to the Status of Refugees* (1951), http://www.unhchr.ch/html/menu3/b/o_ c_ref.htm.

34. For more on Overseas Development Statistics, see Development Co-operation Directorate (OECD), "Development Aid at a Glance 2007," http://masetto.sourceoecd .org/vl=3495881/cl=12/nw=1/rpsv/devaid2007/s-1-1.htm. For more on Immigrant Remittances, see the International Fund for Agricultural Development report, "Sending Money Home: Worldwide Remittance Flows to Developing Countries," http:// www.ifad.org/events/remittances/maps/brochure.pdf.

35. Migrants and refugees often bear the burden of a humanity living in tension between the land of likeness to God (*regio similitudinis*), which fosters the dignity of every person, and the land of unlikeness to God (*regio dissimilitudinis*). The concept of *regio dissimilitudinis* has its origin in Platonic thought, but it has parallels in the Scriptures. Mystics like Bernard of Clairvaux and others in the Middle Ages also used the concept when speaking about the movement of people away from the divine image and likeness toward a state of alienation. For more on this topic, see Etienne Gilson, "Regio dissimilitudinis de Platon à Saint Bernard de Clairvaux," *Medieval Studies* 9 (1947), 109–17.

36. Georges Didi-Huberman, *Fra Angelico: Dissemblance and Figuration*, trans. Jane Marie Todd (Chicago: University of Chicago, 1995), 45.

37. As the International Theological Commission (ITC) notes, in Christ "we find the total receptivity to the Father which should characterize our own existence, the openness to the other in an attitude of service which should characterize our relations with our brothers and sisters in Christ, and the mercy and love for others which Christ, as the image of the Father, displays for us" (ITC, *Communion and Stewardship*, 53).

38. Aquinas notes that the basic principle of the moral life, the natural law, and all of creation are dynamic by nature in that everything comes from God and returns to God (*exitus et reditus*). Migration names what it means to be human before God: the movement from God the Creator, the return to God, and the condition of that return in Christ the mediator. See Aquinas, ST 1-2, q. 92.

39. Karl Barth, *The Doctrine of Reconciliation: Church Dogmatics*, trans. G. W. Bromiley, ed. G. W. Bromiley and T. F. Torrance (New York: Continuum, 2004), 157–210.

40. Ibid., 159.

41. Hans urs von Balthasar, *Love Alone: The Way of Revelation*, 5th ed. (London: Sheed & Ward, 1992), 84.

42. Jesus was rejected by many in his day including Herod, who feared losing his power (Mt 2:1–13); Jesus' family, who thought he was out of his mind (Mk 3:20–21); his neighbors, who failed to understand his origins (Mt 13:54–57; Mk 6:1–4; Lk 4:13–30); the rich young man, who had great wealth but did not want to share it (Mt 19:16–22; Mk 10:17–22; Lk 18:18–23); the religious leaders, who envied Jesus' popularity with the people (Mt 26:3–4; Jn 11:47–53); Judas, who exploited Jesus for money and favor with those in power (Mt 26:14–16, 47–50, Lk 22:4–6, Jn 18:2–5); Peter, who feared the ramifications of association with him (Mt 26:69–75, Mk 14:66–72, Lk 22:54–62, Jn 18:15–18, 25–27); and the crowds, who shouted "crucify him" and did nothing to redress injustice (Mt 27:15–18, 20–23; Mk 15:6–14; Lk 23:13–23; Jn 19:5–7, 14–15).

43. Karl Barth, *The Doctrine of Reconciliation*, 184.

44. Ibid., 192.

45. Ibid., 171.

46. Ibid., 180.

47. Ibid., 170.

48. Ibid., 208.

49. David Power, in his book *Love without Calculation*, examines in depth the notion of kenosis, which has many ramifications for our discussion on migrants and refugees. He notes that the self-emptying of Christ prompts the church to a greater identification with the poor and to wait in hope for the gratuitous gift of life. He observes that "for humankind to be united in one . . . the web of hatred, injustice, and sin has to be broken. . . . Humans need to know how to face death in the hope of life, be it personal, generational or cultural. In self-giving, in being for others, in seeking freedom from a global Babel, belief in both human community and in transcendent gift are needed and possible. In Jesus Christ we are given a way to be free from evil, a way to pass to life through death lived as self-gift and witness." David Noel Power, *Love without Calculation: A Reflection on Divine Kenosis*, "He Emptied Himself, Taking the Form of a Slave," Phil 2:7 (New York: Crossroad, 2005), 4.

50. Jesuit Ignacio Ellacuría, who was murdered in 1989 by a military death squad, referred to the poor as "the people crucified in history" (Ignacio Ellacuría, "The Crucified People," in *Mysterium Liberationis: Fundamental Concepts of Liberation Theology*, ed. Ignacio Ellacuría and Jon Sobrino [Maryknoll, N.Y.: Orbis, 1993], 580–604, at 580). See also Jon Sobrino, "La teología y el 'Principio de Liberación,'" in *Revista latinoamericana de teología* 12 (May–August 1995): 115–40; and Michael E. Lee, "Liberation Theology's Transcendent Moment: The Work of Xavier Zubiri and Ignacio Ellacuría as Noncontrastive Discourse," *Journal of Religion* 83 (2003): 226–43; Kevin Burke and Robert Lassalle-Klein, *Love That Produces Hope: The Thought of Ignacio Ellacuría* (Collegeville, Minn.: Liturgical, 2006). See also Gioacchino Campese, "¿Cuantos Más? The Crucified Peoples at the US/Mexico Border," in *A Promised Land, A Perilous Journey: Theological Perspectives on Migration*, ed. Daniel G. Groody and Gioacchino Campese (Notre Dame, Ind.: University of Notre Dame, 2008), 271–98; and Daniel G. Groody, *Border of Death, Valley of Life: An Immigrant Journey of Heart and Spirit* (Lanham, Md.: Rowman & Littlefield, 2002). See also Daniel G. Groody, "Jesus and the Undocumented: A Spiritual Geography of a Crucified People," *Theological Studies* 70 (2009), 298–316.

51. Augustine, *Teaching Christianity*, trans. Edmund Hill, ed. John E. Rotelle, Works of Saint Augustine: A Translation for the 21st Century (Hyde Park, N.Y.: New City, 1996), 120–21.

52. Gustavo Gutiérrez has contributed greatly to reflection on the poor from a theological perspective and the ethical demands that flow from the gratuitous nature of God's love for the world and outreach to those most in need. He notes: "The condition of the poor, because it is deeply tied to inhumanity, is a radical challenge to the human and Christian conscience. No one—no matter their geographical or social location, their culture or religion—can pretend that they are not gripped by it. To perceive the condition of the poor, it is necessary to see poverty in all its depth and breadth. It is a challenge that extends beyond the social field, becoming a demand to think about how we proclaim the Gospel in our day and how we might present the themes of the Christian message in new ways. . . . The Christian is a witness to the resurrection, the definitive victory over all forms of death" (Gutiérrez, "Memory and Prophecy," in *Option for the Poor in Christian Theology*, 17–40, at 28).

53. Pope Paul VI, *Populorum Progressio (On the Development of Peoples)* 42 (1967).

54. Pope Paul VI, *Lumen Gentium (The Light of Nations)* 9 (1964).

55. Robert Schreiter outlines five distinctive elements of a Christian understanding of reconciliation in light of the migrant reality: (1) God is the agent of reconciliation; (2) healing begins with the victim; (3) the healing brought about in the reconciliation process takes the victim to a new place; (4) the migration story has to be reframed; and (5) the healing process of reconciliation is never complete. He notes that one of the common denominators in the ministry of reconciliation to migrants is dealing with trauma caused by leaving one's homeland, traveling to a new place, and settling in an unfamiliar location. For more on mission and migration, see: Robert J. Schreiter, "Migrants and the Ministry of Reconciliation," in *A Promised Land, A Perilous Journey*, 107–23; Robert J. Schreiter, *The Ministry of Reconciliation: Spiritual-*

ity and Strategies (Maryknoll, N.Y.: Orbis, 2008); Daniel G. Groody, *Border of Death, Valley of Life,* 115–36; Stephen Bevans, "Mission Among Migrants, Mission of Migrants: Mission of the Church," in *A Promised Land, A Perilous Journey,* 89–106. For more on mission from a variety of cultural and continental perspectives, see Robert J. Schreiter, *Mission in the Third Millennium* (Maryknoll, N.Y.: Orbis, 2002).

56. An important work on public policy and Christian values is Dana W. Wilbanks, *Re-Creating America: The Ethics of U.S. Immigration Refugee Policy in a Christian Perspective* (Nashville: Abingdon, 1996).

57. Aquinas understood "law" as "an ordinance of reason for the common good, promulgated by him who has the care of the community" (ST 1–2, q. 90). The eternal law governs everything in the universe: the divine law corresponds to the Old Law and New Law of the Hebrew Scriptures and New Testament; the natural law deals with ethical norms and human behavior; and the civil law deals with human codes used for social order. For an overview of natural law and its development within Catholic tradition, see Stephen J. Pope, "Natural Law in Catholic Social Teachings," in *Modern Catholic Social Teaching: Commentaries and Interpretations*, ed. Kenneth R. Himes (Washington: Georgetown University, 2005), 41–71. For a more extended treatment, see John Finnis, *Natural Law and Natural Rights* (New York: Oxford University, 2001).

58. For interdisciplinary perspectives on rights in Africa, see David Hollenbach, ed. *Refugee Rights: Ethics, Advocacy, and Africa* (Washington, D.C.: Georgetown University, 2008).

59. For more on Catholic social teaching regarding migration, see Michael A. Blume, "Migration and the Social Doctrine of the Church," in *Migration, Religious Experience, and Globalization,* ed. Gioacchino Campese and Pietro Ciallella (New York: Center for Migration Studies, 2003), 62–75.

60. S. Jonathan Bass, *Blessed Are the Peacemakers: Martin Luther King, Jr., Eight White Religious Leaders, and "The Letter from the Birmingham Jail"* (Baton Rouge: Louisiana State University, 2001), 244. Cardinal Roger Mahony, addressing the failure of Congressional leadership to pass comprehensive immigration reform in June 2007, appeals to a law that supersedes the particular laws of a nation: "Today, we don't have a law on the part of our House of Representatives and the Senate. We don't have a civil law, but we are following a better law, the law of God. We are following the teachings of God in the Old Testament. Also, we are following the teaching and example of Jesus in the Gospel. This law for me is a higher law, and we will keep following it" (Cardinal Roger Mahony, Statement regarding the Failure of the Senate's Comprehensive Immigration Reform Bill, Archdiocese of Los Angeles, Office of Media Relations, June 29, 2007).

61. While "entry without inspection" has long been a criminal offense, it has traditionally been treated as an administrative violation, leading to civil deportation proceedings. In recent years, however, the Department of Homeland Security has referred for criminal prosecution increasing numbers of immigrants who have entered illegally and committed other immigration violations. "Immigration crimes" now represent more than one-half of all federal criminal prosecutions, more than all the cases

referred by the Federal Bureau of Investigation, the Drug Enforcement Administration, and other federal agencies combined. See Doris Meissner and Donald Kerwin, "DHS and Immigration: Taking Stock and Correcting Course" (Washington, D.C.: Migration Policy Institute, February 2009), 40-41, http://www.migrationpolicy.org/pubs/DHS_Feb09.pdf.

62. For the text of the "Convention and Protocol relating to the Status of Refugees," see http://www.unhcr.org/protect/PROTECTION/3b66c2aa10.pdf.

63. See in particular Terry Coonan, "There Are No Strangers among Us: Catholic Social Teaching and U.S. Immigration Law," *Catholic Lawyer* 40 (2000), 105–64, at 105.

64. Luke Bretherton, *Hospitality as Holiness, Christian Witness amid Moral Diversity* (Burlington, Vt.: Ashgate, 2006), 128.

65. Norman Perrin, *Rediscovering the Teaching of Jesus* (San Francisco: Harper & Row, 1976), 102.

66. Robert J. Karris, *Luke: Artist and Theologian* (New York: Paulist, 1985), 47.

67. Michael Guinan, "Davidic Covenant," in *The Anchor Bible Dictionary*, ed. David N. Freedman (New York: Doubleday, 1996), 72; Guinan, "Mosaic Covenant," in ibid., 909. See also Walter Brueggemann, *Solomon: Israel's Ironic Icon of Human Achievement* (Columbia: University of South Carolina, 2005), 58–59, 219.

68. Raymond E. Brown, *The Book of Deuteronomy: Introduction and Commentary, Old Testament Reading Guide* 10 (Collegeville, Minn.: Liturgical, 1965).

69. Cathy Ross, "Creating Space: Hospitality as a Metaphor for Mission," unpublished paper, October 16, 2007, http://www.cms-uk.org/Resources/CrowtherCentre home/Missiologyarticles/tabid/191/language/en-GB/Default.aspx.

70. Bernard McGinn points out that throughout the tradition *visio Dei* holds in tension two apparently contradictory biblical claims: some texts affirm that God can be seen (Gen 32:30; Isa 6:5; Mt 5:8); others deny it (Gen 32:30; Exod 33:20; Jn 1:18; 6:46; 1 Jn 4:12; Mt 11:27; 1 Tm 6:16). Like *imago Dei*, *visio Dei* is also much debated through history, particularly about how the vision of God deals with the relationship between this life and the next. Innocent III spoke of three kinds of "vision of God": corporeal, veiled, and comprehensive. "The corporeal vision belongs to the senses; the veiled to images; the comprehensive to the understanding" (Innocent III, Sermon 31, PL 217, coll. 598–96). McGinn traces the various ways in which this concept has been considered throughout the tradition by writers such as Clement of Alexandria, Augustine, Dionysius, Eriugena, Gregory of Nyssa, Albert the Great, Thomas Aquinas, and Meister Eckhart. McGinn notes that, even though many debate the relationship between *visio Dei* in this life and the next, there is general agreement that the vision of God is the goal of Christian life. My focus here is to examine the social implications of such a vision. See Bernard McGinn, "Visio Dei: Seeing God in Medieval Theology and Mysticism," in *Envisaging Heaven in the Middle Ages*, ed. Carolyn Muessig and Ad Putter with Garth Griffith and Judith Jefferson (New York: Routledge, 2007), 15–33; see also McGinn, "Visions and Visualizations in the Here and Hereafter," *Harvard Theological Review* 98 (2005), 227–46; and McGinn, "Seeing and Not-Seeing: Nicholas of Cusa's De visione Dei in the History of Western Mysticism," in *Cusanus: The Legacy of Learned Ignorance*, ed. Peter Casarella (Washington: Catholic University of America, 2005), 26–53.

71. Bernard McGinn, "Visio Dei: Seeing God in Medieval Theology and Mysticism," 24–27.

72. The notion of *visio Dei* is integrally related to evangelical poverty. For more on the relationship between poverty and the direct awareness of God, and poverty as a response to material prosperity in medieval society and the purification of self, see David Linge, "Mysticism, Poverty and Reason in the Thought of Meister Eckhart," *Journal of the American Academy of Religion* 46 (1978), 465–88.

73. "The more ardently we love God," Augustine wrote, "the more certainly and calmly do we see him, because we see in God the unchanging form of justice, according to which we judge how one ought to live" (De Trinitate 8.9.13). See McGinn, "Visio Dei: Seeing God in Medieval Theology and Mysticism," 17. One way of describing Augustine's notion of the blinding disfigurement of the image of God is to say the image is deformed by pride, that is, the love of power over justice (Trin. 13.17). Faith in the incarnation is the beginning of a transformation of the image, reformed by Christ's preference for justice over power, and this transformation of the image tends toward the vision of God (Trin. 14.23; 15.21). For more on this topic, see John C. Cavadini, "The Quest for Truth in Augustine's De Trinitate," *Theological Studies* 58 (1997), 429–40.

74. *LG*, 36.

75. Christine D. Pohl, "Biblical Issues in Mission and Migration," *Missiology* 31 (2003), 3–15.

76. John Henry Newman, "An Essay on the Development of Christian Doctrine," 6th ed. (Notre Dame, Ind.: University of Notre Dame, 1989), 375.

77. The Hebrew letters for "Egypt" are those found in Psalm 116:3: "the snare (literally "the oppressive confinement" or "narrow straits") of Sheol" and Psalm 118:5: "out of my distress (literally "strait," "narrow confinement," "tight place") I called on the Lord." There is an exact match between the unvocalized Hebrew "Egypt" and "narrow straits" as it is spelled in Lamentations 1:3: "All her persecutors come upon her where she is narrowly confined." The author is clearly using a play on words here between "narrow confinements" and Egypt. See Laurel A. Dykstra, *Set Them Free: The Other Side of Exodus* (Maryknoll, N.Y.: Orbis, 2002), 58. I am grateful to Lisa Marie Belz for this insight.

78. Terry Coonan, "There Are No Strangers Among Us," 110–11.

79. For more on different ways in which Matthew 25:31–46 has been interpreted throughout history, see John R. Donahue, S.J., "The 'Parable' of the Sheep and the Goats: A Challenge to Christian Ethics," *Theological Studies* 41 (1986), 3–31.

80. Robert McAfee Brown, *Unexpected News: Reading the Bible with Third World Eyes* (Philadelphia, Penn.: Westminster, 1984), 127–41.

81. Cardinal Roger Mahony, in his Templeton Lecture, "The Challenge of 'We the People' in a Post 9/11 World: Immigration, the American Economy and the Constitution," http://www.la-archdiocese.org/news/pdf/news_884_TempletonFinalMay_8_07 percent20_2_.pdf, addresses the immigration issue in light of the root meaning of "economy" (Gk oikonomia, defined as the arrangement of a household). He notes that in the early Church "oikonomia collectively referred to the way in which God's household is ordered or administered, and in that sense economized. God's household, God's

grand economy, is one in which holiness and truth, justice and love, and above all, peace (eirene or shalom) prevail." He argues that what makes for a sound economy is "the full flourishing of everyone who is part of God's economy, household, or community."

82. Josef Pieper, *A Brief Reader on the Virtues of the Human Heart* (San Francisco: Ignatius, 1991), 39.

83. Gil Loescher, "The PRS Project," unpublished paper, presented at Queen Elizabeth House, Oxford University, November 22, 2007.

84. David Hollenbach, *Claims in Conflict: Retrieving and Renewing the Catholic Human Rights Tradition* (New York: Paulist, 1979), 204.

85. Elie Wiesel, "The Refugee," in *Sanctuary: A Resource Guide for Understanding and Participating in the Central American Refugee's Struggle*, ed. Gary MacEoin (New York: Harper & Row, 1985), 9.

Chapter Two

International Migration: Social, Economic, and Humanitarian Considerations

Mary DeLorey

INTRODUCTION: MIGRATION AS A GLOBAL PHENOMENON

To the Catholic Church, major migration flows constitute "signs of the times," reflecting broader social, economic, and political realities. They implicate economic development and trade relations, shifting demographics and labor markets, security, and human rights concerns. For many of the same reasons, migration receives considerable attention from international bodies and governments.

The number of international migrants (those living outside of their countries of origin) has more than doubled in the past 30 years to close to 200 million worldwide. The vast majority are economic migrants, many with few options to escape grinding poverty and to remain in their countries of origin. Contrary to common belief, nearly a third of today's migrants move from one developing country to another, with an equal proportion moving from developing to developed countries.[1] Globally, international migrants still comprise only three percent of the world's population. However, an increasing number of countries are experiencing emigration rates as high as one quarter of their population. Many nations host large foreign-born populations, in excess of twenty percent of the total population in a number of small countries. Large-scale immigration significantly impacts both sending and receiving nations, particularly affecting local development, integration, and the boundaries of national identity.

This chapter describes the factors that influence people's decisions to migrate and the connections between migration and development, in both economic and social terms. Additionally it highlights new vulnerabilities and human rights concerns in this era of large-scale migration.

WHAT MAKES CONTEMPORARY MIGRATION DIFFERENT?

Trade Agreements Move Jobs across Borders; People Follow

Globalization, which is characterized by interconnected and interdependent economic and social relations, has created levels of wealth and new opportunities barely imagined in the past. Yet it has also exacerbated economic inequalities between and within countries. For example, the ratio of the average purchasing power of the five richest countries to the five to ten poorest in 1900 was 9 to 1; by 1960 it was 30 to 1; and today it is 100 to 1.[2] Migrants moving from lower to higher income countries can earn 20 to 30 times as much as they could obtain in their home countries. Favorable exchange rates between countries of destination and origin also create a powerful incentive to migrate; that is, conversion of stronger currency such as American dollars to the currency in the home country significantly increases the purchasing power of migrants or their families there.

The liberalization of trade (generally characterized by the reduction of governmental intervention through such policies as taxes on imports and subsidies on exports) makes it possible for goods, capital, and entire employment sectors to cross borders with increasing freedom. Yet opportunities are very limited for workers, particularly low-skilled workers, to migrate legally and safely to areas where jobs have been created as a result of globalized economies. This reality undermines the potential for greater positive economic impacts of free trade agreements and creates considerable imbalances in labor markets. Finally, the movement of workers, often without required residency and work documents, makes them vulnerable to a range of exploitation and abuse.

Decisions regarding trade, national and regional development, labor markets, and foreign aid rarely are analyzed in terms of their impact on migration in any serious or systematic manner, yet they often are the largest contributors to subsequent dislocation and migration.

In the words of *Erga Migrantes Caritas Christi (The Love of Christ Towards Migrants),* issued in 2004 by the Pontifical Council for the Pastoral Care of Migrants and Itinerant People, globalization has "flung markets wide open but not frontiers, has demolished boundaries for the free circulation of information and capital, but not to the same extent for the free circulation of people."[3] As the former director general of the International Labor Organization, Juan Somavia, states, "If you look at globalization from the point of view of people's concerns, its single biggest failure is its inability to create jobs where people live."[4]

Aging Populations in Receiving Countries;
Growing Populations in Developing Countries

Industrialized countries are increasingly characterized by aging populations and low fertility rates. Consequently, they experience a substantial decline in "replacement workers" entering the workforce. Simultaneously, these post-industrial economies create greater demand for service sector jobs and both high- and low-skill employment. The result is a greater reliance on migrants in many wealthier nations to fill labor gaps in their economies and to shore up the tax base that provides the necessary resources for social benefits expected by aging workers. As such, migrants generally have a disproportionately positive impact on national productivity in the countries where they work.

These demographic shifts are receiving increasing attention at the global level. Without additional immigration, the total labor force in Europe and Russia, the high-income countries of East Asia and the Pacific, China, and to a lesser extent, North America, is projected to be reduced by 29 million people by 2025 and by 244 million by 2050. In contrast, the labor force in the South is projected to add some 1.55 billion, predominantly in South and Central Asia and in Sub-Saharan Africa. From 1990 to 2000, international migration accounted for 56 percent of the population growth in the developed world and, within Europe, accounted for 89 percent.[5]

The high demand for labor in some countries and regions and the large supply of potential workers in others would suggest that a win-win situation potentially exists between developed and developing nations. However, migration and labor policies have always been more complicated than a simple cost-benefit decision-making process. National policymakers need to consider the social, political, and cultural concerns of their populations. Issues of social cohesion, displacement, and national identity have been effectively and repeatedly used to derail attempts to develop more beneficial immigration policies in the United States and European countries. Debates fueled by concerns and fear of cultural and ethnic change have been incorporated into anti-immigrant political movements such as Jean Marie Le Pen's Front National party in France. These concerns are also reflected in controversial analyses by academics such as Samuel P. Huntington, in his article "The Hispanic Challenge," published in *Foreign Policy Magazine*.

In large measure, these social, political, and cultural considerations have led to migration policies that are out of sync with current economic and demographic realities. Indeed, migration policies have taken on a decidedly restrictive nature in much of the world in recent years. Consequently, they often result not in sound migration management or even narrowly defined "migration control," but rather in increasing levels of irregular migration and the exposure of more migrants to exploitive, dangerous, and even life-threatening conditions.

Feminization of Migration

As migration patterns change over time, new characteristics need to be identified and understood to improve migration management. One of these factors is the increase in female migration throughout the world. Although migration flows in the past have been dominated by men, as of 2005, women accounted for 49.6 percent of global migrants. The percentage of women migrating now exceeds that of men in North America, Europe, Australia, the former Soviet Union, Latin America, and the Caribbean.[6] According to the UN Global Commission on Migration, this trend "will continue in the years to come," responding to the push factor of limited economic and social opportunities for women. Divorced, widowed, childless, and single women in some countries of origin are more likely to be drawn by the pull of enormous worldwide demand for labor traditionally associated with women: domestic work, nursing and personal care services, and the sex trade.[7] Additionally, it is important to point out that women are disproportionately impacted when employment options and social safety nets decline or disappear, leading to their greater impoverishment, a critical factor in increased migration.

Impact on Sending Countries

Large-scale migration is also redefining issues of national development in both sending and receiving countries. The worldwide flow of remittances is conservatively estimated to exceed $200 billion a year, with more than 60 percent going to developing countries.[8] Remittances globally outstrip international aid funding, and have become a central aspect of the economic calculus of a number of developing countries. However, migrant remittances primarily help to meet the basic needs of families, and have a more limited impact on local development; they are not a panacea or alternative to much needed local, national, and regional economic development.

The social impact of current rates of migration merits attention. The scale of migration from many countries has brought about significant demographic changes in communities of origin. Migration of the most economically produc-

A child who had managed to board the train while it was moving ran atop the cars, happy to continue his journey, and tried to jump to the next train car. He didn't make it, fell, and was crushed by the train. I saw his foot cut off and tried to climb down at the moment he fell but was unable to because of the speed of the train. Throughout my journey I thought of this child who moments earlier had told me he was traveling in search of his mother who was in Los Angeles. "Because I am fair-skinned, I'll easily cross the border," he told me. I don't remember his name but he said he was from El Salvador. I got off the train and instead of continuing north I am going to return to Honduras. I can't take the things I have seen.

—*Juan Alberto*, Honduran Immigrant

tive age groups or disproportionate rates of migration of one gender can render sending communities little more than "nurseries and nursing homes." Consequently, home communities experience lower productivity, disintegration and division of families, and unexpected cultural and economic dislocation.

Large-scale family separations have been shown to have long-term ramifications for family members as well as serious social impacts in sending countries. Sending countries see increasing numbers of "social orphans," when family networks are insufficient to meet the needs of children whose parents have migrated. The high rate of children left behind is more often than not a reflection of the lack of safe, legal options for families to migrate together. Some of these children are housed in state institutions or end up on the street. They experience higher rates of depression and delinquency and are more likely to migrate unaccompanied.

Current migration is also characterized by advances in technology, which facilitate linkages between countries of origin and destination. In the past, international migration resulted in long-term, if not permanent, separations with limited subsequent contact with home countries. Today, much more fluid connections may be maintained. Advances in communication and transportation have made it possible for frequent contact with family members, travel between home and destination countries, and substantial levels of economic, social and political interactions that would not have been possible in the past.

To conclude, the scale of migration and its impact on the economic and social development of migrant-sending countries merit greater attention by sending and receiving governments and communities to ensure protection of migrants and promotion of the common good.

LOOKING A LITTLE DEEPER:
WHAT IS DRIVING MIGRATION?

Princeton sociologist Douglas Massey, along with Jorge Durand and Nolan Malone, have set forth four questions necessary for understanding the multi-dimensional nature of migration and its relationship to humanitarian and development concerns:

- What are the forces in sending societies that promote out-migration and how do they operate?
- What are the forces in receiving societies that create a demand for immigrant workers, and how do they function?
- What are the motivations, goals, and aspirations of the people who respond to these forces by migrating?
- And what are the social and economic structures that arise in the course of migration to connect sending and receiving societies?[9]

Factors Driving Migration from Countries of Origin

In the 1980s and 1990s, conventional wisdom held that an expanded global market would in and of itself decrease the income gap between rich and poor countries. In fact, income disparities narrowed for only a small number of countries, despite the prevalence of efforts by developing countries to open trade and financial systems to the global market. Yet in 2005, 185 million people worldwide were unemployed, 550 million of the employed survived on less than one dollar a day, and half the world's workers earned less than two dollars a day.[10]

Agricultural competition often factors into decisions to migrate. Nearly half of the work force in developing countries is employed in agriculture. Small producers throughout the world are finding it difficult if not impossible to remain on land worked by their families and communities for generations. Weak physical and financial infrastructures, low levels of investment in rural development, and increasing levels of environmental degradation create limited opportunities for competitive farm production in developing countries. Moreover, given the framework of current free trade agreements, these farmers now find themselves in competition with highly subsidized agricultural products from wealthy countries.

Although international migration receives the greatest attention globally, the majority of large-scale migration today remains internal to countries from rural to urban areas. According to the United Nations Population Fund (UNFPA), in 2008—for the first time in history—more than 50 per-

> Our efforts to help family farmers improve their incomes and living conditions in Mexico have been substantially limited by the impact of international trade policy. Hundreds of thousands of family farmers throughout Mexico have been severely affected by the flood of cheap corn imports from the United States after the passage of the North American Free Trade Agreement. The price of corn in Mexico has been driven below the cost of production, leaving farmers with a crop literally not worth harvesting. The Mexican government's cuts to vital support and subsidy programs for farmers has only made matters worse. After generations of farming corn, families are giving up, abandoning their farms, and heading north.
>
> —*Erica Dahl-Bredine,*
> Catholic Relief Services/Mexico Country Manager

cent of the world's population lived in urban rather than rural areas. That percentage is projected to increase to two-thirds by 2030, with more than 90 percent of this growth taking place in developing countries. In and of itself, this internal migratory pattern deserves attention. Additionally, urban migration is increasingly the first step in a progression toward international migration.

A diversity of factors drive migration between regions and countries, but the example of Latin America—one of the regions producing the highest rates of migration—is illustrative. The basic economic framework that has been promoted within Latin America since the 1980s (generally referred to as neoliberal economic policies)[11] has not improved the living conditions or prospects for a large percentage of the region's population. This model has been characterized by a radical modification of economic structures and primary economic actors, including: the reduction of the role of the national government in the economy in favor of the private sector; privatization, more generally (including of service sectors); market-determined exchange rates; and the removal of tariffs and subsidies as a hallmark of free trade. (It should be noted, however, that the United States and Europe have not concurrently eliminated their own subsidy programs in key agricultural sectors.) Priority in this period has been given to foreign trade over economic development within countries, and small and medium enterprises and agricultural production have been reduced in favor of industrial farms and large-scale enterprise. The model has resulted in a reduction in government expenditures, which often has included reduction in social welfare protections. Concurrently, employment and real wages have declined in many areas.

The Catholic Church has expressed its concerns about this economic model as it has been applied in the Western Hemisphere. As Pope John Paul II stated in *Ecclesia en America (The Church in America)*:

> More and more, in many countries of America, a system known as "neoliberalism" prevails; based on a purely economic conception of man, this system considers profit and the law of the market as its only parameters, to the detriment of the dignity of and the respect due to individuals and peoples. At times this system has become the ideological justification for certain attitudes and behavior in the social and political spheres leading to the neglect of the weaker members of society. Indeed, the poor are becoming ever more numerous, victims of specific policies and structures which are often unjust.[12]

Moreover, trade policies of high-income countries, which are particularly sensitive to domestic pressures, are often at odds with their stated commitments to promote development and poverty reduction. Trade rules and trade agreements to date have disproportionately benefited some nations, and sectors within those nations, and negatively impacted if not devastated others. The Catholic Church has taken the position that trade needs to be structured in a manner that is fair; that prioritizes the reduction of poverty; and that protects the interests of the most vulnerable. This is not, however, the principle driving current trade policy. Rather, current policy emphasizes the market's ability to create wealth, not the distribution of the wealth created by trade. The latter is seen as the purview of social policymaking and responsibility.

Although agreements to liberalize trade and the movement of goods and capital have become more numerous, they have rarely addressed the movement of workers, other than entrepreneurs and the highly skilled, across borders.

A variety of approaches have been taken in response to international economic integration and its consequences. The European Union (E.U.) strategy, for example, has included substantial financial and technical investment in weaker economies prior to their integration into the E.U. The E.U. approach of strengthening would-be members improved their growth rates and employment, thereby reducing the pressure for large-scale migration and maximizing the advantages of a liberalized system of labor migration among E.U. members. Western Hemisphere free trade agreements, including the North American Free Trade Agreement (NAFTA) and the Central American Free Trade Agreement (CAFTA), by contrast, were preceded by very limited investment in and preserved few protections for smaller, weaker economies. In addition, economic integration in the Western Hemisphere is occurring between countries with far more unequal economies and wage disparities than in Europe, further increasing pressure to migrate and expanding the possible benefits of migration.

An analysis that only considers poverty or demographic pressures as the motivation for migration is an oversimplification of a far more complex dynamic. It has been documented that economic development and growth (particularly if the growth and distribution are modest), does not necessarily reduce migration, at least in the short term, particularly in the face of a broader array of social factors.

Factors Promoting Migration in Countries of Destination

As previously noted, many developed countries are experiencing low or declining birth rates, leading to smaller and older populations. Without considerable adaptations (including additional immigrant labor) these demographic changes have the potential to retard economic growth, to undermine the viability of pension and social security funds (which generally require ongoing contributions by younger workers), and to diminish labor sectors that are facing greater demand (e.g., care for children and the elderly, and domestic services).

As the 2006 UN Report, *Globalization and Interdependence: International Migration and Development* states:

> Many advanced economies need migrant workers to fill jobs that cannot be outsourced and that do not find local workers willing to take them at available wages. . . . As younger generations become better educated, fewer are content with low paid and physically demanding jobs.[13]

In addition to these demands, highly skilled workers are in demand across the globe. Few national education systems can adapt quickly enough to produce a sufficient number of highly trained workers for the labor markets of advanced economies in areas of technology and knowledge management. By necessity, therefore, they seek to recruit from among the highly skilled workers of a global labor pool.

Despite this demonstrated economic demand, new immigrants more often than not are confronted with antagonism rather than gratitude. In many receiving countries, the public is concerned that immigration will negatively impact national labor markets, reduce job opportunities, or decrease wages. However, empirical studies have demonstrated that in general, immigrants— whether documented or undocumented, temporary or permanent—have a small impact on wages and employment. Both unskilled and highly skilled immigrants typically complement the skill sets and educational attainment of native-born workers.

Individual and Collective Decision Making:
Reflections on Theories of Migration

It is worth reviewing some basic theories of why people migrate, if only to highlight the complexity of this phenomenon. Jose Luis Rocha succinctly summarizes many of the core elements of prevailing theories of migration.[14]

(1) *Departure based on cost-benefit analysis:* People choose to migrate because the potential benefits outweigh the investment, hardship, risk to life, and potential rejection or exploitation in the destination country. Even if income increases in the country of origin, continuing wage disparities would exert a considerable influence on the decision to migrate. (For example, in Haiti, the average per capita income is $400 per year. Nearby in the United States, an unskilled day laborer can earn that much in less than one week.)

(2) *Migration as part of a family strategy:* Migration not only maximizes earnings but also reduces risks. Families in many nations lack access to credit, insurance, unemployment benefits, and social welfare support. In countries of origin, salaries do not compensate for this heightened exposure to risk. The unit of analysis here is the household, which may distribute family members between the local community, to urban areas (in the same country), and to international locations in order to minimize risk and distribute assets. Wage-earning members of a family are less likely to be simultaneously impacted in the event of unexpected crises (such as natural disasters, national economic decline, or declining employment options) if they are distributed in different locations and labor markets.

(3 & 4) *Supply and demand of labor, and problems of the structural demand for labor in industrialized societies:* These two overlapping theories of migration underline the reality that globally, large labor forces exist where there is limited capital, and limited labor forces where there is significant capital. The theory suggests that greater economic and labor equilibrium will occur as a result of labor moving to capital rich (wealthier) areas, and wages will subsequently increase in countries of origin as the labor supply shrinks.

(5) *Moving from the periphery to the center:* The creation of bi-national linkages tends to increase migration and to serve as a catalyst for migration, whether these linkages were created under a colonial relationship, military actions, or (as has occurred more recently) as a result of multinational presence and trade ties. While it may seem counter-intuitive, the flow of merchandise and capital into new areas is typically followed by flows of labor in the opposite direction. Economic investment in areas where bi-national migration has become established is often insufficient to deter continued migration, either because the investment offers benefits that still remain below what could be gained by migration or because it only addresses economic but not social and cultural motivators of migration. This dynamic tends to occur *un-*

til there is a sufficient increase in employment in the source community, a significant decrease in the wage gap, or shifts in other demographic factors, such as fertility or mortality rates.

(6) *Perpetuation theory:* The establishment of an immigrant diaspora tends to facilitate future migration, as costs and risks are lowered by the established family or network. The establishment of family or community members overseas provides a network that affords newcomers knowledge, contacts, resources, and social support, thus easing economic and personal costs to migration.

(7) *Culture of migration:* Once migration becomes large scale and continues over time, it tends to become normative and even a cultural expectation.

I live in Mexicali in Baja California, Mexico. My brother José died this summer crossing the Arizona desert. He was twenty-five and had two children, ages seven and one. José had been working in construction in Sonora and was not able to make enough to support his wife and children and our mother. He moved to Mexicali earlier this year to try to find work in a maquiladora plant. That was his dream, to find a job in a maquiladora. I went with him to the factories to look for work, but no one would give him a job. Finally, he gave up and decided to go to the United States with our brother Jaime to try to find work. He told me he had to do something to support his family and especially to pay for his children's school expenses.

He and my brother Jaime paid a smuggler (U.S.) $1,000 each to take them across the border. The next day, my brother Jaime called us in Mexicali and told us that José was lost. Jaime said that at the end of the first day he was too exhausted and sick to keep going. He tried to talk José into going back with him, but José refused and wanted to go on. Jaime decided to go for help. He said he wanted to find the Border Patrol and send them to arrest José so they would save him. When they finally got back to where they had left the group, they were gone. They found José's backpack nearby and various sets of footprints, but nothing else. I came with some other family members and friends and we started searching everywhere for José. We searched on both sides of the border. We went to police departments and jails and put up signs with José's picture everywhere. We put out jugs of water on the highway, hoping José would make it out of the desert and find the water.

Four days later, on June 22, they told us that José's body had been found, along with another man in the group. Three other migrants in the group are still missing. My mother still won't accept that José is dead. Since she hasn't seen his body, she says he must be in prison somewhere.

(continued)

They said they identified José by his fingerprints, since it was not possible to identify the body.

What would I tell other migrants who want to cross? I came to pick up José's body, in a truck that a friend lent us. When I was crossing the border back into Mexico with the coffin in the back of the truck, I passed a group of migrants getting ready to start crossing the desert. I stopped and got out of the truck, and I was crying and I said to them, "Why do you want to risk your lives like this? Come and look at my brother in his coffin. Please don't do this. It's not worth it. If you make it across, they won't treat you well there. Please don't try it." I made them come and look at José's body in the coffin. That's what I would tell other migrants who want to try what José did. It's better to stay here eating nothing but beans and bread than to leave your children fatherless.

What I would tell people in the United States is to support the migrants, and to tell our president to create jobs in Mexico. People in my country who aren't able to finish their education can't find a job, and they need a way to live. We have so many people who come to Mexicali (after having) borrowed huge amounts of money to come north. The smugglers cheat them of what little they have, and they end up alone and begging for food, or risking their lives to cross into the U.S. These are good, hard-working and honest people—they just have no way to make a living. My brother's dream was to work in a maquiladora plant, even if he only made 700 pesos a month (U.S. $70). With that he would have been happy to stay in Mexico with his family. But he couldn't find a job.

—*Sonia G.*, sister of deceased migrant

Migrants' Impact on the Development of Their Home Countries

Not only do micro- and macroeconomic considerations impact the decision to migrate, but migration impacts micro- and macroeconomic development. The overall economic impact of migration receives the greatest degree of research attention, perhaps because it is easier to quantify than other significant political and social dimensions. The volume of money sent home to family members (remittances) significantly affects migrant sending communities and countries, as do, to greater and lesser degrees, migration-related foreign direct investment, philanthropy, and collective remittance transfers.

As particular sectors of the labor market move between developed and developing countries, they impact the economy of both sending and receiving countries. The issues of "brain drain," or what is more recently referred to as "care drain" (the mobility of care-giving services), and "brain circulation" (the value of more fluid movement of professionals between wealthy and developing nations), are discussed in chapter 3.

In addition to their economic impact, diaspora communities also influence the political and social dimensions of their countries of origin. Voting rights and, in many cases, dual citizenship, have been extended to diaspora communities, which are increasingly sought out by national and local politicians from their countries of origin. The economic contributions of diasporas have created new centers of political influence and leverage.

In 2005, remittance flows were estimated to have exceeded U.S. $233 billion worldwide, with U.S. $167 billion going to developing countries. Much of the remittance flow is concentrated in a limited number of countries, with Latin America and Asia receiving the lion's share of these funds and a third of global remittances going to only three countries: India, China, and Mexico.[15]

The distribution and impact of remittances vary greatly between and within countries. Remittances are often used for subsistence needs, but a smaller proportion is also used in various forms of investment. For example, in Ecuador, 75 percent of households received remittances;[16] and one-fifth of the capital invested in Mexican microenterprises is associated with remittances.

Remittances can significantly improve a family's standard of living. Between 15 and 20 percent of remittances are spent on medicines and to pay for medical help as the need arises. Remittances thus play an important role in improving the health of the family members of migrants and to a degree, combating disease in local communities. Additionally, remittances have a positive impact on the attainment of universal primary education. Children in families receiving remittances stay in school longer because they do not need to work to support themselves and their families.[17]

Remittances have also been cited for their multiplier effect. Some estimates suggest that every dollar from remittances may create two to three additional dollars of income in communities of origin because remittances are spent on goods and services supplied by others in the local economy.

Much of the attention that remittances receive is focused on how to transform what is essentially household income into a "resource for development" or productive projects (i.e., wealth generating). Although there is certainly much potential in these resource flows, concern has arisen among immigrant organizations and advocates that governments, multilateral organizations, and NGOs have taken on an "extractive approach to remittances." They argue that this approach places a disproportionate burden on migrants to meet not only family needs but also to contribute to needs of communities in areas where neither the public nor private sectors opt to invest. Indeed, often the very factors that push migrants to leave (such as poor infrastructure, limited market access, weak institutions, and failed or non-existent development strategies) limit the investment potential of migrant-sending communities.[18]

In addition to remittances, foreign direct investment, migration economies, philanthropy and collective contributions of immigrant organizations all provide economic benefits to migrant-sending communities.

Direct investment by migrants helps to multiply the benefits of a diaspora's financial growth to the migration source country. In the case of China, for example, remittances are relatively modest—approximately U.S. $4 billion between 1991 and 1998. Meanwhile Foreign Direct Investment (FDI), half of which is believed to originate with Chinese immigrant diasporas, was over $40 billion in 1998 alone. In this case, a focus on remittances alone would miss the largest component of the economic impact of migration. The manner in which the Indian software industry has benefited from high-tech immigrants in the United States, who have played a significant role in spurring greater trade and investment in India, provides another example of direct investment and job creation by emigrants.[19]

Various factors combine to create what some have termed "migration economies" in sending countries. Manuel Orozco, Senior Associate and Director of Remittances and Development at the World Bank, has set forth "the five T's of economies that grow up around . . . the migration phenomenon itself." These include transfers of remittances, transportation, tourism, telecommunication, and nostalgic trade. The combined share of these factors in some cases exceeds half of the country's GDP. In terms of nostalgic tourism and transport, Salvadoran, Dominican, and Mexican migrants constituted 50 percent, 30 percent, and 20 percent, respectively, of tourists to their countries of origin.[20] Nostalgia markets (created by diaspora demand for food and products of their countries of origin) create substantial new markets and can spur increased productivity in countries of origin.

Migrant philanthropy contributions to home countries and communities may come from Home Town Associations (HTAs), returnee associations (as in Jamaica), and charitable foundations (as in Egypt and the Philippines). HTAs have received particular attention in the United States. HTAs are diaspora communities that organize in order to finance projects for the betterment of their home communities. They generally carry out activities to respond to a common concern or need in the hometown and raise money, collect in-kind donations, or advocate for specific projects.[21] Involvement in HTAs allows immigrants to maintain their ties with their communities of origin and connections to other immigrants from the same region.

More than 650 Mexican HTAs exist in the United States, primarily in California and the Chicago metropolitan area. Similarly, more than 350 HTAs of Salvadorian migrants provide direct aid to their home communities. Although some of the associations date back decades, the majority have been constituted since the late 1990s. These associations, which can be as small as ten people or as large as 2,000, often become part of much larger federations. As of 2005, there were approximately twenty-five federations of Mexican associations in the United States. Annual collections by each association average $10,000 and rarely exceed $20,000 annually. In areas where a small town's municipal budget may be less than $50,000, an HTA investment can represent a considerable infusion of funds.

The Mexican government has taken the lead in promoting matching grants with U.S.-based HTAs for community projects. The Iniciativa Ciudadana 3x1 is a matching grant program started in 2002 between Mexican associations and all three levels of government.[22] For each dollar remitted, three are invested by the government—one by the local, one by the state, and one by the federal government. The matching process is usually financial, but in several cases the municipalities contribute in-kind with equipment and paid laborers. In areas with populations under 1,000, where nearly 50 percent of all hometown donations are sent, the contributions may be as much as seven times the budget allocated for public works in that community.[23]

HTAs have also played a valuable role in transforming the political culture in migrant source communities. For example, they have pressured governments to meet higher standards for transparency and accountability by making demands for the projects they fund.

An expanding array of disapora actors and organized efforts throughout the world use different models for their philanthropy. African diaspora associations in Europe have a similar intent, if not structure, to the Latin American HTAs. Filipino-American philanthropy, which includes HTAs and a variety of Filipino diaspora professional groups, utilize intermediary Filipino-based organizations, which offer services such as due diligence and grant monitoring.

The degree to which many national governments are analyzing the relationship between their emigrant communities (diasporas) and development is illustrated in the findings of a recent U.N.-sponsored poll. Of the 42 national governments who responded, including both developed and developing countries, 95 percent stated they were formally involved in cooperation with diasporas abroad, and 76 percent with foreign diasporas on their own territories. Sixty-nine percent of the respondent governments stated that migration is a part of their official development agenda, including 77 percent of developing countries, and (notably) 55 percent of developed countries.[24]

While the development potential of remittances and diaspora philanthropy sheds a positive light on the future of developing countries, the departure of many of the most talented and entrepreneurial people leaves researchers to ask, at what cost? Moreover, this reality increases the dependence of developing nations on migrant-receiving countries.

As the following insert illustrates, understanding the links between migration and development and creating legal avenues for labor migration are two of four critical gaps in the world's response to migrants; the other gaps involve internally displaced persons and other populations with particular vulnerabilities.

Four Gaps in the World's Response to Migrants

With only one exception, the four most prominent gaps in the world's response to migration involve *international* migrants. The one exception is *internally* displaced persons, who of course, have not crossed a border out of their own country. The gaps are not presented here in priority order: they are all pressing.

Gap 1: Internally Displaced Persons (IDPs) and Stateless Persons

The IDP and stateless gap is of critical importance. First, in sheer numbers, the U.N. High Commissioner for Refugees (UNHCR) tells us that there are over 25 million IDPs, and more than 15 million people not recognized as nationals by any government, called "stateless persons." (It is useful for the sake of comparison to note that there are currently an estimated 14 million refugees worldwide.) Yet no legal or institutional infrastructure exists for IDPs and stateless people. Second, the numbers of IDPs and stateless people—especially the stateless—are rising at a shocking pace. Third, precisely because these are people either displaced within their own countries due to serious problems there or have no country at all, there is tremendous global concern about what to do. Finally, and perhaps inevitably, with international institutions beginning to take organized action in response to this concern, there are serious questions about the effect of such action on the capacity of the international community to respond to other gaps.

Until recently, the world's response to IDPs had been almost entirely *ad hoc*. All too often over-resourced and under-coordinated U.N. and aid groups have been the only advocates for the world's IDP and stateless.

Gap 2: Especially Vulnerable Populations

This category includes victims of human trafficking; migrants in peril during transit; and "irregular" or unauthorized migrants. Many hundreds of
(continued)

thousands of migrants in the world today actually meet all three of these descriptions. However, there is no international framework of consistent, coherent, and rights-based responses when people are exploited or otherwise suffer because of these vulnerabilities. Such responses must begin with protection, but they should also entail humanitarian alternatives to detention, basic humanitarian and post-arrival services, rehabilitation, and durable solutions, including appropriate integration support.

Gap 3: Labor Migration

The gap in legal mechanisms for labor migration is immense, immediate, and startling. Of the world's 200 million international migrants, the vast majority of the adults are workers. Moreover, a large (but unknown) percentage of the 200 million actually migrated *for* work and are needed by their new countries. And therein is the cue that there is more to this modern migration than the archetypal "pull" factors, so much more in fact that we would miss the truth—and trends of global importance—if we did not look at modern labor migration more closely. For in an age of globalization accompanied by unprecedented demographics of *late death–low birth* in destination countries, it is impossible to maintain traditional "push-pull" analyses of international migration. The more accurate paradigm is one of mutuality—a matching of mutual need: of destination countries for millions of workers, and of migrants for jobs.

Gap 4: Understanding the Links between Migration and Development

A significant gap of knowledge and action remains regarding the linkages between migration and development. It is a gap framed by the following questions: What are the effects of migration on development, and what should be done to yield the best results? In turn, what are the effects of development on migration, and what should be done there? What are causal linkages between the two concepts? How do remittances impact development of sending and receiving countries? What are the impacts of migration on social development? Given its deep local involvement and international network, as well as its faith conviction, the Church is well-poised to address links and gaps between migration and development.

But there is a significant challenge in trying to link the two at the intergovernmental level. There, the knowledge-discussion-action gap is best demonstrated by the utter newness of even international *consultation* (much less collaboration) on this linkage: for the first time in U.N. and global history, the nations of the world gathered in 2005 specifically to

(*continued*)

discuss migration and development. The governments came together for this purpose twice between 2006 and 2007. First at the U.N. General Assembly, which dedicated its once-a-year High Level Dialogue of 2006 entirely to the subject. Secondly, at the direct follow-up to the High Level Dialogue: the intergovernmental Global Forum on Migration and Development, held in Brussels in July 2007. Defying the skeptics and exceeding expectations, the Global Forum was attended by 155 governments. Moreover, this effort at filling the gap on intergovernmental cooperation will continue. The Philippines hosted the Global Forum in 2008, and there is every sign that the international community is eager to address the intersection of migration and development.

—*John K. Bingham*, Head of Policy,
International Catholic Migration Commission

MIGRANT RIGHTS ARE HUMAN RIGHTS: NEW VULNERABILITIES AND CONCERNS

The limited options for legal migration have led to a well-documented increase in abusive and dangerous migration conditions throughout the world. Roughly 30 to 40 million unauthorized migrants live in the shadows of host countries, comprising around 15 to 20 percent of the world's immigrant population. The irregular status of these migrants limits their ability to access civil or labor rights and the systems designed to enforce such rights. Thus, they remain outside the protection and support of authorities and often are dependent on smugglers and potentially exploitive employers. Countries of destination may also view the unauthorized as security risks, making it even less likely that they will come forward when abuses occur, given the negative consequences they expect to encounter by doing so.

The litany of suffering and abuse experienced by migrants, particularly irregular migrants, includes drowning and suffocation in over-crowded and dangerous boats and cargo transport; mutilations from falling or being pushed from trains; deaths from exposure or dehydration in border crossings; high rates of physical and sexual violence in transit; detention under inhuman conditions; and very little recourse to protection, legal representation, or services. (There is a shelter specifically for "mutilated" migrants who have fallen from trains in southern Mexico.)

There is also very little in the way of services or reintegration programming for migrants who are deported or repatriated. Migrants may be repatriated with little prior warning, potentially after years of established residence in destination countries. The dislocation and obstacles they face to reintegra-

Picture the following: A county medical examiner's office has so many bodies piling up, it has to rent a refrigerated truck and park it out back to store them. A pauper's cemetery no longer has room to bury the bodies, so it begins to cremate them. A consular office sets up a special team and database to identify human remains and respond to the hundreds of missing persons requests flooding its office. Then we fade to the desert at night, where men, women, and children are tracked by infrared cameras and helicopters as they run desperately searching for a place to hide. If we didn't know better, we might think this was some kind of an apocalyptic film plot. But these scenes are playing out right here and now in southern Arizona where I live along the border, where at least 3,000 migrants are known to have died in the past ten to twelve years. Since many border crossers tell us about having passed bodies in the desert, we know that the actual number is probably higher.

—*Erica Dahl-Bredine*, CRS/Mexico Country Program Manager

tion can be considerable. Without reintegration opportunities, they may be more likely to attempt to migrate again or to become part of criminal activity leading to additional social problems in their home communities.

One of the most severe forms of abuse that has burst into global awareness in recent years is human trafficking,[25] commonly referred to as "modern day slavery." It is estimated that 700,000 to 2 million people are victims of human trafficking annually. The majority of trafficking victims begin as economic migrants or refugees and displaced persons who are seeking safer or more economically viable alternatives for themselves or their families. These would-be migrants often become victims of trafficking after being deceived by persons whom they believed to be smugglers, employment contractors, or even friends or relatives. Because of the dearth of safe and legal options for migration, families often must stagger their migration. Thus, women and children are increasingly migrating by themselves, increasing their risk. In gender-segregated fields such as domestic work or child care, jobs which tend to be poorly regulated, migrant women are at higher risk for exploitation, labor slavery, and slavery-like conditions. Women and children (particularly those unaccompanied by parents) face heightened risk of trafficking with all its dangers, including sexual abuse or violence. When victims of sex trafficking escape traffickers, they may be further stigmatized upon return to their communities of origin.

Finally, immigrant workers—particularly unauthorized migrants—are vulnerable to a variety of health concerns in transit and in destination sites.

GLOBAL COMMISSION ON INTERNATIONAL MIGRATION

Analysis and Recommendations for an International Response

Among those institutions that have recognized the opportunities, as well as challenges, in migration is the Global Commission on International Migration. The commission was established by U.N. Secretary General Kofi Annan to produce a study and concrete recommendations to the U.N. on responding to modern global migration. Issued at the end of 2005, their landmark report, the *Report of the Global Commission on International Migration* (available at www.gcim.org), is a comprehensive analysis of global migration. It offers thirty-three clear, and at times provocative, recommendations. Several of the recommendations speak of the need to consider *without delay* the creation of a new U.N. body for *migration*—i.e., neither with a mandate focused principally on refugees, as with the U.N. High Commission for Refugees, nor operating outside the U.N. system. The purpose of the new entity would be to organize better international systems and standards for labor migration. Over and above the specific recommendations, the report almost single-handedly changed the international debate on migration in three critical aspects.

First, migration could no longer be "just" a "'*dirty*' word" for governments, international engagement, and media. In its studied analysis, its scrupulous attention to real economic and social data—including the new paradigm of the mutual need of migrants for jobs and of destination countries for workers—the Global Commission succeeded at rebalancing the debate with the *positives* of migration.

Second, the report infused the international community with the ethic, and contributed to an emerging consensus, that *"migration should be by choice and not by necessity."* Working front-line everywhere with heartbroken refugees and migrants forced for survival to leave their lands, countries and often families, the Catholic Church couldn't agree more. But it is striking how widely that simple phrase has been embraced and articulated: in the halls of the U.N. in New York and Geneva, in formal statements of States of the global north and south, in policy positions of non-governmental as well as government institutions. On a subject not given to consensus, even the convergence of language of that kind gives rise to hope.

—*John K. Bingham*, Head of Policy,
International Catholic Migration Commission

Unauthorized migrants, for example, suffer a disproportionate level of work-place injuries and often face unhealthy work conditions related to contact with toxic chemicals, pesticides, and contamination. These problems go hand in hand with the dangerous and poorly regulated jobs. These same persons may also be exposed to illnesses by virtue of living in marginal areas with limited access to health care.

CONCLUSION

In 2003, the U.S. Conference of Catholic Bishops and Mexican Episcopal Conference took the unusual step of issuing a joint pastoral letter on migra-tion, reflecting the significance and considerable concern they share about migration, which transcends their national borders. In *Strangers No Longer: Together on the Journey of Hope*, the bishops wrote:

> Catholic teaching has a long and rich tradition in defending the right to migrate. Based on the life and teachings of Jesus, the Church's teaching has provided the basis for the development of basic principles regarding the right to migrate for those attempting to exercise their God-given human rights. Catholic teaching also states that the root causes of migration—poverty, injustice, religious intol-erance, and armed conflicts—must be addressed so that migrants can remain in their homeland and support their families.[26]

Additionally, in the Papal Exhortation, *Ecclesia en America (The Church in America)*, Pope John Paul II called upon the Church in the Western Hemi-sphere to re-envision itself as one Church in the Americas, and to work to-gether in solidarity for the common good, including on the issues that have led so many migrants in the region to leave their homes:

> Taking the Gospel as its starting-point, a culture of solidarity needs to be pro-moted, capable of inspiring timely initiatives in support of the poor and the out-cast, especially refugees forced to leave their villages and lands in order to flee violence. The Church in America must encourage the international agencies of the continent to establish an economic order dominated not only by the profit motive but also by the pursuit of the common good of nations and of the inter-national community, the equitable distribution of goods and the integral devel-opment of peoples.[27]

The Church's approach to migration has and will continue to include both the reduction of the need to migrate and the protection of those who have little choice but to do so. The long-term goal is equitable development for all peoples, so that migration is a choice rather than a necessity. Finally, the needs of the most vulnerable in our societies remains the overriding principle for economic and social development.

NOTES

1. United Nations, "Globalization and Interdependence: International Migration and Development," Report of the Secretary General Sixtieth Session Agenda, item 54C (May 2006).

2. Nancy Birdsall, "Global Demographic Change: Economic Impacts and Policy Challenges" (paper presented at a Symposium sponsored by the Federal Reserve Bank of Kansas City, Jackson Hole, Wyoming, Aug. 2004), 2, http://www.kansascityfed .org/PUBLICAT/SYMPOS/2004/pdf/Birdsall.Paper.0914.pdf.

3. Pontifical Council for the Pastoral Care of Migrants and Itinerant People, *Erga Migrantes Caritas Christi (The Love of Christ Towards Migrants)* 9 (2004).

4. Patrick Taran, "Human Mobility: An Imperative for Development and Welfare in the Age of Globalization" (paper presented at the V. Caritas Europa Migration Forum, Lisbon, Sept. 2007).

5. Global Commission on International Migration, *Migration in an Interconnected World: New Directions for Action* (Geneva: Report of the Global Commission on International Migration, 2005).

6. International Catholic Migration Commission, "Signs of the Times: Document in preparation for ICMC Members meeting" (July 2006).

7. Global Commission on International Migration, 14.

8. Remittances refer to the money migrants send back to their home countries, usually to support basic family living. Collectively, they often represent a significant portion of the funds entering developing economies.

9. Douglas S. Massey, Jorge Durand, and Nolan J. Malone, *Beyond Smoke and Mirrors: Mexican Immigration in an Era of Economic Integration* (New York: Russell Sage Foundation, 2002).

10. Global Commission on International Migration, 11.

11. There is no absolute consensus on the definition and parameters of neoliberalism and neoliberal economic policies. Generally speaking, they refer to economic policies that seek to limit government intervention in and power over the economy. Neoliberal policies are characterized by, among other things, free trade; the privatization of previously publicly owned enterprises; minimal governmental regulation; market-determined exchange rates; and reductions in government expenditures.

12. Pope John Paul II, *Ecclesia en America (The Church in America)* 56 (January 22, 1999).

13. *Globalization and Interdependence: International Migration and Development*, item 54 C, sec.50, 12.

14. Jose Luis Rocha, "Why Do They Go? Theories on the Migration Trend," *Revista Envio* (July 2003), 34–48.

15. Global Commission on International Migration, sec. 54.

16. Kevin O'Neil, "Using Remittances and Circular Migration to Drive Development," Migration Information Source (Washington, D.C.: Migration Policy Institute, 2003), http://www.migrationinformation.org/Feature/display.cfm?ID=133.

17. However this positive impact of increased numbers of children remaining in school tends to alter aspirations for improved livelihood options in environments where opportunities for better jobs or salaries may remain unchanged.

18. *Globalization and Interdependence: International Migration and Development*, sect. 220–23.

19. Ibid., sect. 241.

20. Manuel Orozco, "Remittances, the Rural Sector, and Policy Options in Latin America," Migration Information Source, (Washington, D.C.: Migration Policy Institute, 2003) http://www.migrationinformation.org/Feature/display.cfm?ID=133.

21. These organizations do not collectively gather individual family remittances, but rather fundraise to obtain the support needed.

22. Manual Orozco, "Mexican Hometown Associations and Development Opportunities," *Columbia Journal of International Affairs* (Spring 2004), 21.

23. World Bank, *Global Economic Prospects 2006: Economic Implications of Remittances and Migration* (Washington, D.C.: World Bank, 2006), 27.

24. International Organization for Migration, *Mainstreaming Migration into Development Policy Agendas* (IOM Migration Policy, Research, and Communications Department, IOM 2005), 115–23. The statistics are based on an IOM questionnaire to member states entitled, "Engaging diasporas as agents of development for home and host countries." Forty-two countries responded to the questionnaire.

25. According to the *UN Convention Against Transnational Organized Crime* and the *Protocol to Prevent, Suppress and Punish Trafficking in Persons, Especially Women and Children*, "Trafficking in persons (is defined as) the recruitment, transportation, transfer, harboring or receipt of persons, by means of the threat or use of force or other forms of coercion, of abduction, of fraud, of deception, of the abuse of power or of a position of vulnerability or of the giving or receiving of payments or benefits to achieve the consent of a person having control over another person, for the purpose of exploitation. Exploitation includes, at a minimum, the exploitation of the prostitution of others or other forms of sexual exploitation, forced labor or services, slavery or practices similar to slavery, servitude or the removal of organs."

26. U.S. Conference of Catholic Bishops and Conferencia del Episcopado Mexicano, *Strangers no Longer, Together on the Journey of Hope* (Washington, D.C.: U.S. Conference of Catholic Bishops, 2003), 28.

27. Pope John Paul II, *Ecclesia en America (The Church in America)* 52 (1999).

Chapter Three

But the Laborers Are . . . Many?
Catholic Social Teaching on Business,
Labor, and Economic Migration

John J. Hoeffner and Michele R. Pistone

The migration of people who leave their homelands in order to work some-place else occurs in many contexts. Often such migration is temporary; some-times, it is not. Often it is compelled by circumstances; sometimes, it is a mat-ter of free choice. In many instances, it is authorized and even encouraged by U.S. domestic law; in other instances, it is discouraged and takes place with-out legal authorization. Some forms of it are controversial; others forms en-gender little or no controversy. This chapter will provide an overview of busi-ness, labor, and economic migration, its place and purpose in today's world, and Catholic social teaching's views on it.

GLOBALIZATION AND DEVELOPMENT

Catholic social teaching's views on migration take place against a backdrop of two complex and controversial topics: globalization and development. The Church considers the topics in various senses. For example, both globaliza-tion and development are accepted as facts—as part of the "signs of the times"—that cannot be ignored by commentators upon modern social condi-tions and issues, and both are also understood as goals. In neither case, how-ever, does the "fact" that must be acknowledged correspond exactly to the goal that must be worked toward and proclaimed. Thus, for the Church, the globalization we see is only partly the globalization we seek (and is often the globalization we should not welcome). Likewise, the development we see is only partly the development we seek (and, again, is often development of an unwelcome sort).

The Church's various understandings of globalization and development constitute an essential—and long-standing[1]—background to its teaching on migration, especially to its treatment of economic-based migration.

GLOBALIZATION

Globalization is hard to define, but impossible to deny. Anyone old enough to remember even the 1980s knows that our ability to communicate, especially with people far away, and our ability to access information easily and cheaply, have increased exponentially over the last several decades. These developments, which have had such noticeable effect on the personal level, also have enabled notable changes on a larger scale, such as an increased intertwining of financial systems. Technological advances and changes in financial systems, accompanied and even propelled by massive political changes, also have produced a marked increase in the extent and reach of international trade. And all of these various changes, having in common that they appear to reduce the relevance of traditional national borders, have tended to reinforce each other and encourage further action along the same lines, such as the increasing establishment by corporations of factories, offices, and research centers beyond the borders of the corporations' traditional domiciles (a process known by the descriptive if not always literally correct term, "offshoring").

The result has been a change in mindset, such that even globalization critics like the Uruguayan writer, Eduardo Galeano, have recognized our era as one of "mandatory globalization."[2] To some—those who see the story of globalization mainly as one of welcome progress—the implications of "mandatory globalization" may seem thrilling. To others—those who view globalization's destabilizing effects as primarily negative in character—the phrase may seem chilling. Catholic social teaching endorses neither of these strong positions in their entirety. Why not?

First, to the extent that strong support or opposition to globalization is based upon and presupposes a strong preference for a particular model of political and economic organization, Catholic social teaching—by its own acknowledgment—has no special competence to judge the matter. "The Church has no models to present";[3] it does not "propose economic and political systems."[4]

Nor does looking beyond globalization's modes of organization and focusing instead on its effects offer the Church any basis for a definitive, overall conclusion about globalization. Concerning the extent of the progress that has been made in underdeveloped territories, the evidence is mixed. Certainly one should start with the understanding that, until recently, even in successful societies, most people lived at or barely above subsistence levels (in unsuccessful societies, people lived below subsistence levels, which means that they tended not to live very long).[5] Recent troubles notwithstanding, the economic progress of the last forty years is thus truly remarkable—indeed, "the rapid and accelerating growth in per capita income" experienced in developing countries in that time period is "without precedent in history."[6] In recognition of this growth, John Paul II emphasized that globalization was "not to be dismissed, since it can create unusual opportunities for greater prosperity."[7]

John Paul II also noted, however, that while "the processes which are globalizing markets and communications do not in themselves possess an ethically negative connotation," the "processes [of globalization] that, in principle, appear as factors of progress can have, and in fact already have had, ambivalent or decidedly negative consequences, especially to the detriment of the very poor."[8] The late pope's reference to "ambivalent or decidedly negative consequences" is well taken, for there are many to choose from. Consider, for example, the fate of the very poorest countries in the age of globalization. Even in the face of strong overall growth in developing countries, the poorest countries in the world, with a combined population of over one billion, have had essentially no growth since 1970;[9] indeed, in many of these places conditions continue to worsen.

Moreover, the "ambivalent or decidedly negative consequences" of globalization are not limited to the most troubled countries. Examples of this kind include the following:

- The globalization of agriculture has had a negative impact upon small farmers in many developing countries, as these farmers find it difficult to compete with large agricultural corporations who enjoy massive advantages of scale as well as the newest technologies. The small farmers' difficulties are compounded by the extensive availability of agricultural subsidies in the developed world; over $300 billion a year in such payments are currently made to farmers in Europe, Japan, and the United States.[10] In many developing countries, the difficulties of small farmers constitute a large societal problem, because small farmers constitute a sizable portion of the national labor force.
- The economic growth facilitated by globalization has resulted in an intensification of the global search for natural resources of all kinds. The results can benefit national economies; however, it can devastate local ones. Mining operations, for example, not only can upset traditional economic arrangements, in some cases they can obliterate them due, among other

things, to the environmental damage they can cause. On the Guajira penin-
sula of Colombia, for example, the world's largest open-pit coal mine—30
miles in length and 5 miles wide, with its own 90-mile-long railroad to the
sea—has devastated the local economy and disrupted the social fabric of
indigenous tribes and others. Often in concert with the Colombian government, the consortium of European companies that own the coal mine
have polluted and closed off traditional hunting and fishing grounds,
blocked access to roads, bulldozed some villages and otherwise forced removal of residents in others, confiscated productive farmland to make
room for mine operations, and reduced the air quality due to the sometimes
visible coal dust.[11]

• The mobility of capital is a defining feature of globalization, but the same
restlessness in the pursuit of ever-greater productivity that can motivate
capital to enter a country also can cause it to flee elsewhere. The risk is the
creation of a "race to the bottom," as capital uses its mobility as leverage to
demand ever more advantageous conditions concerning labor standards,
taxation, environmental regulation, and the like. To the extent that this risk
materializes, globalization's promise to raise global living standards is un-
dermined. Moreover, at the same time, globalization's inherently destabilizing effects are extended and reinforced, as multinational employers
move in and move out, remaking labor markets both as they come and as
they go. In addition, underscoring both the leverage of multinational corporations and the damage that their departure can do is the unfortunate fact
that once traditional economic arrangements are dismantled they, like
Humpty Dumpty, are not easily put back together again.

The common element in these examples is the disruption of local labor
markets. One of the consequences of such disruption is migration, as workers
move to where jobs can be found. In developing countries, the flow of internal migrants is predominantly from rural areas to large cities; internationally,
the flow is largely to developed countries. The lure of paid work is the *sine
qua non* of most of this migration, of course, with the extent and direction of
the movement a function not only of disparities in economic development but
also of the mirror-image demographics of developed and underdeveloped nations. (In short, while "virtually all of the world's population growth is taking
place in developing countries," the so-called birth dearth in developed countries "threatens their ability to sustain current levels of economic growth and
to maintain their existing pensions and social security systems," i.e., developed countries need workers born elsewhere.)[12] The current demographic pattern (which is expected to endure for at least several more generations) suggests that the globalization of labor—its movement from the underdeveloped

to the developed world—is, economically at least, a mutually beneficial arrangement. However, while relatively positive consequences can flow from this movement, further decidedly negative ones do as well. For example:

(1) Because paths of legal immigration are limited, despite the economic and demographic need, migrants seeking work often must proceed without official travel authorization. Several consequences result, the first being that their migration journeys to and across borders often expose them to great danger. With the usual travel routes closed to them, undocumented travelers seek out persons engaged in the business of human smuggling. The animal names used to refer to such smugglers—snakeheads and coyotes—fairly suggest the danger of the environment undocumented migrants must enter. Indeed, thousands of people die each year attempting clandestine border crossings, including several hundred per year at the U.S.-Mexico border, while others are robbed, assaulted, or severely injured.[13]

(2) Beyond the risks of death, crime, and serious injury, undocumented migrants also suffer from numerous forms of exploitation. One of the worst forms is trafficking, in which persons are enticed to migrate by lavish promises, only to find themselves upon arrival in situations of forced or bonded labor or sexual servitude. Approximately 800,000 people per year are trafficked across international borders. The U.S. Department of State has attributed at least part of the recent expansion of the trafficking problem to "[t]he globalization of markets and labor forces, and the concomitant relaxation of travel barriers."[14]

(3) Even migrants who are not trafficked are subject to exploitation after they arrive at their destination. Undocumented immigrants of every nationality, for example, often fall prey to fraudulent legalization schemes promulgated by unscrupulous persons who hold themselves out as legal specialists, perhaps even as lawyers. These operators, known as "notarios" in Spanish-speaking communities, charge clients thousands of dollars for non-existent or hopelessly futile services, such as filing legalization claims pursuant to legislative proposals that have not been enacted. Notarios are also notorious for losing difficult or impossible to duplicate paperwork essential to filing legitimate claims.

(4) In another example of post-arrival exploitation, in law as well as in fact, undocumented migrant workers are subject to lower labor and employment standards and have fewer health and wage protections than other workers. The disproportionate concentration of undocumented workers in dirty and dangerous jobs compounds the difficulties—not to say the injustices—that these lower standards can create, even as those difficulties are perpetuated by undocumented workers' restricted ability to challenge the circumstances of their employment through organization or through the judicial system.

(5) In addition, migrations that avoid the worst forms of exploitation (and even those that might otherwise be regarded as "successful") are not lacking in negative consequences. For instance, migrations of every kind tear persons away from the comforts of a familiar culture and separate husbands from wives and parents from their children, while substantial migrations additionally can split and even decimate communities. To the extent that globalization necessitates and facilitates migration, these decidedly negative consequences are appropriately attributed to it.

(6) Finally, while undocumented immigration by relatively unskilled workers is one characteristic of migration in the current age of globalization, another is the largely legal immigration of skilled workers. There is no question that individual members of this second, significantly smaller but very important group of migrants, for the most part avoid the worst hardships faced by undocumented migrants. And there also is very widespread agreement that skilled migration economically benefits receiving countries, as it also delivers many benefits to skilled migrants themselves.[15] Sending countries, however, and the people left behind in them, may sometimes suffer—at least in the short term—when a substantial number of their population's most skilled workers depart. This is particularly true of poor countries and their inhabitants, as poor countries are more likely than rich ones to lack qualified substitute workers.

Given all this, and given that there is no compelling reason to believe as of yet that the "decidedly negative consequences" of globalization are mere growing pains—perhaps they are more the proverbial canary in the coal mine—there is ample cause to be wary of globalization's effects, even as benefits of globalization are recognized. Accordingly, as to the "fact" of globalization, as to the globalization *that is*, Catholic social teaching is appropriately neither an enemy nor a cheerleader of the phenomenon taken as a whole.[16]

And yet there is a sense in which the Church is and must be the foremost advocate of globalization. It believes, after all, in a universal natural law, and it declares itself a universal church to whom no person is a stranger. It has been charged by its founder with a universal evangelizing mission—to go and make disciples of all the nations (Mt 28:19). It recognizes that the communications revolution that is part of the globalization *that is* provides an unsurpassed opportunity to fulfill its worldwide evangelizing mission (thus, to take best advantage of this revolution, the Vatican engaged in a sustained and difficult effort to win its own internet ".va" suffix, rather than the Italian ".it" that it was initially assigned). It recognizes the rewards of other cultures and the benefits of exposure to them, and thus values the increased exposure to other peoples that globalization necessitates and its tools facilitate. It proclaims the uniqueness and immeasurable worth of every human life, and sees in the economic productivity potential of globalization an opportunity to lessen the material deprivations that tragically shorten many lives, as well as offend the dignity of many more. In sum, rightly understood, the Church *is* a cheerleader for globalization, but a globalization of a very particular sort. Exactly what that globalization, rightly understood, entails and requires demands a more extensive examination into the subject of development.

DEVELOPMENT

As St. Paul suggested (1 Cor. 12:13), and modern cognitive science confirms, we all see the world imperfectly, through conceptual frameworks, which influence and limit our perceptions.[17] One of the joys—and discomforts—of Catholic social teaching is that it does not conform to established partisan frameworks of which we are all familiar and to which many of us tend to adhere. (Limiting ourselves only to life and health issues, would any political party be comfortable endorsing the Church's positions on war *and* assisted suicide, abortion *and* the death penalty, and health care *and* stem cell medical research?) Rather than subscribe to any purely partisan view, Catholic social teaching aims to provide "a broader horizon" that inspires and benefits the world as people apply it to their lives and work.[18]

On the topic of development, for persons in the developed world the key (perhaps discomforting) insight of Catholic social teaching is that one must not think of development merely as something that must happen "out there," in the nether regions of China or India, or in poor nations one hears about only when natural disasters or man-made brutalities turn particularly costly. To think about development only in this way—even when accompanied by wishes and sympathies for, and the occasional donation to, the less fortunate—is to have a diminished understanding of what it means to be human, and leads as inevitably to distortions in developed countries as it does to hardships in underdeveloped ones.

Sollicitudo Rei Socialis (*On Social Concern*), a 1987 encyclical by John Paul II, is the primary teaching document on "the development of individuals and peoples,"[19] along with *Populorum Progressio* (*On the Development of Peoples*), a 1967 encyclical by Paul VI. *Sollicitudo Rei Socialis* (which was intended to commemorate and update *Populorum Progressio*) does not offer—in fact, it states that the Church does not have—technical solutions "for the problem of underdevelopment."[20] Following *Populorum Progressio*,

Sollicitudo Rei Socialis does offer, however, two conceptions regarding development that tend to expand the frame through which the issue is typically viewed.

First, John Paul II repeatedly insists that underdevelopment is not only or even mainly an economic reality; there is "cultural, political and simply human" underdevelopment as well.[21] Indeed, John Paul II suggests, "a too narrow idea of development, that is, a mainly economic one," bears some responsibility for "the sad reality of today."[22]

The second conception follows from the first. John Paul II seeks to give "'development' its fullest meaning,"[23] but if "authentic development" (John Paul II uses "authentic" as well as "true," "genuine," and "integral" to distinguish his idea of development from the narrower economic view) requires more than mere economic advancement, then it also subjectively must be a worldwide concern, extending even to the most economically secure persons and nations, for their development in the full sense of the word can be misshapen or incomplete as well. John Paul II's conceptual broadening of development thus implies a spatial or geographic broadening as well. John Paul II aptly summarizes his more expansive conception of development by quoting Paul VI's memorable call for "development of the whole human being and of all people."[24]

By conceiving of authentic development as a goal and as a necessity for all persons, John Paul II places a premium on the content of the conception. *Sollicitudo Rei Socialis* provides some indicators of authentic development. Among other things, authentic development demands religious freedom, the right to life, justice in employment relationships, the freedom to organize and to form unions, the right to free and responsible political participation, the right to economic initiative, the rule of law, and a basic education, as well as fairness in trade relationships.[25] It also demands "a lively awareness of the value of the rights of all and of each person,"[26] including the value of those persons " — the many who have little or nothing — who do not succeed in realizing their basic human vocation because they are deprived of essential goods."[27]

By some of these criteria, the globalization *that is* has made advances toward authentic development, but the advances have been intermittent and incomplete and, as we saw earlier, there have been losses and reversals, too. *Sollicitudo Rei Socialis* explains that an indicator of the human and moral development of well-off persons in the developed countries and elsewhere is to recognize this reality, and to try to do something about it — not merely because that reality reveals economic hardships for "them," but also because it reveals a moral challenge for those never deprived of essential goods. Referring to children brought up in refugee camps, Pope Benedict XVI recently asked, "How can we not think that these little beings have come into the world with the same legitimate expectations of happiness as the others?"[28] Indeed—*how* can we not think it, of these children and others in similarly distressing circumstances? Is it not piercing to treat the question not merely as a rhetorical flourish, but rather as an accusation demanding an answer? Authentic development in the—dare we still use the word?—developed countries demands a globalization that has such questions at its start and at its center, and then makes its aim the development of those "who have little or nothing." The globalization *that is* proceeds largely on a different basis, one that at best assumes such development as an incidental, one might even say as an accidental, benefit. The problem is, as Thoreau wrote, that "[i]n the long run, men hit only what they aim at."[29] Catholic social teaching agrees that the globalization it seeks will not happen by accident, but only upon a conscious awakening of "solidarity, based upon the principle that the goods of creation are meant for all."[30]

To some, a world that places the energy, the tools, and the effects of globalization in the conscious service of a global solidarity that has as its aim the authentic development of all may seem an unrealizable goal. Perhaps, although we note that John Paul II cautioned against pessimism of this sort.[31] In all events, however, that goal will become less of a dream and more of a reality as the developed world comes to view the lack of economic development in other parts of the world not merely as an economic problem, but also as a test of, or a proving ground for, its own authentic development. That goal will become less of a dream and more of a reality as the communications advances characteristic of globalization come to assume importance in developed (and underdeveloped) countries not merely because they entertain and connect us to those we know, but also because the same advances provide the developed world with better knowledge of material deprivations elsewhere, and thus provide an enhanced opportunity for the human development of the fortunate and unfortunate alike.[32] And that goal will become more of a reality as the economic prosperity that developed economies have achieved in this age of globalization comes to assume importance in developed countries not mainly because of the material comforts it can deliver at home, but because of the unremitting hardships it can elsewhere relieve. A globalization permeated by attitudes such as these is the globalization that Catholic social teaching has urged and a globalization that it could endorse. And, to be sure, this vision of globalization in pursuit of authentic development has implications for Catholic social teaching's views of the migration issues that will be the direct focus of the remainder of this chapter.

PATHS TO IMMIGRATION IN A GLOBALIZED WORLD

Immigration is both a cause and effect of globalization, as it is with development—or its lack—as well. Because different types of immigration raise different moral questions, and because they have different relationships to globalization and development, it will be helpful to outline the many types of immigration there are, and how American law characterizes them.

Permanent Legal Immigration

Other than being born a citizen, there are four broad paths to permanent legal status in the United States. Each of the paths starts with the grant of lawful permanent resident (LPR) status. At the immigrant's choice, after a waiting period of five years (less in some cases), LPR status can lead to naturalized citizenship, assuming no disqualifying acts have occurred in the interim (such as the commission of a crime) and no irregularities have been uncovered in the original application for LPR status or in the petition for citizenship.

The first of the four broad paths to LPR status requires a showing of certain specified family relationships and is based on the principle of family reunification. The second path requires either a general or a specific showing of employability and is based largely on grounds of enhancing economic productivity. The third path requires establishing that one is a refugee entitled to asylum protection or refugee resettlement. This path is based on humanitarian grounds. Finally, the fourth path allows individuals from certain countries with relatively low levels of immigration to the United States to apply for permanent residency through what is essentially a lottery. Diversity is the justification for this final path. Combined, slightly more than one million people take advantage of these paths each year. For the U.S. government fiscal years 2005–2007, family sponsorships accounted for 62 percent of the successful applications, employment-based preferences accounted for about 17 percent (this figure includes spouses of workers as well as dependent children), recognition of refugee or asylee status accounted for an average of 14 percent, and the diversity lottery accounted for about 4 percent.[33]

Although the admission of immigrants or refugees for family reunification, humanitarian, or diversity purposes is not justified on economic grounds, and employment is not the primary expressed objective for any of these three migration paths, migrants of sufficient age who fall within these three categories are entitled to work legally upon or soon after their arrival or grant of legal status. With regard to work, however, there are two notable differences among these groups.

The first difference arises before the application for permanent residence is granted, and concerns the immigrant's present capacity for employment. In short, refugees, asylees, and family-sponsored applicants do not need to prove their employability, while diversity immigrants must show that they possess a high school diploma (or its equivalent) or specified work experience. There is less to this difference than initially appears, however, for many refugees, asylees, and family-sponsored applicants come to the United States with significant education, skills, and work experience.

The second difference arises after permanent status has been granted. Refugees and asylees are eligible to receive federally funded financial support for eight months, while members of the other groups typically are not. Indeed, should family-sponsored immigrants require public assistance before either working for ten years or becoming a U.S. citizen, the government is empowered to recoup the cost of any welfare payments from the sponsoring family member.[34]

Family-sponsored and diversity immigrants, as well as asylees and refugees, thus not only affect the economy generally, they also often directly affect the labor market. So, of course, do employment-based permanent immigrants—indeed, that is the main and expressly articulated point of their admission. The availability of employment-based permanent visas decidedly favors highly educated persons, especially those with a demonstrated record of "exceptional" or "outstanding" ability (one type of visa of this kind requires a documented showing of "extraordinary ability"). High-level corporate executives, academics, scientists, artists, writers, engineers, and members of other professions—dubbed "superstars" and "stars" by one prominent immigration scholar[35]—accordingly are allocated slightly more than half of the available employment-based permanent visas. Except for visas reserved for persons of "extraordinary ability," all of these visas require an existing job offer from a U.S. employer—in fact, the employer is technically the applicant—and some require a certification from the Secretary of Labor that American workers will neither be displaced nor have their wages adversely affected by the proposed immigrant hire.

Another 28.6 percent of allocated employment-based permanent visas are reserved mainly for professionals and skilled workers of less notable accomplishment, and one-quarter of this 28.6 percent (approximately 10,000) can go to relatively unskilled workers. This is the only category of employment visa that consistently sees applications well above its allocated amount, which is approximately 40,000 per year. This category also requires an existing job offer and a certification by the Secretary of Labor; substantial processing delays are ameliorated to some extent by the Secretary's blanket certification of labor shortages in some professions, such as nursing and physical therapy.

The remainder of the allocated employment-based permanent visas are divided among certain types of "special immigrants," such as ministers, religious workers, and persons who work or worked for the U.S. government abroad, and "investors" who create companies and jobs in the United States. The allocation for investors is severely underused, and has been since it was first authorized in 1990.[36]

Temporary Legal Immigration

Let's begin here with a brief word on terminology. In the subsection immediately above, we referred to permanent immigrants as . . . "permanent immigrants." It may surprise you to learn that U.S. lawyers use the same common sense terminology (though they are equally likely to speak of "permanent residents" or of people with "lawful permanent resident" or "LPR" status). With temporary immigrants, however, lawyers (we are two of them, so we know whereof we speak!) revert to form and speak of "temporary nonimmigrants" instead. There are technical reasons for this (there always are), stemming from peccadilloes in the statutory and regulatory law, as well as the desire to efficiently distinguish permanent immigrants from all other non-citizens, including short-term visitors for whom the word "immigrant" is manifestly unsuited, such as vacationers. But given the apparent contrariness of the common and the legal terms, the unfortunate result is that the technical legal term is likely to appear confusing if not nonsensical to the non-lawyer. We seek to avoid this confusion, and offer this solution. We will utilize "temporary immigrants" as a broad term encompassing everyone that the lawyers refer to as "nonimmigrants," except that we will exclude from our definition travelers for pleasure.[37]

So defined, temporary immigration illustrates in a nutshell the dynamism and the scope of the globalization *that is*. Thus, globalization is characterized by the proliferation of multi-national corporations—the purpose of the L visa is to authorize immigration by executives of multi-national corporations who have received an intra-company transfer into the United States. Globalization is characterized by trade and the transfer of capital across borders—the B-1 visa allows business executives to travel to the United States for negotiations with American companies and others, and the E visa is expressly intended to allow immigrants to oversee U.S. business investments and to conduct "substantial trade." Globalization places a premium on having world-class talent— the O visa authorizes entry of people with "extraordinary ability" in a broad variety of fields, as well as their assistants. Globalization has highlighted the importance of science and technology—the H-1B visa, famously supported by high-tech Silicon Valley executives and one of the few temporary visas that are numerically restricted, provides for the entry of college graduates in "specialty occupations," defined as occupations requiring the "theoretical and practical application of a body of highly specialized knowledge." More generally, globalization also has highlighted the importance of education— F-1 visas are used by persons seeking full-time undergraduate or graduate study, while M-1 visas are for persons seeking to enroll in vocational schools.

Globalization also stresses and demands cross-cultural understanding— Q visas are expressly designed to facilitate cultural exchange programs "providing practical training, employment, and the sharing of the history, culture, and traditions of the country of the [immigrant's] nationality." P-2 visas similarly foster cultural exchange, by allowing the entry of artists and entertainers engaged in reciprocal exchange programs, while P-3 and R visas specifically authorize the entry of "culturally unique" artists and entertainers to teach or perform, and the entry of members of religious groups. Combining science, education, and culture, as well as childcare, the J-1 visa authorizes the entry of professors, researchers, students, and au pairs.

The U.S. immigration system, through a combination of deliberate intent and historical coincidence, reflects the reality and the needs of our globalized world in other ways as well. Has the communications revolution accompanying globalization enabled a globalization of news and entertainment? The I visa is reserved for foreign journalists, and the P-1 visa is for athletes and entertainers. Does globalization increase the importance of quasi-governmental organizations able to develop and enforce common legal standards across international borders? The G visa was introduced for the officers and employees of such organizations, e.g., the United Nations, the World Trade Organization, and the International Monetary Fund. Have fears of a globalization of crime, including international terrorism, heightened in recent years? The S-5 and S-6 visas, established as a part of a temporary pilot program designed to encourage the testimony of persons with critical information regarding criminal or terrorist organizations, were revived and made permanent less than three weeks after they expired on September 13, 2001. And recall this chapter's earlier citation to the U.S. State Department's noting of the connection between globalization and the expansion of human trafficking—the government responded to concerns about increased trafficking by establishing in 2000 the T visa, which can be provided to trafficking victims who agree to assist in the prosecution of their traffickers.

Many of these temporary visas, including the E, H-1B, L, S-5, S-6, and T (and sometimes the J-1), are valued and sought not only because of the temporary privileges that they grant, but also because they can lead directly to permanent status. Indeed, in recent years, a majority of immigrants acquiring permanent status were already within the United States on temporary visas, at the time that they had their status adjusted.[38]

Most temporary visa categories generate little controversy. Exceptions to this rule exist, however, including the H-1B visa and the various visas for foreign students, and two temporary worker visas not discussed above—the H-2A visa for seasonal farm-workers, and the H-1C visa for nurses. The H-1B and H-1C debates—of which there have been many—repeatedly find one side (often U.S.-based labor organizations) arguing that the availability of a particular visa drives down American wages and costs American citizens jobs. Meanwhile, the other side (mainly businesses and business groups) argues that there is a labor shortage in a particular field and that dire consequences (damage to U.S. economic competitiveness and technological innovation or a deterioration in healthcare) will result if the visa is not retained or even expanded.

Other interests assert themselves as well, and they illustrate the range of issues raised even by temporary immigration. For example, the foreign student visa debate has featured an economic competitiveness versus national security dynamic, with the latter interest raised in the H-1B debate as well.[39] The H-1C issue additionally is controversial because of a concern that the immigration of healthcare workers can devastate healthcare in the developing world. Finally, regarding the H-2A farm-worker visa, a visa that has no numerical limitation but is relatively unused, the debate features charges by employers that the visa is impractical and that the bureaucracy administers it inflexibly, while labor groups contend that the visa leads to worker abuse and exploitation, as well as to harm to American workers. According to its participants, the H-2A debate also proves either that the United States needs undocumented workers to keep food from rotting on the vine (as there is no other practical way to find the needed workers), or it proves that the United States doesn't really need undocumented workers at all (because the relative disuse of the *unlimited* H-2A program simply shows that the employing farmers' main concern is not a fear of an unavailability of workers, but an aversion to paying the higher wages and benefits mandated by the H-2A program, which sets wages that are high enough so as not to undercut native labor).

Undocumented Immigrants

For immigrants in the United States and many other countries, regularization of status, especially the grant of permanent status, constitutes a powerful legal incentive to migration. Conversely, the prospect of irregular status—with its attendant string of legal sanctions and disabilities (for example, the threat of deportation, ineligibility for many government programs, limited employment options and labor rights, and greatly circumscribed political rights)—is a powerful legal disincentive. But as the legal incentives do not always compel migration, so too the legal disincentives do not always deter it.

Other forces are at play as well. Migration researchers find that the flow of international migrants is maintained largely by the lure of work, which is reinforced and augmented by demographic pressures and the desire to escape repressive regimes.[40] Because researchers do not expect these forces to moderate any time soon, they do not see migration in general moderating, either.

To the extent that U.S. immigration law is designed to attract talented and educated persons from around the world—and, as we have seen, to a significant extent, it is—the expected persistence of the general trend toward migration should provide many benefits to the United States. However, the expected persistence of the trend also highlights a considerable problem for U.S. immigration policy. In particular, a discrepancy exists between the strength of the forces propelling migrants into the United States and the ability of the current law to recognize in some official way the reality of their presence. Hence, the problem of the undocumented immigrant.

Recent efforts to reduce this discrepancy have proceeded on two separate and very different tracks. The first track, exemplified by the Kennedy-McCain bill that was defeated in the Senate in 2006,[41] would in a sense legalize the reality, by providing many undocumented immigrants a path to legalization and perhaps citizenship, through the payment of fines and adherence to other requirements. The second track, by contrast, seeks to roll back the reality, by continuing a several-decade emphasis on ever-increasing border enforcement efforts, additionally combined with a new focus on what has been termed an "attrition" strategy. The attrition strategy, which has seen a number of local legislative successes but some judicial defeats, expressly aims at making life unbearable for undocumented migrants. Its preferred methods for doing so include the introduction of locally implemented steep fines and license suspensions for hiring undocumented immigrants or for renting housing to them.

The reality that the first track seeks to recognize and the second track seeks to reverse is a considerable one. Undocumented migrants are estimated to constitute approximately four percent of the total U.S. population, or more than 11 million people. Until the economic recession beginning in 2007, this population was increasing by about 500,000 annually in the United States.[42]

THE U.S. IMMIGRATION SYSTEM IN LIGHT OF CATHOLIC SOCIAL TEACHING

Does the immigration system outlined in the previous section work toward the globalization sought by Catholic social teaching? Does it facilitate a culture of solidarity and authentic development? Addressing the system as a whole, the answer is mixed. This answer is somewhat misleading, however, in the same way that it is misleading for a man standing with his head in an oven and his feet in a bucket of ice water to say that, overall, the temperature is quite comfortable, thank you. Our mixed overall appraisal similarly hides wide discrepancies. In the discussion that follows, we shall see that Catholic social teaching views U.S. immigration law as deeply problematic in some ways and quite unobjectionable, if not imitable, in others.

The previous section noted many different categories of immigration. For purposes of measuring these categories against the demands of Catholic social teaching, we propose to place the categories into the following framework, which is of our own device but has ample if implicit support in the teaching. In particular, we will look at immigration—as Catholic social teaching does—from three temporal perspectives: (1) the (unacceptable) present; (2) the near-to-middle-term future; and (3) the long term. All types of migration may be viewed from every one of these perspectives, of course, but for any one type of migration, one perspective or the other usually stands out as the most important one to consider for that particular type of migration. In all events, as we shall see, one's emphasis of a particular temporal perspective for a particular type of migration influences but does not necessarily determine one's assessment of that migration.

Undocumented Immigration: Facing the Unacceptable Present

There are many ways to approach the topic of Catholic social teaching's views on undocumented migration. With great legitimacy, one could claim human dignity as the essential starting point for the discussion, or human dignity and the common good (or the universal common good) together. One could begin with the preferential option for the poor or the universal destination of goods, or both. Each of these characteristic principles of Catholic social teaching can be applied to migration issues, and each can yield rich insights.

Because this chapter is uniquely focused on economic migration, however, we thought we might take another tack; namely, we begin by considering Catholic social teaching's outlook on work. As the privileged expression of human dignity, work has "a special place in Catholic social thought."[43] In fact, said John Paul II, "work is a key, probably the essential key, to the whole social question."[44] In Catholic social thought, work is not regarded solely as an instrument of production, but rather has the three-fold value of being a way to "[achieve] fulfillment as a human being," a way to provide "a foundation for the formation of family life" ("since the family requires the means of subsistence . . . normally gain[ed] through work"), and a way to contribute to the common good.[45] For these reasons, "[i]t is the ethical responsibility of an organized society to promote and support a culture of work."[46]

When work is unavailable, or insufficiently satisfies the purposes of work, authentic development is jeopardized. Catholic social teaching takes it for granted that serious material deprivation places a person in such jeopardy, for it takes the very realistic view that access to a certain level of material goods is necessary not only to support oneself and one's family, but also is "absolutely indispensable" to "attain the highest purposes to which [one] is called,"[47] including the purpose of contributing to the common good.

A broad conception of the migratory right flows from these conclusions. John Paul II summarized that conception by stating that a person "has the right to leave his native land for various motives—and also the right to return—in order to seek better conditions of life in another country."[48] The logic of Catholic social teaching plainly demands that this right be extended above all to the world's poor (as well as to asylum seekers), for as a rule it is they who will possess the greatest and most urgent need for "better conditions."

Is this migration—"the migration of the desperate,"[49] in John Paul II's memorable phrase—unlimited in its moral claim? The answer is no; Catholic social teaching recognizes the right of a state to regulate migration in furtherance of the common good of the receiving community. This sovereign right is itself circumscribed, however, in several respects. Generally, immigration cannot be impeded for narrow or insubstantial reasons; rather, only "grave requirements of the common good, considered objectively," can justify impeding the right to migration.[50] More specifically, the grave requirements standard is not met when immigration is restricted "merely for the purpose of acquiring additional wealth;"[51] in fact, at least for highly economically developed countries, even the protection of one's current level of prosperity cannot be the sole basis for excluding needy migrants.[52]

Given the Catholic conception of the importance of work for authentic development, and the widespread acknowledgment that undocumented workers are driven to migrate by their desire to, and material need for, work, meeting the standard for exclusion set by Catholic social teaching is no easy task for persons in the developed world. Indeed, the task seems insurmountable if one focuses on the immediate and unacceptable present, in which billions of people are left to languish with severely diminished, if not non-existent, hopes of developing their human potential.[53] And, with respect to undocumented migrants, this *is* the focus of Catholic social teaching. Hence, the repeated efforts in the teaching to heighten the immediacy of our unacceptable present, by noting the great stakes *on every side* that a decision to exclude entails: "How can the baptized claim to welcome Christ if they close the door to the foreigner who comes knocking?" asked John Paul II in one of his annual migration messages.[54] The undocumented immigrant, he stated in another, is "like that stranger in whom Jesus asked to be recognized. To welcome him and to show him solidarity is a duty of hospitality and fidelity to Christian identity itself."[55] Reiterating the point again, a third message states that

> Jesus' demanding assertion: "I was a stranger and you welcomed me" . . . retains its power in all circumstances and challenges the conscience of those who intend to follow in his footsteps. . . . [I]n every human being [the believer] knows he is meeting Christ, who expects to be loved and served in our brothers and sisters, especially in the poorest and neediest.[56]

Many more citations could be made to the same effect. In all of them, the unmistakable point is that by refusing to aid in the development of those trying "to escape from a life with no future,"[57] who even beyond the limits "imposed by law"[58] legitimately "expect our help in fulfilling their human potential,"[59] we not only guarantee others' lack of authentic development, we concomitantly reveal distortions in our own development.

Even more disturbingly revelatory, from the perspective of Catholic social teaching, is the recent popularity of "attrition" legislation expressly designed to make life unbearable for undocumented immigrants. Catholic leaders have criticized such legislation in unusually sharp language. Edward J. Slattery, the Bishop of Tulsa, for example, condemned one such law—Oklahoma's House Bill 1804—as creating "an atmosphere of repression and terror."[60] From the perspective of the unacceptable present, it is easy to see why House Bill 1804—which, among other obstacles to assistance and welcome, made it a felony to knowingly shelter or transport undocumented migrants and set up barriers to hiring them—was the target of such highly charged criticism. A staple of Catholic social thought is to emphasize the necessity for seeing and not ignoring the poor; the Gospel parable of the rich man who failed to note the beggar Lazarus at his gate is commonly cited to illustrate the point.[61] At its worst, attrition legislation would by force of law command the conduct that the parable forbids while, at its best, the legislation would merely encourage the forbidden behavior. It would do this, moreover, in an attempt to discourage a population that overwhelmingly consists not of beggars, but of laborers, able, eager, and willing to work in pursuit of their own human development.

How far this treatment is from Catholic social teaching, which demands not only engagement with the poor immigrant and an attempt to help him, but also nondiscrimination, so that the immigrant is not "placed at a disadvantage in comparison with the other workers . . . in the matter of working rights."[62]

How different is this punitive approach, which seeks to make the undocumented immigrant an untouchable in various ways, to the U.S. Bishops' support for providing undocumented immigrants a pathway to full political and social participation, activities necessary for authentic development. And this fierce determination to drive the migrant away by depriving him of work and housing—how removed it is from the Church's commitment to stand in solidarity with those "without rights, without any security," who "are unable to find a stable home anywhere."[63] We said earlier that Catholic social teaching finds itself in opposition to some aspects of U.S. immigration law and in agreement with some others; nowhere is the gap between the two viewpoints any greater than it is with undocumented migration. And as attrition legislation proliferates, the gap continues to widen.

What can justify such treatment and such legislation? Proponents of attrition legislation typically state that they are not opposed to immigrants, they are opposed only to illegal immigrants. In an effort to demonstrate the strength and legitimacy of this rationale, proponents sometimes add a statement along the lines of "it does not matter if we are talking about farm workers from Mexico or wealthy English Lords: illegal is illegal." The effect is thus to dismiss distinctions that, according to Catholic social teaching, should make all the difference. The argument calls to mind Anatole France's famous statement mocking "the majestic egalitarianism of the law, which forbids rich and poor alike to sleep under bridges, to beg in the streets, and to steal bread." Catholic social teaching says it matters that undocumented workers come not in search of a respite from the duties of the manor, but in search of work they otherwise cannot find, in order to overcome the material deprivations that otherwise would thwart their human potential.[64] The majestic egalitarianism of "illegal is illegal" treats these realities as irrelevant.

The discounting of the unacceptable present is in the service of a different concern—maintaining the primacy of the rule of law—and stresses a different time horizon. The fear is the development over time of a culture of disrespect for the law. Such a development would indeed have serious and unwelcome consequences, which should not be understated.[65] It is by no means clear, however, that failures of compliance threaten the law more than the law's failure to come to terms with the consequences of the global jobs crisis. To the extent that the era of Prohibition saw the law fall into disrepute, for example, the judgment of history is that the root problem lay more in the Eighteenth Amendment itself than with the speakeasies and bootleggers who evaded it. In all events, the commercial imperatives of many businesses that employ large numbers of undocumented immigrants—landscaping, housekeeping, and various forms of caretaking, for example, among others that require a nontrivial level of intimacy and trust—are entirely inconsistent with the development of a community reputation for law-breaking. This fact alone suggests that, if the law generally should fall into disrepute, the source of the trouble will not be traced to communities dominated by those workers.

Indeed, the clear position of the American Catholic Church is that it is the immigration status quo itself that breeds disrespect for the law and risks bringing it into disrepute.[66] The Church's position is based not only on a recognition of the untenable discrepancy between the law as it is and the strength of the forces that drive migration, but also on the recognition that—at least to some extent and in some instances—the realities that drive poor persons to migrate stem from the economic globalization that the United States and other developed nations have created and shaped to their benefit. Given this latter ground, the Church's advocacy for a legislative solution that would regularize the status of most undocumented immigrants is accordingly justifiable as a matter of restorative as well as distributive justice. These justified concerns and the legitimacy of undocumented migrants' yearning for authentic development lend great support to the Church's position that such regularization would best assure continued respect for the general rule of law, by making the specific law of immigration more worthy of respect.

Skilled and Educated Migrants: Toward Authentic Development Everywhere and a Future of Equals

While a gross mismatch exists between the U.S. immigration law and the supply of, and demand for, unskilled and lesser-skilled workers, the alphabet soup of visas noted in the previous section suggests the U.S. legal system does a much better, if not a perfect, job of accommodating market realities with regard to the immigration of skilled and educated workers. In its analysis of this migration, compared to its treatment of undocumented migration, Catholic social teaching focuses less on the circumstances of the immediate situation and more on future consequences.

Migration by skilled and educated persons to the United States for the purposes of work occurs in four contexts: (1) temporary migration from another developed country; (2) temporary migration from a developing country; (3) permanent migration from another developed country; and (4) permanent migration from a developing country. As for the first three groupings, Catholic social teaching is generally uncritical and in some respects favorable. In these cases, relevant Church documents tend to reflect mostly pastoral concerns, such as how to minister effectively to migrants and how to meet migrants' spiritual, cultural, and social needs.[67] The fourth context, regarding permanent migration from a developing country to a developed country, is another matter, one that is viewed with a much more critical eye. We begin with the relatively positive assessments.

Temporary migration of all kinds possesses the following advantages. First, as does all migration, it increases cultural awareness and fosters cultural exchange. Especially from developing to developed countries, temporary migration also helps the country of origin after the skilled migrant's emigration ends, as the migrant returns with new skills, new contacts, and new ways of doing and seeing things. Indeed, some new ideas can be transmitted even during the period of temporary migration, as can other benefits, such as remittances. The migrant's work can also be personally fulfilling. Catholic social teaching recognizes all of these advantages. Catholic social teaching also recognizes—and Pope Benedict XVI in particular has stressed—the special case of students who temporarily migrate in pursuit of higher education. Such student migration, Pope Benedict XVI has said, presents "a unique opportunity [for the students] to contribute to the development of their own countries"[68] and to "be enriched in their contact with other students of different cultures and religions."[69]

Compared to temporary migration, permanent migration by skilled and educated persons raises questions of a more troublesome sort. While some of the benefits of temporary migration extend to permanent migration (e.g., cultural exchange and heightened cultural awareness), permanent migration raises the fear for Catholic social teaching that a migrant thus cut off from his homeland will never be able to fulfill his duty to contribute to it.[70] (Poor migrants have the same duty, but the duty does not stand as a substantial barrier to migration when migration is necessary to fulfill the even more fundamental duty to support oneself and one's family.) When the permanent skilled migration is from a developed country to a developed country, however, the Church's cautions are subdued, more along the lines of "think twice" than "don't do it." The latter warning, though—or something quite like it—historically *has* been the Church's message vis-à-vis permanent skilled migration from a developing to a developed country. Consider, for example, the following statements, all taken from authoritative Church documents, and directed both to receiving countries and to potential migrants over the course of more than forty years:

> Even though they have a right of emigrating, citizens are held to remember that they have the right and the duty . . . to contribute according to their ability to the true progress of their own community. Especially in underdeveloped areas where all resources must be put to urgent use, those men gravely endanger the public good, who, particularly possessing mental powers and wealth, are enticed by greed and temptation to emigrate. They deprive their community of the material and spiritual aid it needs.[71]

[T]he special preference afforded by the U.S. to highly skilled persons should be restricted. Our immigration policy should not encourage a flow of educated persons needed for development in other countries. . . . It does not make good sense to direct foreign aid to developing countries and at the same time receive reverse foreign aid in the form of professional persons whose talents are badly needed in the same countries.[72]

[Laws allowing highly skilled immigration] in effect bleed a nation troubled with population problems of its best citizens, leaving behind those who can contribute least to national prosperity. Such ungenerous laws seem to bespeak a spirit of selfishness rather than a genuine desire by a privileged people to help those in need.[73]

[T]he emigration of talented and trained individuals from the poorer countries represents a profound loss to those countries.[74]

To understand why the Church has adopted a strong position against permanent skilled migration from developing countries to developed ones, but not from developed to developed countries, it is necessary only to ask the question, "What do developed countries have that developing ones do not?" The answer is obvious: they already have an adequate level of economic development, so that human development has at least become a widespread possibility. In assessing permanent skilled migration from developing countries, the Church fixes its attention on this difference, with the aim of eliminating it by raising the economic standing of developing countries. The departure of skilled workers is opposed because it is seen as an impediment to achieving this objective as soon in the future as is possible.

This future focus is intended to help make effective what has become customary to state as a leading principle of Catholic social teaching on migration: the right *not* to have to migrate. In recent years, John Paul II, the Pontifical Council for the Pastoral Care of Migrants and Itinerant People, and various conferences of bishops all asserted variations on the theme that people have a "a right not to emigrate," that is, a "right to find in their own countries the economic, political, and social opportunities to live in dignity and achieve a full life through the use of their God-given talents."[75] Giving effect to this right means paying attention to the root causes of migration (a focus beneficial not only to would-be future migrants, but also to the many persons too poor even to migrate), and it is possible to conclude—as Catholic social teaching has—that one such root cause is the departure of skilled and educated personnel who are no longer able to assist their homelands. It also is possible to raise doubts about the current validity of this conclusion, which is a factual one. One might ask, for example, questions such as the following:

What if new developments in technology and communications enabled skilled immigrants to contribute to the growth of their home countries even while abroad? What if, given the new developments, the Church's view that the migrant crosses "an unbridgeable gulf, cutting himself off completely from his homeland, unable and unwilling to contribute to its economic life," no longer is true?[76] Surely such a fact, at the very least, might undermine the foundational belief that elite migration necessarily causes a failure of duty to the home country and its people.

Similarly, what if an imperative of economic growth is increased integration with the global economy? In that case, some migration of its highly skilled workers might be an advantage for a developing country, rather than a disadvantage, as such migrants could foster economic integration in numerous ways—for example, by making or influencing foreign direct investments and through transnational transfers of knowledge—much more easily than non-migrants might.

Consider also this possibility, which again implicates the question of duty. What if it appears that technology-minded immigrants make special efforts to develop technologies that could not be developed at home and that are of special benefit to their home countries? Surely the American Catholic Church's sensitivity to, and responses toward, the problems of people of other nations is favorably advanced by the special efforts of the ten percent of its bishops and the large numbers of its clergy who are immigrants. Is it reasonable to assume that immigrants of a scientific and technical bent are less inclined to use their talents to help address the problems of their home countries?

Numerous other questions might be asked as well. Are the lessons of the past clear in showing that historically a high rate of emigration impedes development? Does the money sent as remittances by migrants to their family and friends who remain back home stimulate the national economic growth of the home countries in addition to increasing the standard of living of the individual recipients? Might the (often unacted upon) possibility of migration create an increased incentive for people in less developed countries to pursue higher educational opportunities that they would not otherwise pursue? And is the phenomenon of return migration by skilled and educated individuals— even those considered "permanent" immigrants—much more prevalent than originally contemplated?

We do not ask these questions randomly; we have explored them all at length elsewhere,[77] and concluded that, whatever the merits of the Church's strong position against the so-called brain drain when the position was first articulated half a century ago, subsequent developments counsel for the formation of a more nuanced policy, one that is more neutral with respect to the skilled migrant's decision to emigrate from a developing country.[78] We hasten to add, however, three additional points.

First, to recommend a policy more open to the mutual benefits of skilled migration from developing countries is not to discount the importance of the right not to migrate. Nor does it diminish the need to accelerate development efforts in poor countries. The principles and goals that shape and direct Catholic social teaching in this area, in other words, remain fully operative.

Second, the suggestion that Catholic social teaching should adapt to new circumstances is not a novel or inappropriate idea. Indeed, Catholic social teaching itself has identified its openness to new facts as a necessity and its adaptability in the face of new developments as a strength. These views, implicit in the call for reading the signs of the times, were made explicit by John Paul II in *Sollicitudo Rei Socialis*:

> [T]eaching in the social sphere . . . [o]n the one hand . . . is *constant*, for it remains identical in its fundamental inspiration, in its "principles of reflection," in its "criteria of judgment," in its basic "directives for action," and above all in its vital link with the Gospel of the Lord. On the other hand, it is ever *new*, because it is subject to the necessary and opportune adaptations suggested by the changes in historical conditions and by the unceasing flow of the events, which are the setting of the life of people and society.[79]

Third, and finally, while the developing (or formerly developing, now developed) nations that have benefited greatly from the emigration of their skilled population—China,[80] India,[81] South Korea,[82] and Taiwan, for instance—contain approximately half the population of the developing world, and many other nations also have received substantial benefits, it must be acknowledged that skilled emigration is no panacea, and can even create obstacles to development under certain circumstances. For example, in the entire debate about the migration of skilled workers, no matter is more problematic for immigration proponents than the migration to the developed world of trained health professionals from the developing world. Rightly or wrongly, poor nations may understandably be thought to offer little in the way of professional challenges or opportunities to engineers or M.B.A.'s, but in the case of doctors and nurses, poor nations might be thought to offer more of a challenge and to represent a greater need. Moreover, from the perspective of Catholic social teaching, the migration of medical personnel from poor nations is doubly troubling, as—much more than other types of skilled migration—it rather starkly appears both to set back the prospects for near-to-mid-term development[83] *and* to deepen the hardships of the unacceptable present. In the face of all this, how can such migration be justified?

The response can legitimately include arguments noting: (1) that the work of some medical professionals cannot be performed in developing countries; (2) that some nations quite deliberately produce more health professionals than their medical infrastructures can support, in the hope that medical personnel will migrate and send remittances when they do; (3) that because of better equipment and more support, health professionals can, by some measures, be more productive in the developed world; (4) that in many developing countries, the pay and working conditions for doctors and nurses is atrocious; and (5) that the work itself often is regarded by health-care workers in developing countries as demoralizing rather than fulfilling, because "the absence of medicines and other supplies leaves [health-care workers] feeling more like hospice and mortuary workers than healers."[84] At least some of these concerns carry weight in any moral calculus. Work is meant to help one achieve fulfillment as a human being and to reach one's human potential. To the extent that one's work instead frustrates and debilitates, and no adequate local alternative appears, a substantial reason for migration is created. Further, a decent respect for human agency and the right of the person to economic initiative suggest that one should be cautious in casting aspersions on decisions to migrate, even decisions by skilled migrants.[85]

Nonetheless, the case that the permanent migration of medical personnel can benefit source countries is a good deal thinner than the case for skilled migration generally, and accordingly creates a greater moral quandary than the migration of skilled workers in general. The quandary is heightened by the absence of any easy practical solution. Singling out health professionals for migration restrictions could backfire by reducing demand for medical education, as the potential for migration is actually an inducement to education in developing countries. The alternative of restricting migration across all disciplines is, one might say, a cure that is likely to be worse than the disease, for such a restriction would risk all the other benefits developing nations can receive from skilled migration. Moreover, as the Global Commission on International Migration has noted, not only would such an approach "not be consistent with human rights principles [and] be very difficult to put into practice," it also would discourage migrants from going back to their own country if they left it without authorization and felt that they would be penalized on their return."[86]

While the issue is thus complex in the extreme, Catholic social teaching can play a very constructive role in addressing it. A more nuanced policy that avoided blanket criticisms of skilled migration would have greater freedom to stress health-care migration as a special case, which it is, due to its unusually potent and negative combination of immediate health effects and longer-term developmental effects. Given these negative consequences, health-care migration and the related crisis of health-care in the developing world deserve special attention from all. Actions in this case truly will speak louder and more eloquently than any words, but words urging action are the next best thing, and Catholic social teaching could fill a very useful role in intensifying the call for governments, businesses, skilled migrants, and health-care organizations, as well as international and non-governmental organizations, to do what they can with persistence, patience, creativity, solidarity, and sacrifice.

And much can be done. Healthcare providers in the developed world, for example, can facilitate in many ways the efforts of immigrant medical professionals to contribute to their homelands. Providers might, for instance, allow their employees flexibility in taking vacation or leave time so that they can travel back home to provide care. Providers could organize such trips themselves. They also might develop programs that allow migrants (and others) to make use of modern technology to remotely serve patients in the homeland. On the remote island of Ginnack, for example, "nurses use a digital camera to record patients' symptoms. The pictures are sent electronically to a nearby town to be diagnosed by a local doctor, or sent to the United Kingdom if a specialist's opinion is required."[87] Replication of programs such as this would provide tremendous opportunities for medical migrants to contribute to their homelands while working in the United States. Perhaps Catholic hospitals can be urged to take a leading role in establishing similarly helpful programs and practices. Immigrant health professionals also can and do make efforts on their own to satisfy their duty to contribute to the common good of their native country, such as by conveying new medical developments to their counterparts back home.[88] Catholic social teaching should more prominently recognize and encourage these individual initiatives.

Governments naturally have a large role to play as well. Catholic social teaching has often expressed support for international agreements such as the International Convention on the Protection of All Migrant Workers and the Members of Their Families.[89] It similarly should call upon governments to support a global orphan drug agreement. In the United States, the Orphan Drug Act provides tax incentives and enhanced patent protection for companies that develop drugs for rare diseases. The result has been a ten-fold increase in the availability of such drugs. A global orphan drug agreement could be similarly beneficial, by "provid[ing] a much-needed push for research on tropical diseases, which also represent small commercial markets—not because they are rare but because they afflict poor people."[90]

Governments in developed countries also must work to increase the domestic supply of healthcare workers to match the domestic demand. A number of approaches might be taken, but it is important that the implementation start as soon as possible, for aging populations in the developed countries suggest that current imbalances will only worsen with time. The range of efforts must be broad, from supporting efforts by domestic medical and nursing schools to expand their teaching capacity, to initiatives that would encourage current medical practitioners, wherever situated, not to leave the field.

The few actions mentioned here by no means constitute an exhaustive list of what might be done. But the situation is such that what might be done must be done. By focusing its discussions of permanent skilled migration on the migration of skilled medical personnel, Catholic social teaching can better help to raise the profile of the issue and inspire concrete and creative action where action is most needed. When the average life expectancy in a nation is less than half of what it is in the developed world, the quest for authentic development in that nation is necessarily distorted. Moreover, to sharpen a point made in a general way much earlier in this chapter, when the developed world treats a health crisis of such magnitude with relative complacency, it does more than raise questions about the limits of its own development—it answers them. Catholic social teaching is well positioned to make both points, and might do so more effectively by discarding its anachronistic criticism of permanent skilled migration in general.

CULTURAL MIGRATION: SECURING THE FUTURE

In one sense, cultural migration is a truism, like wet rain or cold snow. Immigrants cannot help but transmit their cultures to their new surroundings; all migration, accordingly, is "cultural migration." But all migration is not the subject of this subsection. Rather, we are using the term here to encompass a subset of the temporary migration discussed earlier, namely, the migration that has as its very purpose the conveyance of one's culture. Persons traveling on P-2, P-3, and Q visas would be the prime, though not the only, examples of what we mean by cultural migration.

Migration of this kind constitutes a very small portion of total migration. Yet, it is worth singling out for discussion because, from several perspectives, it is the indispensable migration. First, the Church's view is that a satisfactory response to the human needs of migrants and the poor in other countries requires a more widespread commitment to a world of authentic development and a globalization in solidarity. How are these aspirations to be realized? John Paul II stated that "enriching dialogue between cultures . . . is an obligatory path to the building of a reconciled world."[91] Cultural migration, as we have defined it, is the only type of migration whose very purpose is to stimulate dialogue between cultures. It is the only type of migration established on the basis that the migrant will discuss or demonstrate his or her culture for persons who are committed to listening. And it is only through listening that one can rise "above all the differences which distinguish individuals and peoples [and accept that] there is a *fundamental commonality*."[92] There are many obstacles on the road to a globalization in solidarity; the "obligatory path to a reconciled world" needs to be cleared. Cultural migration is valuable because it is a tool specifically designed to do the clearing.

Cultural migration is more, however, than a necessary tool *to* a better world; it also is a necessary tool *in* a better world. Consider, for example, this thought experiment. Let us imagine that the right *not* to migrate has become universally recognized and effective. And let us further imagine that this welcome change came about the only way it ever could: through a widespread commitment to authentic development and to a globalization in solidarity. In such a world, almost all migration is a matter of choice, as the migration of the desperate is no more (except perhaps for refugees fleeing a natural disaster). Further, due to a more equal distribution of goods and opportunities, immigration as a matter of choice—one made for work—has declined, too.[93] What poses the greatest danger to this world?

The danger is a re-emergence of the pride that, according to the story of Babel (Gn. 11:1–9), originally set each nation apart. What has been joined together can be put asunder, and will be put asunder absent dialogue between cultures. Migration fosters this dialogue, which is necessary to "the 'dream' of a future of peace for all humanity."[94] In the relative absence of migration, can the realized dream survive? Only if the dialogue continues. Cultural migration, often overlooked today because its numbers are relatively small and because it has few, if any, opponents to raise its profile through controversy, is the migration for the long term, necessary now to secure the peace and necessary later to preserve the peace, once secured. Cultural migration is the indispensable migration because there will never be a time when its importance fades. Every generation will need to learn anew respect and appreciation for other cultures, in order to either prepare a path to a globalization in solidarity or to safeguard it. In either case, in words emphasized by John Paul II in *Centesimus Annus*, "*a great effort must be made to enhance mutual understanding and knowledge*."[95] Cultural migration now does and always should find favor with the Church, because it can contribute greatly to this effort.

CONCLUSION

Several years ago, the Gallup polling organization committed to conducting a World Poll of more than 100 countries. The first study was on the topic of

"Global Migration Patterns and Job Creation." Its results were published in 2007, and they included what Gallup's CEO described as "one of the single biggest discoveries Gallup has ever made." What was this startling discovery? We quote: "What the whole world wants is a good job."[96] Reading this, we couldn't help but think, if they had only read more Catholic social teaching in the Gallup offices, they might have saved themselves a lot of effort.

Catholic social teaching's apparent prescience in this regard is no mere lucky guess. Rather, it indicates that the Church's social teaching on migration is based on a true understanding of the importance of work, a true understanding of the yearning for authentic development, and a true understanding of the desperate conditions in the world that far too often render such development a practical impossibility. Given this, it is ironic that Church teaching on migration is sometimes dismissed as unrealistic. The critics need to take care that they are not simply blind to the realities that Catholic social teaching articulates and confronts. John Maynard Keynes once buttressed his skepticism about long-range economic planning by famously noting that "[i]n the long run we are all dead." What should it mean to us, in assessing Catholic social teaching's views about the right to migrate and the right not to migrate, that in the *short* run of today, tomorrow, and the next, so many will die never having had a chance at life? Immigration, it is true, is a complex and challenging phenomenon, "a never-ending subject of debate."[97] There is plenty of room for multiple points of view. But in light of the stakes, no one familiar with the current system can be satisfied with it. Can we do better, especially for the suffering poor? For the sake of authentic development—ours and theirs—we must try.

NOTES

1. Catholic social teaching recognized the importance of globalization and global economic development before or roughly contemporaneously with their recognition in the wider world community. Thus, in his 1991 encyclical *Centesimus Annus*, John Paul II expressly discussed "globalization," Pope John Paul II, *Centesimus Annus (One Hundred Years)* 58 (1991), and eight years later he referred to it as a "pervasive phenomenon." Pope John Paul II, "Holy Father's Speech to the Centesimus Annus-Pro Pontifice Foundation," Sept. 11, 1999, 2. Significantly earlier references to the processes of globalization can be found as well. In 1978, for example, in a major document on migration, the Pontifical Commission for the Pastoral Care of Migrants and Itinerant Peoples discussed the implications of the fact that "[t]he economy ha[d] become global." *Letter to Episcopal Conferences on the Church and People on the Move*, May 4, 1978. As for global economic development, the U.N.'s optimistic labeling of the 1960s as the "Development Decade" at the decade's start reflected an

enormous change that had crystallized only a few years before, a change that saw worldwide economic development for the first time widely regarded not only as important and desirable, but as possible as well. See also Michele R. Pistone & John J. Hoeffner, *Stepping Out of the Brain Drain: Applying Catholic Social Teaching in a New Era of Migration* (Lanham: Lexington Books, 2007), 76. The Church's social teaching swiftly reflected this change. John XXIII's 1961 encyclical *Mater et Magistra* (*Mother and Teacher*) was "the first social encyclical to deal extensively with global poverty." Thomas Massaro, *Living Justice: Catholic Social Teaching in Action* (Franklin: Sheed & Ward, 2000), 143. Six years later, Paul VI unequivocally placed development at the forefront of the Church's concerns by devoting an encyclical to the topic, and expressly declaring in that encyclical that "development [was] the new word for peace." Pope Paul VI, *Populorum Progressio* (*On the Development of Peoples*) 76 (1967).

2. Eduardo Galeano, "Civilization's Discontents," *Los Angeles Times*, May 23, 1999, 4. See also Barack Obama, *The Audacity of Hope: Thoughts on Reclaiming the American Dream* (New York: Crown Publishers, 2006), 175 (stating that it is "hard to deny" that "we can't stop [globalization]").

3. *CA*, 43.

4. Pope John Paul II, *Sollicitudo Rei Socialis* (*On Social Concern*) 41 (1987).

5. See, e.g., Robert William Fogel, *The Escape from Hunger and Premature Death, 1700–2100: Europe, America, and the Third World* (Cambridge: Cambridge University Press, 2005). Fogel, an economist and a winner of the Nobel Prize, details the near-Malthusian equilibrium that bedeviled even the wealthiest societies until relatively recently, noting, among other things, that in the eighteenth century average life expectancies in Western Europe were less than half of what they are today. Sadly, life expectancies in some of the poorest countries in the world today, such as Botswana and Zimbabwe, approximate eighteenth-century life expectancies in Europe.

6. Paul Collier, *The Bottom Billion: Why the Poorest Countries Are Failing and What Can Be Done About It* (Oxford: Oxford University Press, 2007), 8–9.

7. *CA*, 58. See also Pope John Paul II, *Ecclesia in America* (*The Church in America*) 20 (1999) (noting that "economic globalization . . . brings some positive consequences, such as economic efficiency and increased production").

8. Pope John Paul II, "Holy Father's Speech to the Centesimus Annus-Pro Pontif= ice Foundation," Sept. 11, 1999, 4. http://www.vatican.va/holy_father/john_paul_ii/ speeches/1999/september/documents/hf_jp-ii_spe_11091999_centesimus -annus_en.html. Eight months earlier, in *Ecclesia in America* (*The Church in America*) (n20), John Paul II had detailed what some of the "decidedly negative consequences" could be: "the absolutizing of the economy, unemployment, the reduction and deterioration of public services, the destruction of the environment . . . the growing distance between rich and poor, [and] unfair competition which puts the poor nations in a situation of ever increasing inferiority."

9. Collier, *The Bottom Billion*, 9–10.

10. Global Commission on International Migration, *Migration in an Interconnected World: New Directions for Action* (2005), 21.

11. For more information on the impact mining can have, and has had, on the Guajira region and places like it, see www.minesandcommunities.org.

12. Global Commission on International Migration, *Migration in an Interconnected World: New Directions for Action* (2005), 13.

13. Ibid., 34 (stating that 2000 Africans seeking to migrate are estimated to die in the Mediterranean each year, while 400 Mexicans die trying to cross the U.S. border). See also U.S. Gov't Accountability Office, *Illegal Immigration: Border-Crossing Deaths Have Doubled Since 1995; Border Patrol's Efforts to Prevent Deaths Have Not Been Fully Evaluated*, GAO-06-770 (Aug. 2006), 1 (stating that "since fiscal year 1998, there has been an upward trend in the number of migrant border-crossing deaths annually, from 266 in 1998 to 472 in 2005"). Forced by their circumstances to cross borders at unpatrolled and sparsely populated areas, migrants often travel across rivers, seas, and deserts. As a result, many migrant deaths occur due to drowning and various heat-related causes. Sometimes, migrants die after being abandoned en route by smugglers. Cases of murder have also been documented among migrant trails, including murders by criminal gangs who prey on both smugglers and the smuggled.

14. United States Department of State, "Trafficking in Persons Report" (June 2007), 7–8, http://www.state.gov/documents/organization/82902.pdf.

15. Thus, even George Borjas, a leading academic advocate for a more restrictive U.S. immigration policy, acknowledges that skilled immigration economically benefits the United States. *The Economic Case for Skilled Immigration: Hearing Before the S. Comm. On Health, Education, Labor and Pensions*, 109th Cong. 3 (2006) (testimony of Prof. George J. Borjas), http://help.senate.gov/Hearings/2006_09_14/Borjas.pdf (stating that "there is little doubt that high-skill immigration is a good investment").

16. John L. Allen. Jr., "The Word from Rome," *National Catholic Reporter*, May 7, 2004. (Illustrating the Church's continuing overall perspective, Bishop Giampaolo Crepaldi, Secretary of the Pontifical Council for Justice and Peace, stated in 2004 that globalization "is among the signs of the time, [but] it is neither good nor bad in itself."—Presentation, Conference on Globalization and Development, Centesimus Annus—Pro Pontifice Foundation.) See also United States Conference of Bishops and Conferencia del Episcopado Mexicano, *Strangers No Longer: Together on the Journey of Hope: A Pastoral Letter Concerning Migration from the Catholic Bishops of Mexico and the United States* (2003), 1 ("globalization . . . brings with it great promises as well as multiple challenges").

17. George Lakoff, *Whose Freedom? The Battle over America's Most Important Idea* (New York: Picador, 2006), 10–13 (discussing developments in cognitive science and cognitive linguistics showing that while the establishment and utilization of conceptual frameworks, i.e., "mental structures of limited scope," are a universal characteristic, they tend to limit our ability to observe what is outside of or inconsistent with our particular conceptual framework). See also Nicholas Wolterstorff, "Public Theology or Christian Learning?" in *A Passion for God's Reign*, ed. Miroslav Volf (Oxford: Blackwell Publishers, 1998), 65, 84 (describing the partial and perspectival nature of human knowledge).

18. *CA*, 59; see ibid. at 57 ("the social message of the Gospel . . . above all else [must be considered] a basis and a motivation for action"). See also Pope John Paul II, *Message for the 85th World Migration Day 1999*, 1 (stating the intent "to broaden the horizons of believers, so that they will see things in the perspective of Christ: in the perspective of the Father who is in heaven") (internal quotation marks omitted).

19. *CA*, 3.

20. *SRS*, 41.

21. Ibid., 15.

22. Ibid.

23. Ibid., 27 n. 50.

24. Ibid., 30 (quoting Pope Paul VI, *Populorum Progressio* (*On the Development of Peoples*) 42 (1967).

25. *SRS*, 15, 33, 43, 44.

26. Ibid., 33.

27. Ibid., 28.

28. Pope Benedict XVI, *Message for the 94th World Day of Migrants and Refugees* (2008).

29. Henry David Thoreau, *Walden*, in *Walden and Civil Disobedience* (New York: Penguin Classics, 1986), 69. Continuing a happy agreement with Catholic social teaching, the Thoreau quote continues: "Therefore, though they should fail immediately, they had better aim at something high."

30. *SRS*, 39.

31. Ibid., 47.

32. See Pope Benedict XVI, *Deus Caritas Est (God is Love)* 30(a) (2005) (noting that mass communications technologies that enable us "to know almost instantly about the needs of [different peoples] challenges us" to respond charitably to them).

33. Kelly Jefferys and Randall Monger, Dep't of Homeland Security, Office of Immigration Statistics, "U.S. Legal Permanent Residents 2007" (March 2008). Numerous other paths account for about 2.5 percent of successful applications for permanent residence, with many of these other paths created by special legislation targeted at and limited to specific groups of people, e.g., the Nicaraguan Adjustment and Central American Relief Act (1997), the Haitian Refugee Immigration Fairness Act of 1998, and the Vietnam, Cambodia and Laos Adjustment Act (2001).

34. An immigrant becomes eligible to apply for naturalization to become a U.S. citizen after receiving lawful permanent residence and then either living in the United States for five years or being married to a U.S. citizen for three. Department of Homeland Security, U.S. Citizenship and Immigration Services, I-864 Affidavit of Support under Section 213A of the Act, http://www.uscis.gov/files/form/I-864.pdf.

35. Stephen H. Legomsky, *Immigration and Refugee Law and Policy*, 4th ed. (2005), 293.

36. Ibid., 334–36.

37. In the lawyers' defense, definitional issues and quirks plague the migration field generally. The problem has been noted by Archbishop Agostino Marchetto, the Secretary of the Pontifical Council for the Pastoral Care of Migrants and Itinerant People, who stated in 2003 that even "when we use the term 'migration,' it is not im-

mediately clear what is meant." Indeed, Archbishop Marchetto has suggested that migration—considered broadly—occurs in so many different contexts it might be better to think in terms of movement or human mobility. See Archbishop Agostino Marchetto, "Flows of Human Mobility Worldwide: Consequences and Expectations" (2003) (citing in support a researcher's conclusion that "[i]t does not make sense to think in terms of rigid categories, nor to place 'migration' at some defined point on the mobility continuum").

38. Kelly Jefferys and Randall Monger, Dep't of Homeland Security, Office of Immigration Statistics, "U.S. Legal Permanent Residents 2007" (March 2008), Table 1 (indicating that for the U.S. government fiscal years 2005–2007, more than 63 percent of those persons receiving permanent status were already living in the United States).

39. Michele R. Pistone and John J. Hoeffner, "Rethinking Immigration of the Highly-Skilled and Educated in the Post-9/11 World," *Georgetown Journal of Law & Public Policy* 5: 495 (2007) (arguing that economic development of underdeveloped nations is crucial to U.S. national security, and that student and skilled worker immigration can advance such development).

40. Thus, the Global Commission on International Migration has referred to the "global jobs crisis" and explained the persistence and direction of global migration as being a function of differentials and disparities in the "3D's," i.e., development, demographics, and democracy. Global Commission on International Migration, *Migration in an Interconnected World: New Directions for Action* (2005), 11–14.

41. Secure America and Orderly Immigration Act of 2005, H.R. 2330, 109th Cong. (2005).

42. Jeffrey S. Passel, "The Size and Characteristics of the Unauthorized Migrant Population" (Washington, D.C.: Pew Hispanic Center, 2006).

43. U.S. Conference of Catholic Bishops, Office of Social Development and World Peace, *Minimum Wage* (February 2004), http://www.usccb.org/sdwp/national/bkgrd04.htm.

44. Pope John Paul II, *Laborem Exercens (On Human Work)* 3 (1981).

45. Ibid., 8–10.

46. Pope John Paul II, *Ecclesia in America (The Church in America)* 54 (1999).

47. Pontifical Council for Justice and Peace, *Compendium of the Social Doctrine of the Church* (Washington, D.C.: U.S. Conference of Catholic Bishops, 2005), 171. See Pope John Paul II, *Message for World Migration Day 2000*, 3 (noting that the poor "do not have easy access to the resources needed for adequate human development").

48. Pope John Paul II, *Laborem Exercens (On Human Work)* 23 (1981).

49. Pope John Paul II, *Message of the Holy Father for the World Migration Day 2000*, 2.

50. Sacred Congregation for Bishops, *Instruction on the Pastoral Care of People Who Migrate* (Washington, D.C.: U.S. Catholic Conference, 1969), 8, 7.

51. United States Conference of Bishops and Conferencia del Episcopado Mexicano, *Strangers No Longer: Together on the Journey of Hope: A Pastoral Letter*

Concerning Migration from the Catholic Bishops of Mexico and the United States (2003), 36.

52. Pope John Paul II, *Message of the Holy Father for the 87th World Day of Migration 2001*, 3.

53. In *CA,* 33, John Paul II discussed how widespread a problem it was for work to lose its potential as an instrument of authentic development:

> The fact is that many people, perhaps the majority today, do not have the means which would enable them to take their place in an effective and humanly dignified way within a productive system in which work is truly central. They have no possibility of acquiring the basic knowledge which would enable them to express their creativity and develop their potential. They have no way of entering the network of knowledge and intercommunication which would enable them to see their qualities appreciated and utilized. Thus, if not actually exploited, they are to a great extent marginalized; economic development takes place over their heads, so to speak.

54. Pope John Paul II, *Message of the Holy Father for the World Migration Day 2000*, 5. John Paul II continues by quoting the first epistle of John: "If anyone has the world's goods and sees his brother in need, yet closes his heart against him, how does God's love abide in him?" 1 John 3:17.

55. Pope John Paul II, *Undocumented Migrants: Message for World Migration Day 1996*, 6.

56. Pope John Paul II, *Message for World Migration Day* (1998), 3 (quoting Matthew 25:35).

57. Pope John Paul II, *Message of the Holy Father for the World Migration Day 2000*, 4.

58. Pope John Paul II, *Undocumented Migrants: Message for World Migration Day 1996*, 5. See also Pope John Paul II, *Ecclesia in America (The Church in America)* 65 (1999), 65 ("Attention must be called to the rights of migrants and their families and to respect for their human dignity, even in cases of non-legal immigration").

59. Pope John Paul II, *Message for World Migration Day* (1998), 6.

60. Edward J. Slattery, "The Suffering Faces of the Poor Are the Suffering Face of Christ," The Diocese of Tulsa (Nov. 25, 2007), 6, http://migrante.com.mx/pdf/BISHOP.pdf.

61. See, e.g., *SRS,* 42 (discussing the parable and citing Luke 16:19–31).

62. *LE,* 23.

63. Pope John Paul II, *Message for the World Migration Day 2000*, 6.

64. E.g., Pope John Paul II, *Message for the 85th World Migration Day 1999*, 8 ("When speaking of migrants, we must take into account the social conditions in their countries of origin").

65. "The rule of law is the necessary condition for the establishment of an authentic democracy." Pope John Paul II, *Ecclesia in America (The Church in America)* 56 (1999), (internal quotation marks omitted). On the other hand, however, "there is no authentic and stable democracy without social justice." Ibid (internal quotation marks omitted).

66. Kaitlynn Riely, "Catholic leaders react to Senate's failed immigration bill," *The Catholic Standard and Times* (July 5, 2007), 18.

67. "[A]ttention to migrants and refugees [is] one of [the Church's] pastoral priorities." Pope John Paul II, *Message for World Migration Day* (1998), 2. See Pope John Paul II, *Message for the 87th World Day of Migration 2001* (on the topic of "The Pastoral Care of Migrants"); Pontifical Council for the Pastoral Care of Migrants and Itinerant People, *Erga Migrantes Caritas Christi* (*The Love of Christ towards Migrants*) (2004); Pontifical Council for the Pastoral Care of Migrants and Itinerant People, "II World Congress for the Pastoral Care of Foreign Students: Final Document," Dec. 13–16, 2005.

68. Pontifical Council for the Pastoral Care of Migrants and Itinerant People, "II World Congress for the Pastoral Care of Foreign Students: Final Document," Dec. 13–16, 2005 (reporting Benedict XVI's remarks to the World Congress).

69. Pope Benedict XVI, *Message for the 94th World Day of Migrants and Refugees* (2008). In a probable reflection of his background as a university professor, Benedict XVI has heightened the attention given to student migration. Among other notable demonstrations of this, he devoted a paragraph or more to the topic in each of his first three annual messages on migration.

70. Thus, Archbishop Agostino Marchetto's sharp distinction between students who return to their home countries after graduation and those who do not: "If they return, they would be a resource for their home countries. If they stay, they are 'brains' that are 'drained'" Archbishop Agostino Marchetto, "Flows of Human Mobility Worldwide: Consequences and Expectations" (2003).

71. Sacred Congregation for Bishops, *Instruction on the Pastoral Care of People Who Migrate* (Aug. 22, 1969), 8 (citations and internal quotation marks omitted), reprinted in *People on the Move, A Compendium of Church Documents on the Pastoral Concern of Migrants and Refugees* (U.S. Catholic Conference, 1988), 85.

72. National Conference of Catholic Bishops, *The Pastoral Concern of the Church for the People on the Move* (1976), 14.

73. National Catholic Welfare Conference Administrative Board in the Name of the Bishops of the United States, *World Refugee Year and Migration* (Nov. 19, 1959), 31, in *People on the Move, A Compendium of Church Documents on the Pastoral Concern of Migrants and Refugees* (U.S. Catholic Conference, 1988), 19.

74. U.S. Catholic Bishops, *Welcoming the Stranger Among Us* (2000), 8.

75. Pope John Paul II, *Message of the Holy Father for the 90th World Day of Migrants and Refugees 2004*, 3 (proclaiming "first of all *the right not to emigrate*, that is, the right to live in peace and dignity in one's own country"); United States Conference of Bishops and Conferencia del Episcopado Mexicano, *Strangers No Longer: Together on the Journey of Hope: A Pastoral Letter Concerning Migration from the Catholic Bishops of Mexico and the United States* (2003), 34. See Pontifical Council for the Pastoral Care of Migrants and Itinerant People, *Erga Migrantes Caritas Christi* (*The Love of Christ towards Migrants*) 29 (2004) (affirming "the right of the individual not to emigrate . . . that is, the right to be able to achieve [one's] rights and satisfy [one's] legitimate demands in [one's] own country." See also Pope John Paul II, *Message of the Holy Father for the 87th World Day of Migration 2001*, 3 (noting "the right to have one's own country, to live freely in one's own country"); Pope John Paul II, *Message of the Holy Father for the World*

Migration Day 2000, 6 ("noting everyone's right to be able to live peacefully in his own country").

76. Andrew M. Yuengart, *Catholic Social Teaching on the Economics of Immigration*, (Spring 2000) www.acton.org/publicat/m_and_m/2000_spring/yuengert.html.

77. Michele R. Pistone & John J. Hoeffner, *Stepping Out of the Brain Drain: Applying Catholic Social Teaching in a New Era of Migration* (Lanham, Md.: Lexington Books, 2007).

78. A very partial list of sources supporting various aspects of our conclusion includes the following: United Nations Development Programme, *Human Development Report 2001: Making New Technologies Work* (2001), 30 (noting that technological changes "radically [alter] access to information and the structure of communication—extending the networked reach to all corners of the world"); B. Lindsay Lowell, *International Migration Papers 46: Some Developmental Effects of the International Migration of Highly Skilled Persons* (International Labor Office 2002), 22 (noting that migration of highly skilled persons can "yield a flow back of new technologies that can boost" the growth of the sending country); AnnaLee Saxenian, "Brain Circulation: How High-Skilled Immigration Makes Everyone Better Off," *Brookings Review* (Winter 2002: 28), 30 (explaining how "transnational communities provide the shared information, contacts and trust that allow local producers to participate in an increasingly global economy"); AnnaLee Saxenian, *Local and Global Networks of Immigrant Professionals in Silicon Valley* (San Francisco: Public Policy Institute of California, 2002), 29, 37 (indicating that the foreign-born entrepreneurs in California's Silicon Valley participate in several forms of direct foreign investment in their home countries, noting, in particular, that half of them "have set up subsidiaries, joint ventures, subcontracting or other business opportunities" in their home countries and that eighteen percent have invested in either start-up businesses or venture capital funds in their home countries); B. Lindsay Lowell, *Skilled Migration Abroad or Human Capital Flight?* Migration Information Source, Migration Policy Institute, at 2, www.migrationinformation.org (June 1, 2003) (noting "support for the notion [called 'optimal brain drain' theory] that the possibility of emigration for higher wages induces more students in the sending country to pursue higher education"); G. Jasso and M. R. Rosenzweig, "How Well Do U.S. Immigrants Do? Vintage Effects, Emigration Selectivity and Occupational Mobility of Immigrants," in *Research in Population Economics*, ed. P. T. Schultz (1988), 229–253 (finding that skilled immigrants have a higher probability of return migration). See also Michele R. Pistone and John J. Hoeffner, *Stepping Out of the Brain Drain: Applying Catholic Social Teaching in a New Era of Migration* (Lanham, Md.: Lexington Books, 2007), 158–63 (discussing technological advances in agriculture, communications, pharmaceuticals, and other areas, tailored to or directed mainly at problems of the developing world, made by emigrant scientists from Nigeria, Kenya, and India, among other places).

79. *SRS*, 3 (emphasis in original).

80. While China's phenomenal economic growth is well known, the role played by the Chinese diaspora in that success has received less attention. As the Global Commission on International Migration has noted, however, that role has been a substantial one. For example, among other things, Chinese emigrants living abroad are

responsible for approximately 45 percent of the foreign direct investment in China. Report of the Global Commission on International Migration, *Migration in an Interconnected World: New Directions for Action* (2005), 30.

81. See Michele R. Pistone & John J. Hoeffner, *Stepping Out of the Brain Drain: Applying Catholic Social Teaching in a New Era of Migration* (Lanham, Md.: Lexington Books, 2007), 138–40 (discussing the critical role played by the Indian diaspora in the United States in establishing India's large and vibrant information technology industry). See also Paul Collier, *The Bottom Billion: Why the Poorest Countries Are Failing and What Can Be Done About It* (Oxford: Oxford University Press, 2007), 93 (noting the importance of the Indian diaspora "in India's breakthrough into the world market for e-services").

82. Walter Adams, "Introduction," in *The Brain Drain* 1, ed. Walter Adams (New York: Macmillan Company, 1968): A book, published in 1968 and titled *The Brain Drain*, identified South Korea on its first page, along with Taiwan, as the world's greatest victims of skilled emigration. At the time South Korea was approximately as wealthy as Ghana and Chad, and Taiwan was about as wealthy as the Congo. In subsequent years, the chief victims of the suspected economic plague known as "brain drain" grew their economies at unprecedented rates, to the point that large numbers of skilled South Koreans and Taiwanese began to return home in the 1980s; indeed, to the extent that there is currently a "brain drain" of South Koreans, it mainly involves students, not qualified graduates. Anne Marie Gaillard and Jacques Gaillard, *International Migration of the Highly Qualified: A Bibliographic and Conceptual Itinerary* (Staten Island: Center for Migration Studies, 1998), 27 and n.30: Today, the economies of South Korea and Taiwan are 50 times larger than they were fifty years ago, while other economies that experienced less skilled emigration grew substantially less, or even remained stagnant.

83. While it once was the conventional wisdom that "health would improve in tandem with general economic development," it now is widely believed "that disease in tropical and desperately poor countries [is] itself a critical impediment to development and prosperity." Laurie Garrett, "The Challenge of Global Health," *Foreign Affairs* 86: 14–38 (Jan./Feb. 2007), 20.

84. Ibid., 28.

85. For a discussion of the right to economic initiative and its relation to human dignity, see Michele R. Pistone & John J. Hoeffner, *Stepping Out of the Brain Drain: Applying Catholic Social Teaching in a New Era of Migration* (Lanham, Md.: Lexington Books, 2007), 177–87.

86. Global Commission on International Migration, *Migration in an Interconnected World: New Directions for Action* (2005), 25.

87. United Nations Development Programme, *Human Development Report 2001: Making New Technologies Work for Human Development* (2001), 33.

88. Alejandro Portes and Ruben G. Rumbaut, *A Portrait of Immigrant America*, 3d ed. (Berkeley: University of California Press, 2006), 4 (noting such efforts by two Indian doctors).

89. See, e.g., Pontifical Council for the Pastoral Care of Migrants and Itinerant People, *Erga Migrantes Caritas Christi* (*The Love of Christ towards Migrants*) 6

(2004). See also Pope Benedict XVI, *Message for the 93rd World Day of Migrants and Refugees* (2007).

90. United Nations Development Programme, *Human Development Report 2001: Making New Technologies Work for Human Development* (2001), 100.

91. Pope John Paul II, *Message for the 90th World Day of Migrants and Refugees 2004*, 5 (internal quotation marks omitted).

92. Pope John Paul II, *Message for World Migration Day* (1998), 6 (emphasis in original).

93. Archbishop Agostino Marchetto, "Flows of Human Mobility Worldwide: Consequences and Expectations" (2003), 12 ("To a high degree . . . migration would not take place if local conditions could guarantee the dignified life of a person and his/her family").

94. Pope John Paul II, *Message for the 90th World Day of Migrants and Refugees 2004*, 5.

95. *A, 52*.

96. Jim Clifton, "Global Migration Patterns and Job Creation," http://media.gallup.com/WorldPoll/PDF/GallupWorldPollWhitePaperGlobalMigration.pdf.

97. Pope John Paul II, "Address of the Holy Father Pope John Paul II to Congress on Pastoral Care of Migrants" (1998), 5.

Chapter Four

Rights, the Common Good, and Sovereignty in Service of the Human Person

Donald Kerwin

The Catholic Church does not have an immigration policy so much as it has a person policy. Its singular contribution to the global debate on immigration lies in its reverence for the human beings at the heart of this phenomenon. "[T]he human person," as Pope Benedict XVI put it, "must always be the focal point in the vast field of international migration."[1]

The anthropologist Olivia Ruiz Marrujo identifies "risk" as central to competing migration paradigms.[2] In Marrujo's view, to conceive of immigrants "as" a risk leads to an analysis of immigration through the lens of sovereignty, national security, and national interest. By contrast, to see immigrants "at risk" places them in a human rights framework, focusing on their hopes, needs, and suffering. Catholic teaching insists that concepts like "sovereignty," "national security," and the "rule of law," which are often used to impede the legitimate aspirations of migrants, must instead be put in service to them. Moreover, it moves beyond the "risk" paradigm, urging that immigrants be treated as agents in their own lives and as full participants in the lives of their communities.[3]

This chapter attempts to reclaim some of the core concepts that for better (human rights and the common good) or often worse (sovereignty, national security, and the rule of law) frame the immigration debate. As Catholic teaching understands and would apply these concepts, they offer a hopeful way to respond to this timeless human phenomenon.

HUMAN RIGHTS

Elie Weisel has characterized human rights as the world's secular religion.[4] If so, one must recognize the intense disagreement over the source of this religion's beliefs, its content, and its utility in resolving deeply rooted social conflicts. Catholic social teaching answers these challenges with an expansive view of rights that is rooted in its distinctive understanding of the human person.

In the Catholic tradition, rights derive from the God-given dignity and equality of each person. Human beings are made "in the image and likeness of God." (Gn. 1:26–27). Their dignity consists in their capacity to give freely of themselves to God and to others.[5] When a person migrates in order to support her children, for example, she seeks to become the person that God calls her to be. Most people do not leave their native countries for selfish or trivial reasons. With migrants, "the reality of the disinterested gift of self is almost always found."[6] Rev. Daniel Groody, C.S.C. finds that self-sacrifice informs the spirituality of many migrants:

> "We abandon everything," said Mario, "our families, our children, and our people. I'm [migrating] more than anything for them." It is a sacrifice often mixed with guilt. For all their good intentions, there is often an underlying regret in not being there to see children grow up, in not being able to return home for a funeral, in not being there for one's spouse. Their spirituality is first and foremost about relationships and providing for others, sometimes through their presence but often in their absence.[7]

Pope John XXIII linked the human person and rights in this way:

> [E]very human being is a person, that is, his nature is endowed with intelligence and free will. Indeed, precisely because he is a person he has rights and obligations, flowing directly and simultaneously from his very nature. And as these rights and obligations are universal and inviolable so they cannot in any way be surrendered.[8]

Similarly, the Universal Declaration of Human Rights conceives of human beings as "born free and equal in dignity and rights," "endowed with reason and conscience," and with duties to the community "in which alone" their "free and full development" can be attained.[9] The Declaration's authors shared the Church's belief "that human nature was everywhere the same and that the processes of experiencing, understanding, and judging were capable of leading everyone to certain basic truths."[10]

"Illegal alien" has become a favored term in U.S. public discourse, with its implication of people totally outside the law's protections and obligations. Anti-immigrant groups claim that "illegals," by definition, have no rights. Sadly, many immigrants have internalized this sacrilegious view of themselves. Certainly, citizenship or membership in a political community can be decisive to safeguarding human rights. Reflecting on the stateless, displaced, and denaturalized following World War I, Hannah Arendt wrote:

> The Rights of Man . . . had been defined as "inalienable" because they were sup-
> posed to be independent of all governments; but it turned out that the moment
> human beings lacked their own government and had to fall back upon their min-
> imum rights, no authority was left to protect them and no institution was will-
> ing to guarantee them. . . . The Rights of Man, supposedly inalienable, proved
> to be unenforceable—even in countries whose constitutions were based upon
> them—whenever people appeared who were no longer citizens of any sovereign
> state.[11]

U.S. Supreme Court Chief Justice Earl Warren borrowed Arendt's definition of citizenship as the "right to have rights."[12] In Catholic thought, however, rights do not *ultimately* derive from "Man" or originate in state membership. Non-citizenship does not deprive a person of "membership in the
human family as a whole, nor from citizenship in the world community."[13] In
the Catholic tradition, states exist to vindicate rights, but they do not create
them. Otherwise, oppressed or stateless people would possess no rights, a notion at odds with core Judeo-Christian and other religious values, the entire
thrust of universal human rights, and particular rights instruments like the
Genocide Convention of 1948.[14]

The Universal Declaration of Human Rights likewise recognizes the "inherent dignity" and the "equal and inalienable rights of all members of the human family."[15] The U.S. Constitution extends its protections to "people" or
"persons," not just to citizens. The U.S. Supreme Court has long recognized
that non-citizens enjoy constitutional rights in matters that do not implicate
the power of the federal government to determine who can enter, who must
leave, and who can stay.[16] Even when the federal government acts pursuant
to its broad power to regulate immigration, it must do so in ways that uphold
constitutional norms. It could not, for example, torture detained immigrants
as a way to force them to abandon their claims to remain or shoot persons as
they attempted to cross the border into the United States.

In Catholic teaching, God ordered all creation according to a rational, objective plan, which is "imprinted" on the human heart (Rm. 2:14–15). Natural
law, whose precepts can be discerned by reason, allows humans to participate
in God's plan in fulfillment of their nature. Thus, natural law has been defined
as the rules of conduct "prescribed . . . by the Creator in the constitution of
[our] nature,"[17] and "the objective order established by God which determines
the requirements for human fulfillment and flourishing."[18] Speaking from this
tradition, Pope Benedict XVI has lauded the rights and principles enshrined

in the Universal Declaration of Human Rights for being "founded on what is essential and permanent in the human person."[19]

According to natural law, rights reflect *objectively* well-ordered or just relationships. For this reason, many scholars find "natural law" to be incommensurable with *subjective* human rights, the idea that certain powers or faculties inhere in human beings. Catholic teaching attempts to reconcile these two ways of conceiving of rights based on its understanding of the human person. It maintains that under God's (objective) plan, human beings are endowed with dignity that, in turn, gives rise to subjective rights. As Pope John Paul II put it:

> The comprehension of the human being, that the Church acquired in Christ, urges her to proclaim the fundamental human rights and to speak out when they are trampled upon. Thus, she does not grow tired of affirming and defending the dignity of the human person, highlighting the inalienable rights that originate from it.[20]

The medievalist Brian Tierney argues that natural law's precepts can be viewed as subjective rights from the perspective of the beneficiary of a just relationship.[21] By way of example, he offers the Commandment "Thou shalt not steal." This precept could be seen to reflect an objectively "right" relationship between people, or it could be viewed as a subjective right to the proceeds of one's work.[22] Similarly, natural law requires parents to support their children. This requirement reflects an objectively well-ordered community, but it also creates a subjective right or claim by children to sustenance. Tierney demonstrates that as early as the Middle Ages, canon lawyers believed that natural law grounded subjective rights, like the right to self-preservation.

Rev. William O'Neill, S.J. places the Church's natural law/rights tradition in the middle ground between traditional liberal and communitarian theories of rights. Catholic teaching diverges from liberalism's view that rights arise from purely private conceptions of the "good" secured by a social duty of "forbearance" or tolerance, and from the communitarian sense that rights are the established or "positive" law of a particular community. To the Church, rights cannot be conflated with whatever laws a particular state passes, nor should they be reduced to individual expressions of the "good" life.

The Rights of Migrants and Newcomers

Migration has less to do with movement, however wrenching individual journeys may be, than with the complex, often painful conditions that lead people to uproot and that greet them in their new countries. In Catholic thought, the large, impersonal forces that drive migration should serve and reflect the dignity of the human person.

The Catholic Church teaches that human beings enjoy a "primary right" to live fully human lives in their own nations.[23] They should neither be forced to leave nor prevented from returning by sub-human conditions. A sign at a migrant shelter in San Carlos, Nicaragua, captures this idea perfectly. "Migration is not a crime," it reads. "The crime is that which causes migration." The Global Commission on International Migration has called on states to promote human rights, democratic processes, good governance, and the empowerment of women so that their citizens can "migrate out of choice," not necessity.[24]

The "right not to have to migrate" inspires the Church's overseas development work, its peace-building programs, and its advocacy for debt relief and fair trade. As Pope Benedict XVI said: "The fundamental solution is there would no longer exist the need to emigrate because there would be in one's own country sufficient work, a sufficient social fabric, such that no one has to emigrate."[25] In this sense, the Church favors voluntary, legal migration. It condemns the suffering and hardship that force people to migrate, and supports the creation of conditions in migrant-sending communities that would allow them to remain.

However, when a person cannot realize her fundamental rights at home, whether because of poverty, war, persecution, natural disaster, or gross economic privation, she possesses "the right to emigrate to other countries and take up residence there."[26] Pope John Paul II urged the Catholic Church to be "a vigilant advocate, defending against any unjust restriction on the natural right of individual persons to move freely within their own nation and from one nation to another."[27] The Catholic Church would extend the right to migrate to economic migrants, going well beyond the requirements of international law:

> But where a State which suffers from poverty combined with great population cannot supply such use of goods to its inhabitants, or where the State places conditions which offend human dignity, people possess a right to emigrate, to select a new home in foreign lands, and to seek conditions of life worthy of man.[28]

In an historic joint pastoral statement on migration in 2003, the U.S. and Mexican bishops asserted that due to rampant poverty and persecution in migrant-sending nations, "the presumption is that persons must migrate in order to support and protect themselves and that nations who are able to receive them should do so whenever possible."[29]

While the most desperate people lack the wherewithal and resources to migrate, the bishops' statement accurately reflects the comparative poverty of migrant-sending communities, and the reality that most migrants leave their homes in order to support themselves and their families. Better to die trying to cross, migrants on the U.S.-Mexico border often say, than to die slowly at home. Unaccompanied minors who had been caught by immigration officials expressed sorrow and shame to a delegation of U.S. bishops in 2006 that they had let down their families and would not be able to provide for them.[30] On a separate occasion, a fifteen-year old migrant told Fr. Daniel Groody, C.S.C.: "I'm thirsty out here in the desert but I'm even more thirsty to find work. My family is very poor and they depend on me. We have nothing to eat, really just beans and tortillas, and I am anxious to respond to their needs."[31]

Economic migration, much of it spurred by globalization, has encountered strong public resistance. A 2007 survey of more than 45,000 persons in forty-seven nations, for example, found widespread support for free trade, multinational corporations, and free markets, but large majorities in virtually every nation favored greater immigration restrictions.[32] By its own logic, globalization requires that displaced persons move toward economic opportunities. Yet trade agreements facilitate the flow of goods, services, capital, and information across borders, but do not legalize the flow of those people whom they invariably displace. This anomaly results in part from fear that immigrants will erode the receiving nation's culture and identity.[33] However, it creates great hardship for those who are displaced. In the 12 years following passage of the North American Free Trade Agreement (NAFTA) in 1994, for example, more than two million persons lost their jobs in the Mexican agricultural sector. As a result, many formerly independent, small family farmers joined U.S. migrant labor streams, most without legal status or protection.

Catholic teaching requires a discriminate response by states and individuals in favor of the very poor and the persecuted based on the "preferential option for the poor." This principle does not connote a preference for one group over another or an optional course of conduct. In fact, the term "option" might be better translated to mean a "decision," and the "poor" encompasses all persons whose rights have been threatened or denied. So understood, the "preferential option" speaks to the need for international bodies, states, and individuals to make decisions that restore persons in need to their proper place in the human family. In biblical terms, God "executes justice for the orphan and widow, and befriends the alien, feeding and clothing him" because He "has no favorites." (Dt. 10:17–18). The "preferential option" is not based on an idealized portrait of the poor, but on the universality of God's love which compels action on behalf of those whose rights have been violated or imperiled.

Catholic teaching supports the generous acceptance of persons who have been forced to migrate to realize their rights. International law recognizes the right of persons to leave their nations and to return home, but eviscerates this right by failing to recognize a corresponding right to *enter* another country.[34] By contrast, the Church recognizes "the right in every human person, in its dual aspect of the possibility to leave one's country and the possibility to enter another country to look for better conditions of life."[35]

Migration can be divisive. Demagogues inflame fears that immigrants threaten the security, identity, culture, and economic prospects of the native-born. They deride immigrants as criminals, terrorists, and "invading hordes." Politicians blame immigrants for social problems ranging from high crime, to a broken healthcare system, to the deterioration of public education. Nativists ascribe to all immigrants the crimes of a few, arguing for ever more punitive policy approaches. These tactics terrorize immigrants and appeal to fears that are as well-known to the Catholic Church as its own long history of migration.

In these circumstances, the Church's teaching and policy prescriptions can be seen as counter-cultural. The Church recognizes a right to life and "all that is necessary for living a genuinely human life: for example, food, clothing, housing, the right freely to choose their state of life and set up a family, the right to education, work, to their good name, to respect, to proper knowledge, the right to act according to the dictates of conscience and to safeguard their privacy, and rightful freedom, including freedom of religion."[36] Catholic teaching calls on states to offer political membership to immigrants if consistent with the common good.[37]

Honoring rights, in turn, promotes immigrant integration. The word "integration" derives from the Latin "integratus," which means to make whole. In the United States, discourse on integration tends to be shaped by metaphors like the melting pot, or mosaic, or salad bowl that seek to capture unity based on shared political, civil, and social values, but that also recognize the unique contributions of immigrants. The European Union (E.U.) has adopted a formal definition of integration as a "two-way process based on mutual rights and corresponding obligations of legally resident third-country nationals and the host society which provides for the full participation of the immigrants." In its emphasis on rights, obligations, and participation, the E.U. definition resonates in the Catholic tradition.[38]

Culture and Rights

Culture also plays a distinctive role in Catholic teaching on rights. Nativists often claim that immigrants balkanize receiving nations and undermine their core identities. Other commentators raise more serious concerns related to social cohesion. Catholic teaching recognizes that people cannot express their faith or values in the abstract, but must do so in the context of their particular cultures. To the Catholic Church, migration creates an opportunity to unify people based on the shared values embedded in their distinct cultures.[39] It allows the Church to pursue its mission to be a "sign and instrument" of communion with God and unity among all men.[40] The Church sees migrants as the "purveyors of diversity which contributes to the ultimate unity of the human family."[41]

Catholic teaching does not affirm all cultural practices. It seeks to transform practices that do not respect human rights or further the common good. It recognizes that "no culture is either permanent or perfect," but all need to be "evangelized and uplifted."[42] It rejects cultural practices both in receiving states and immigrant communities that "contravene either the universal ethical values inherent in natural law or fundamental human rights."[43] Acculturation should not lead immigrants or their children to adopt materialistic, anti-family values. Nor should respect for diverse cultures sanitize practices like forced marriage or female genital mutilation. The U.S. bishops have consistently stressed, however, that successive waves of immigrants have renewed U.S. society and culture through their faith, commitment to family, and hard work.

Rights and Values

Catholic teaching employs the rhetoric of rights to mediate its values in a pluralistic world. Rights give the Church a way to describe duties and responsibilities that are consonant with human dignity. However, honoring rights does not satisfy or diminish the human need for love, justice, or charity. As Pope Benedict XVI recently wrote:

> Love—*caritas*—will always prove necessary, even in the most just society. . . . Whoever wants to eliminate love is preparing to eliminate man as such. . . . In the end, the claim that just social structures would make works of charity superfluous masks a materialist conception of man: the mistaken notion that man can live "by bread alone" (Mt. 4:4; cf. Dt. 8:3)—a conviction that demeans man and ultimately disregards all that is specifically human.[44]

In a recent public debate on an ordinance targeting unauthorized immigrants in Prince William County, Virginia, a county resident told his immigrant neighbors that the native-born residents did not hate them, but they did not welcome them either, and that the immigrants should recognize the difference. It is a distinction with little difference to the Catholic tradition. Catholic teaching requires far more than the absence of hate. It insists that the

God-given dignity of each person be honored with a response that goes beyond vindicating their rights.

THE COMMON GOOD

The "common good" structures Catholic teaching on rights and its analysis of immigration. Classic Augustinian and Thomistic theology understands the common good ultimately in terms of communion with God, a standard that no political authority can satisfy.[45] At first blush, this concept can seem amorphous and a less than rigorous analytical tool. In Catholic thought, it refers to the "sum total of social conditions which allow people, either as groups or as individuals, to reach their fulfillment."[46]

Some argue that the generous enumeration of rights in the Universal Declaration of Human Rights and elsewhere should not be understood in juridical terms, but as a way to outline the common good.[47] Under this view, rights give substance to the common good; in fact, they can be viewed as the "good" common to all.[48] In Catholic teaching, "respect for rights, and the guarantees that follow from them, are measures of the common good."[49] Rights do not exhaust the common good, but set forth "the minimum conditions" for "human dignity" and "dignified life in community."[50] They allow people to realize their potential and participate in the "shared life of the human community."[51]

In Catholic thought, human beings are social by nature and realize their humanity in giving of themselves to others. Thus, human rights must be viewed in the context of the good of others, beginning with families and extending to larger circles of association. Likewise, the Universal Declaration locates rights in "real-life relationships of mutual dependency: families, communities, religious groups, workplaces, associations, societies, cultures, nations, and an emerging international order."[52]

The Church rejects the nativist claim that the rights of immigrants can only be realized at the expense of the native-born. Instead, it teaches that rights both protect immigrants and obligate them to contribute to the good of others.[53] In Catholic teaching, the "good" of all "is realized when people gain the power to work together to improve their lives, strengthen their families, and contribute to society."[54]

In the Catholic Church's vision, communities suffer when they fail to safeguard the rights of any of their members. For example, many U.S. states and localities have adopted "deportation-by-attrition" strategies that aim to curb illegal migration through measures that deny housing, employment, healthcare, and other socioeconomic rights to persons without

legal status and, by extension, to their families. In addition, the federal
government increasingly pressures state and local police forces to enforce
immigration law, ensuring that many immigrants will not report crimes or
otherwise assist the police. The trend toward criminalizing work and self-
sacrifice particularly baffles the targeted communities. As one immigrant
lamented:

> We don't understand why Americans treat us this way . . . all we want to do is
> work here legally. . . . Even though we want to work for them, they won't let us.
> We cross over the border, but they make us out to be criminals. It's like being
> poor is a crime.[55]

The U.S. bishops argue that such laws violate human rights and undermine
the common good. They reason that if immigrants cannot access healthcare,
the public health is endangered. If immigrants cannot obtain police protection, public safety is threatened. If immigrant children cannot attend school,
they cannot fully develop their gifts for the good of their communities. If they
cannot work, they cannot contribute their labor. To the Church, "[i]t is against
the common good and unacceptable to have a double society, one visible with
rights and one invisible without rights—a voiceless underground of undocumented persons."[56]

The U.S. Supreme Court recognized the inter-relationship between rights
and the common good in finding it unconstitutional for states to deny public
secondary schooling to unauthorized children:

> It is difficult to understand precisely what the state hopes to achieve by promot-
> ing the creation and perpetuation of a subclass of illiterates within our bound-
> aries, surely adding to the problems and costs of unemployment, welfare, and
> crime. It is thus clear that whatever savings might be achieved by denying these
> children an education, they are wholly insubstantial in light of the costs involved
> to these children, the State, and the Nation.[57]

In describing her life as an immigrant, a young woman from the Border
Network for Human Rights in El Paso made the same point in starkly personal terms:

> Throughout my academic life there is diploma after diploma, trophy after tro-
> phy that symbolize my achievements. . . . It was in seventh grade that I was ac-
> cepted into the National Junior Honor Society at my school. I have also done
> some volunteer work and community service around my community. I have
> gone to retirement homes and helped out there. I also help tutor elementary kids
> a couple of times a week after school; that is when I am not very busy with var-
> sity soccer practices at school or at my city league team.

Now I am seventeen years old and have lived in America for more than a decade—for most of my life. I am a teenager who gives back to my community but with every new law that Congress makes, it seems that they don't want me here. They would rather have kids that were born here and cause mayhem everywhere. They go over me just for the fact that I was conceived in Mexico, which is only a couple of miles away. I can't drive because I am not allowed to get my driver's license. I can't travel out of town with school programs that I would like to participate in and, worst of all, I can't visit members of my family back in Mexico because there is no way for me to come back. My friends are now planning a trip out of town for graduation and it seems like I'm going to be left behind. . . . I would like to go on to college and continue with my studies and become a productive member of society but with every new law that is put against me, my dream seems that much further from happening.[58]

Catholic teaching roots the common good in the God-given "dignity, unity and equality of all people."[59] In the Catholic tradition, the common good means something very different from the "greater good," which connotes sacrificing the interests of individuals or minority groups for the overall good of a community.[60] Immigrant restrictionists often characterize "illegal immigration" as a "quality of life" issue, by which they mean the quality of their own lives.[61] In Catholic teaching, the quality of everybody's life matters; the common good cannot be interpreted to "exclude or exempt any section of the population."[62]

Two extreme examples highlight the difference in vision. On average, more than one migrant per day, most seeking only low-wage work in the United States, perishes while trying to cross the U.S.-Mexico border. In addition, roughly 33,000 immigrants, including those who have fled persecution, languish in the dysfunctional U.S. immigrant detention system on any given night. The plight of border crossers and immigrant detainees troubles some U.S. citizens, but many do not view these migrants as the nation's responsibility. In addition, their treatment does not inconvenience or degrade the quality of life of most Americans. Yet, in the Catholic tradition, their situation undermines the common good.

The common good is not solely an economic concept, but considers persons in their full dignity: "In order to be authentic, [development] must be complete: integral, that is, it has to promote the good of every person and of the whole person."[63] Nor can development be equated with the acquisition of wealth by a few or even the majority. God created the earth "with everything contained in it for the use of all human beings."[64] In Catholic teaching, human need constitutes the primary ethical claim to material goods.

Catholic teaching acknowledges the right to private property. However, because this right must serve the common good, it cannot "hinder others from having their own part of God's gift."[65] Private property "is under a 'social mortgage,' which means that it has an intrinsically social function based upon . . . the principle of the universal destination of goods"; that is, the idea that the goods of creation are meant for all.[66] At the very least, this principle requires nations to set admissions policies that reflect their own resources and the needs of the global community.[67] It also underlies the Catholic response to criticism of those who migrate illegally, but from economic necessity. As it stands, restrictions on migration to wealthy countries like the United States deny people from poor countries "the largest antipoverty intervention available" to them.[68]

According to one critique, the rhetoric of rights in the United States tends to be absolute, individualistic, and divorced from any ethic of duty.[69] As a result, claims taking the form of "rights" have proliferated in public discourse, degrading the language of rights and diminishing its utility as a problem-solving tool. Partisans characterize their preferred social outcomes as "rights" in order to trump competing claims and to stymie debate. In response, the common good can help to identify legitimate rights, to limit them, and to evaluate and even reconcile conflicting positions. An example from the U.S. immigration debate offers a case in point: Migrants fleeing gross poverty claim a right to support themselves and their families. Yet many believe that cheap immigrant labor violates the rights of native-born workers by driving down wages and working conditions. In the circumstances, the common good points to strategies designed to increase wages and to improve conditions for all workers.

The Universal Common Good and the Human Family

A distinctive feature of Church teaching on migration is its recognition of a "universal" or borderless common good. This seems only fitting for a "catholic" (that is, universal) church. Pope Benedict XVI roots of this principle in the parable of the Good Samaritan:

> Until that time, the concept of "neighbor" was understood as referring essentially to one's countrymen and to foreigners who had settled in the land of Israel; in other words, to the closely-knit community of a single country or people. This limit is now abolished. Anyone who needs me, and whom I can help, is my neighbor.[70]

The salience of the "universal" common good has been attributed to the growing inter-dependence of nations. By this view, war, poverty, and environmental degradation cannot be solved unilaterally. These problems require states to "take into account the needs and legitimate aspirations of every other group, and even those of the human family as a whole."[71] They require a more expansive vision of neighbor and family:

> In an increasingly global society, the unit of human community to which the term "common good" applies moves from the national to the international level.
> . . . The universal common good is violated if there are places anywhere in the world where basic needs like clean water, food, shelter, health care, education and livelihood are not available to all or if the rights and dignity of all are not respected.[72]

In Catholic thought, the common good is realized through the virtue of "solidarity." Solidarity requires that we "assume the plight of others . . . as ours."[73] It requires a "firm and persevering determination to commit oneself to the common good; that is to say, to the good of all and of each individual because we are all really responsible for all."[74] Solidarity also places demands on the poor and persecuted who "while claiming their legitimate rights, should do what they can for the good of all."[75] As a practical matter, a commitment by newcomers to the values and well-being of their new communities can mitigate the fear and sense of displacement that large-scale migration instills in many long-settled citizens.

The common good requires states to protect the rights of migrants. Nations can regulate the entry of all immigrants and can turn away those whose admission would not serve the common good. However, the common good cannot be served by rejecting people who are fleeing persecution, violence, or intense privation. Nor can it be achieved by policies that perpetuate a "double" society consisting of citizens with full rights and mere denizens without legal status, security, or a stake in their communities. The "universal" common good extends the duty to safeguard rights across borders. In the words of the Universal Declaration, everyone is entitled to a "social and international order" in which their rights and freedoms can be fully realized.[76]

SOVEREIGNTY

The Catholic Church recognizes the duty and responsibility of sovereign states to regulate their borders in furtherance of the common good. Yet its teaching on sovereignty has been criticized as undeveloped and its policy positions have been attacked as a threat to the security of the state. In its most basic sense, sovereignty refers to the authority of a nation-state to constitute itself, to repel intrusions by other states, and to govern those within its territory. Scholars commonly trace the modern system of nation-states to the Treaties of Westphalia (1648), which established the equality of nations, their authority to determine their own laws, and their right to manage their own affairs without outside interference.

In popular discourse, sovereignty serves as a short-hand way to express multiple concerns related to immigration. Illegal migration implicates two key indicia of sovereignty: the state's power to allow access to its territory, and its authority to confer political membership.[77] Sovereignty also evokes the related concepts of "national security" and the "rule of law."

The Authority and Purpose of the State

The meaning of sovereignty has evolved in our current era based on what many see as a more circumscribed understanding of state authority. Philip Bobbitt has argued that the "market state," spurred by globalization, has supplanted the sovereign nation-state.[78] While this may seem an extreme claim, it cannot be disputed that international trade agreements limit state authority and create challenges to domestic laws that states have been slow to address. In addition, in the global economy, multinational corporations increasingly offer a counterpoint to state power. As Rev. Daniel Groody, C.S.C. has pointed out, private corporations represent fifty-one of the world's 100 largest economic entities (including nations), profoundly influencing the lives of millions.[79] Globalization has paradoxically diminished state authority and increased the need for sovereign states to protect the vulnerable.

At its core, sovereignty helps to identify responsibility for the protection of rights within a particular territory.[80] States remain the primary vehicle for vindicating the universal rights of their own residents for good reason; this is their core purpose and no other entity can satisfy this responsibility. A state's responsibility to its residents, however, does not relieve it of the need to defend the rights of persons who come from nations that persecute or fail to protect them.[81] To the Catholic Church, sovereignty argues for greater collective action to safeguard the undefended rights of persons in other nations. A sovereign state has primary "responsibility to protect" the rights of its members, but when "unable or unwilling to fulfill this responsibility," the international community (of states) must act in its place.[82]

Totalitarian governments view themselves as the exclusive source of rights within their boundaries. By contrast, liberal democracies believe that states have the responsibility to protect rights that inhere in people based on their very humanity. The U.S. Declaration of Independence, for example, speaks to the need to protect the self-evident and inalienable rights that are endowed by the Creator. By this view, states do not create rights; honoring rights legitimizes states. States also voluntarily qualify their own power through adoption of international treaties and other agreements. The Church has frequently urged nations to embrace the international regime of refugee protection, encouraging all nations to adopt its relevant legal instruments.[83]

States can also serve as a bulwark against supranational political movements and belief systems like communism or imperialism that subjugate peoples and negate rights. In our current era, Al Qaeda operates a worldwide terrorist franchise, headquartered in ungoverned, tribal territory in a lawless border region. It targets recruits in failed states. The terrorist attacks on September 11, 2001 in New York and Washington, D.C., on March 11, 2004, in Madrid, and on July 7, 2005 in London have highlighted the threats posed by non-state actors.

Vibrant, democratic states serve as an antidote to terrorist recruitment and entrenchment. In addition, the terrorist threat demonstrates that sovereign states will need to cooperate more fully with each other to prevent catastrophic rights violations against their own citizens. As the International Commission on Intervention and State Sovereignty has put it:

> In an interdependent world, in which security depends on a framework of stable sovereign entities, the existence of fragile states, failing states, states who through weakness or ill-will harbour those dangerous to others, or states that can only maintain internal order by means of gross human rights violations, can constitute a risk to people everywhere.[84]

Catholic Teaching on Sovereignty

Sovereignty has never been understood in Catholic thought to be an expression of unlimited state power. Catholic teaching would limit state power based on the state's "purpose, the common good, by the inviolable rights of the human person, and by the dictates of the natural law and the divine law."[85] Since the state's purpose is to provide for the "common welfare" or "good," it would "transgress the limits set to its power" for a state to violate human rights.[86]

Migration increasingly results from phenomena like trade agreements, natural disaster, war, persecution, and climate change. In these circumstances, human rights cannot be realized without a commitment to the "good" that crosses borders. Economic globalization has both created great wealth and displaced untold millions of persons, pushing entire sectors of workers into illegal migration streams. In his 2008 address to the U.N. General Assembly,

Pope Benedict XVI affirmed the responsibility of the international community to intervene when individual states do not meet their "primary duty" of safeguarding rights, arguing that such actions "should never be interpreted as an unwarranted imposition or limitation on sovereignty."[87] The very purpose of "civil authority" is "not to confine its people within the boundaries of their nation but rather to protect, above all else, the common good of the entire human family."[88]

By this reasoning, sovereign states must honor the rights of migrants in their home countries, protect them on their journeys, provide them safe haven, and integrate those who settle within their territories. Building on ideas developed in the context of corporate responsibility,[89] Rev. David Hollenbach, S.J. has identified four conditions that, in combination, create an ethical responsibility for states to respond to migrant needs: (1) critical need; (2) proximity to that need; (3) ability to respond; and (4) recognition that the state agent may be the last resort for the migrant. Hollenbach refers to these conditions as the Kew Garden principles after the site of an infamous 1964 murder of a young woman whom nobody assisted despite her repeated pleas for help.

A qualified view of sovereignty does not require a state to open its borders or cede its responsibility for deciding who should belong. Catholic teaching recognizes the authority and duty of a state to ensure the orderly entry of migrants and to exclude and remove persons whose presence would not advance the common good. But sovereignty does not immunize states from responsibility for receiving persons who are forced to cross borders to realize their rights. As the U.S. and Mexican bishops put it:

> The Church recognizes the rights of a sovereign state to control its borders in furtherance of the common good. It also recognizes the right of human persons to migrate so that they can realize their God-given rights. These teachings complement each other. While the sovereign state may impose reasonable limits on immigration, the common good is not served when the basic human rights of the individual are violated.[90]

Under this vision, sovereign states retain significant discretion to craft immigration enforcement policies, yet they must also honor their defining purpose by safeguarding the rights of those whose dignity compels them to cross borders. In particular, states can exercise their immigration responsibilities by identifying migrants who are seeking to realize their rights, by ensuring the orderly entry of these migrants and others whose admission would further the common good, and by denying entry to others.

National Security

Like sovereignty, "national security" refers to the responsibility of the state to protect its members from physical harm and encroachment. However, it also speaks to the protection of a state's "vital economic and political interests, the loss of which could threaten [its] fundamental values and vitality."[91] In its thickest sense, "national security" refers to a state's responsibility to defend the lives of its members, and to promote the civic values, economic interests, and democratic institutions that allow its members to flourish.

Archbishop Migliore, the Vatican's representative to the United Nations, has warned that legitimate security concerns can never justify practices that violate the dignity of the human person. As he testified before the U.N. General Assembly:

[E]ffective counterterrorism measures and the protection of human rights are not conflicting goals. Indeed, the former must serve the latter, because the protection of human rights is the primary objective of any counterterrorism strategy. The absolute unacceptability of terrorism lies precisely in the fact that it uses innocent people as a means to obtain its ends, thus showing contempt and utter disregard for human life and dignity.[92]

Following the terrorist attacks of September 11, 2001, the Catholic Legal Immigration Network, Inc. engaged a group of prominent security experts on the vulnerabilities created by the U.S. immigration system and how it might be reformed to increase security, while safeguarding rights. A consensus emerged around several points.

First, security-related measures need to be rigorously evaluated to determine if they advance legitimate goals and can likely accomplish their purposes. Since security cannot be guaranteed and resources are limited, a "risk management" approach is required. Not every policy instituted in the guise of security makes the nation safer. Particularly suspect have been "security-related" immigration measures targeting Haitian boat people, indefinite detainees, Canadian-bound asylum seekers, and certain refugees and asylum-seekers accused of providing "material support" to terrorists.[93] In addition, the attempted deportation of some significant percentage of the nation's unauthorized immigrants would not be a viable or cost-effective security strategy. In a recent survey of 100 security experts, 70 percent identified improved port and cargo security as top priorities for border security, but only 6 percent viewed building a wall on the U.S.-Mexico border as a key goal.[94]

Second, a viable counter-terrorism plan must draw on the nation's full military, intelligence, diplomatic, and law enforcement resources. It must incorporate "a multi-faceted strategy to break the cycle of terrorist recruitment and replenishment through an appeal to the 'hearts and minds' of persons in terrorist-producing states; expedited restructuring of the U.S. intelligence, law enforcement, and homeland security infrastructure; strengthened intelligence collection, mining, analysis, and sharing capabilities; and the full engagement of local police in the attempt to identify, locate and infiltrate terrorist groups."[95]

The U.S. immigration system has important national security responsibilities. As the 9/11 Commission stressed, it should also be able to: (1) collect, disseminate, and analyze intelligence on terrorist travel methods; (2) conduct identity and security checks on those who wish to enter and to secure legal status; and (3) stop persons from entering who appear on watch lists or who meet terrorist profiles based on behavior and timely intelligence. Immigration authorities should be able to locate certain visitors to the country. They should also be able to expedite the admission of persons who contribute to the nation's economic security and safety, particularly scientists and engineers.

Third, immigrant integration provides an antidote to terrorist recruitment and should be a policy priority. However, economic and social integration should not be viewed as a panacea. Home-grown terrorists in Europe and the United States have been well-integrated in many ways, but not committed to democratic principles or loyal to their native countries.

Fourth, persons without legal status do not present a heightened threat. Many unauthorized immigrants have been driven to the United States by human insecurity, but they do not represent a national security threat. If they did present a risk, U.S. citizens would not entrust them (as they do) to care for their children and elderly, to build and to clean their homes, and to prepare and serve their food. Moreover, terrorist recruiters prefer "clean operatives," meaning citizens and legal residents who will not otherwise come to the attention of the authorities.

At the same time, it would enhance security to learn the identity and to run security checks on persons who lack legal status. For this reason, the United States should implement policies that bring immigrants forward, like offering them a path to legal status or drivers' licenses. In addition, expanded legal avenues for entry would reduce illegal entries, allowing immigration officials to concentrate their enforcement resources on those who present the greatest risk.

The Rule of Law

The "rule of law" figures prominently in the global debate on migration. If human rights can be seen as the moral claim to participate fully in the life of a nation, persons seeking membership should, at a minimum, respect their new nation's laws. The rule of law occupies a privileged place in the United States precisely because its membership is not based on nationality or race, but on a commitment to shared values and ideals. At the same time, while the democratic process legitimizes laws, it does not guarantee just or non-discriminatory laws, much less the fair application of those laws to vulnerable persons. Catholic teaching supports an immigration system that honors the rule of law in its richest sense.

In its most basic form, the rule of law refers to a legal system that holds leaders accountable to the law. "Where the law is subject to some other authority and has none of its own," Plato wrote, "the collapse of the state, in my view, is not far off."[96] Thomas Aquinas believed that the law itself must serve the common good, be promulgated and divulged publicly, reflect reason, and issue from a competent authority.[97] In defining the law in this way, Aquinas anticipated modern notions of the rule of law that speak both to the form that laws must take and the ultimate goals that they serve.

Nativist groups typically invoke the rule of law to demand greater enforcement of the law, and passage of stricter laws, many of which would criminalize migration and push more immigrants outside the law's protections. Yet the rule of law means more than "law and order." Police states excel at enforcing the law or ruling *by* law. However, they egregiously violate human rights, subverting a core principle of the Universal Declaration of Human Rights that "human rights should be protected by the rule of law."

According to Brian Tamanaha, in a legal system that honored the rule of law, the laws would take a certain form (they would be written, prospective, and procedurally fair), they would serve some substantive good (particularly respect for human rights), and they would be the product of a credible, legitimate political system. In liberal democracies, according to Tamanaha, these elements "cluster together . . . as a unified, complementary package."[98]

The U.S. immigration system lacks many of these attributes. Legal reform reports have criticized the retroactivity of U.S. immigration laws, their inconsistent application, and their lack of proportionality.[99] In addition, the immigration system can be procedurally unfair in ways that violate fundamental rights. A 2008 study by scholars from Georgetown University Law Center and Stanford Law School demonstrated that the strength of a claim matters far less to the outcome of a political asylum case than the availability of legal counsel and the individual judge assigned to the case.[100]

Deportation proceedings often fail to comport with basic due process norms. These trial-like proceedings can result in a person's permanent separation from family or return to a country where she faces persecution, torture, or even death.[101] Yet more than one-half of the persons facing deportation lack legal representation,[102] a circumstance that makes them anywhere from three to eleven times less likely to obtain political asylum.[103] Detention also significantly reduces the likelihood of success in immigration court.[104] Restrictions on judicial review in immigration cases undermine the separation of powers, the very linchpin of the rule of law in the U.S. constitutional democracy.

In recent years, it has also become more difficult for migrants to secure protection in the United States. Since September 11, 2001, the United States has denied admission to thousands of refugees and denied political asylum to hundreds for providing "material support" to terrorists. The "material support" standard does not distinguish between hardened terrorist supporters and pro-democracy activists or innocent persons who were forced to assist terrorists under threat of death. Migrants have also found it more difficult to reach U.S. borders due to interception, interdiction, and airport pre-inspection programs. The U.S. Commission on International Religious Freedom has found that roughly one-sixth of those migrants who reach a U.S. border and who express a fear of persecution are not referred to the U.S. asylum system, in contravention of international and domestic law.[105]

In the Catholic tradition, people have a right and a responsibility to support their families. If they need to migrate to sustain their families, they have a duty to do so. By one theory, most migrants leave home as part of a family survival strategy.[106] Yet the U.S. immigration system undermines the right to family unity. It does so by deporting long-term lawful permanent residents, by not permitting the legal immigration of otherwise eligible members from low-income families, and by forcing immigrants who have been approved for family-based visas to wait for years, occasionally decades, before they receive them.

An estimated 4.9 million persons, 2.2 million of them living in the United States, have been approved for family-based visas, but have not received them.[107] The latter have opted to remain in the United States with their families, rather than live apart for years while they wait for their visas. When their visas do become available, these immigrants will be required to leave the country, with no assurance that they will be allowed to return due to their past "unlawful presence."

Beginning in 2006, the Department of Homeland Security (DHS) conducted dozens of high-profile raids at work sites, which led to the arrest and deportation of thousands of workers and to several hundred criminal prosecutions. An Urban Institute study found that one-half of the unauthorized workers arrested in three prominent ICE raids in 2006 and 2007 had children in the United States, two-thirds of them U.S. citizens.[108] Overall, 73 percent of the 5.5 million children of unauthorized immigrants are U.S. citizens by birth.[109]

Hundreds of thousands of migrants risk their lives to enter the United States each year. In recent years, nearly 500 have died annually trying to cross the U.S.-Mexico border.[110] Once in the United States, the great majority have found work, primarily in high-growth industries that could not function without them.[111]

The economic crisis beginning in 2007 hit immigrant laborers with particular ferocity. Unauthorized immigrants work disproportionately in the industries most affected by the recession and possess the demographic characteristics of the most vulnerable workers; they tend to be less-skilled, non-white, relatively young, recent labor-market entrants, and with less formal education.[112] While the economic crisis unsettled U.S. labor markets and migration patterns, immigrants have remained a structural reality in the U.S. economy. The United States will particularly need their labor as the economy recovers and the retirement of the 79-million-person Baby Boom generation accelerates.

Rather than come to terms with these deficiencies and anomalies, U.S. policymakers have increasingly embraced a strategy of putting more and more immigrants beyond the protections of the law. A prominent goal of immigration restrictionists has been to deny citizenship to children born in the United States to parents without legal status. The Fourteenth Amendment guarantees citizenship to those born or naturalized in the United States and subject to its jurisdiction. In an effort to avoid having to try to amend the Constitution, The Birthright Citizenship Act of 2007, which 104 Members of Congress co-sponsored, interpreted the phrase "subject to its jurisdiction" to exclude the children of unauthorized persons. If it had passed, the bill would have overturned the U.S. Supreme Court decision in *United States v. Wong Kim Ark*, which held that citizenship extends to persons born in the United States notwithstanding their parents' alienage.

The result would be akin to the discredited practice of the Dominican Republic to deny birthright citizenship (notwithstanding the law) to ethnic Haitians, creating what the Inter-American Commission of Human Rights has termed a condition of "permanent illegality."[113] The United States should not follow suit. It should honor the rule of law, but this will require reform beyond the enforcement of ever more punitive laws. It will require a far different approach than one that would make innocent children permanently "illegal," and create a hereditary underclass of denizens in the country.

CONCLUSION

Many Catholics invoke the concept of "prudential judgment" to question the authority of Church teaching on immigration and to oppose its policy prescriptions. They believe that determining membership in the polity represents a fundamental state responsibility to which the Church brings no particular expertise. While Catholic teaching offers a structure and language to analyze complex social issues, its inter-locking concepts do not dictate specific policy positions. In fact, it can be maddeningly difficult to trace the evolution from Catholic moral principles to the Church's nuanced positions in the public arena. In 2007, the U.S. bishops characterized the nation's "unjust immigration policy" as among the "serious moral issues" that required action in light of Catholic teaching, but left to debate and discussion "how best to respond" to the immigration issue and "other compelling threats to human life and dignity."[114]

Despite these qualifications, Catholic teaching does not cede all complex questions to the realm of "prudential judgment" or immunize private judgments from moral criticism. It defines "prudence" as the virtue that "makes it possible to discern the true good in every circumstance and to choose the right means for achieving it."[115] People of good will can disagree over how to honor the right not to have to migrate and how to protect migrants on their journeys. Yet "prudential judgment" will never be able to justify indifference to the deaths of migrants along the U.S.-Mexico border or to those who perish while trying to reach Spain's Canary Islands by boat.[116] The "good" can be realized in the cases of persons displaced by violence, natural disaster, or economic privation only by offering them protection and status. This is as true for persons who seek to migrate to a developed country, as it is for the 74 million people who have moved from extremely poor nations like Haiti with a per capita income of $480, to less poor nations like the Dominican Republic with a per capita income of $2,850.[117]

To the Catholic Church, the "good" argues for extending citizenship to hardworking, family-oriented persons who have left their native lands by necessity or by some combination of necessity and choice, and who have made their lives in their new nations. "Don Chuy," for example, left Mexico as a young man to support his mother and six siblings. When he arrived in the United States, he knew nobody and spent his days walking from house to house looking for work. After a few weeks, he was offered a job as a handyman in an automobile garage. He worked from 6 a.m. to 8 p.m., trying to demonstrate that he was a trustworthy man. He considered himself fortunate because, unlike other immigrants, he worked for a fair boss and did not "suffer any discrimination."

"Don Chuy" took additional jobs as a waiter and janitor, and sent money to his mother every week. He married and raised a family. After nearly ten years of work, he received legal status under the 1986 "amnesty" bill. At that point, he decided to "work harder to better himself." He borrowed money to start his own business, ultimately establishing three successful restaurants. As the years passed, he took pride in "what he was becoming: a good person, a good man, a good provider but most importantly . . . he [was] proud of making the hardest decision of his life: to immigrate to the United States and become everything he was once told he couldn't be." "Don Chuy's" four children have now graduated from college. He tries to hire people, like himself, "that are willing to work and become better persons in society." He reveres "the nation that opened its arms and helped him get where he is now."

Catholic teaching urges states to be open to the aspirations, values, and contributions of people like "Don Chuy." The Catholic Church views migrants from the "standpoint of Christ, who died to gather together the dispersed children of God (cf. Jn. 11:52), to rehabilitate the marginalized and to bring close those who are distant."[118] It supports policies that would allow immigrants, even unauthorized immigrants, to become full participants in the lives of their nation. It believes that such policies respect human rights, serve the good of host communities, and honor the very purpose of sovereign states.

NOTES

1. Pope Benedict XVI, *Message on World Day of Migrants and Refugees 2007.*

2. Olivia Ruiz Marrujo, "Immigrants at Risk, Immigrants as Risk: Two Paradigms of Globalization," in *Migration, Religious Experience, and Globalization*, ed. Gioacchino Campese C.S. and Pietro Ciallella C.S. (Staten Island, NY: Center for Migration Studies, 2003), 17, 19–24.

3. Most Rev. Nicholas DiMarzio, Bishop of Brooklyn, "Migration Today: A Social Justice Issue," St. Vincent DePaul Chair of Social Justice Lecture (Jan. 31, 2008). ("The migrant is never an object of migration, but rather its subject. It is free will that is exercised in the act of migration.")

4. Elie Weisel, "A Tribute to Human Rights," in *The Universal Declaration of Human Rights: Fifty Years and Beyond*, ed. Yael Danieli, Elsa Stamatopoulou, and Clarence Dias (Amityville, NY: Baywood, 1999), 3.

5. *Catechism of the Catholic Church* (Washington, D.C.: United States Catholic Conference, 2000), 357. ("Being in the image of God the human individual possesses the dignity of a person, who is not just something, but someone. He is capable of self-knowledge, of self-possession and of freely giving himself and entering into communion with other persons. And he is called by grace to a covenant with his Creator, to offer him a response of faith and love that no other creature can give in its stead.")

6. Most Rev. Nicholas DiMarzio, Ph.D., D.D., "John Paul II: Migration Pope Teaches on Unwritten Laws of Migration," *Notre Dame Journal of Law, Ethics & Public Policy* 21 (May 1, 2007), 191, 197.

7. Daniel G. Groody, "Jesus and the Undocumented: A Spiritual Geography of a Crucified People," *Theological Studies* 70 (2009).

8. Pope John XXIII, *Pacem in terris (Peace on earth)* 9 (1963).

9. Universal Declaration of Human Rights ("Universal Declaration"), (1948), Arts. 1 and 29 (1).

10. Mary Ann Glendon, *A World Made New* (New York: Random House, 2001), 230.

11. Hanna Arendt, *The Origins of Totalitarianism* (New York: Schocken Books, 2004), 370, 372.

12. *Perez v. Brownwell*, 356 US 44, 64 (1958). (Warren, Black, and Douglass dissenting.)

13. *PT*, 25.

14. *Convention on the Prevention and Punishment of the Crime of Genocide*, adopted by the United Nations General Assembly on 9 December 1948.

15. *Universal Declaration*, Preamble.

16. Donald Kerwin, "Immigrant Rights, Integration and the Common Good," in *Securing the Future*, ed. Michael Fix (Washington, D.C.: Migration Policy Institute, 2007), 45–53.

17. *Our Sunday Visitor's Catholic Encyclopedia*, ed. Rev. Peter M.J. Stravinskas, Ph.D., S.T.L. (Huntington, Ind.: Our Sunday Visitor, Inc., 1991), 674.

18. *New Advent Catholic Encyclopedia* (2008), http:///www.newadvent.org/cathen/09076a.htm.

19. Pope Benedict XVI, *State of the World Address* (January 7, 2008), 8, 10.

20. Pope John Paul II, *Message of the Holy Father for the World Day of Migration 2001*, 3.

21. Brian Tierney, *The Idea of Natural Rights* (Grand Rapids, Mich.: Eerdmann's Publishing Company, 1997), 302–304.

22. Ibid., 33.

23. U.S. Conference of Catholic Bishops and Conferencia del Episcopado Mexicano, *Strangers No Longer: Together on the Journey of Hope* (Washington, D.C.: United States Conference of Catholic Bishops, 2003), 59.

24. Global Commission on International Migration, "Migration in an interconnected world: New directions for action" (2005), 26–27.

25. Words from His Holiness, Pope Benedict XVI, During His Apostolic Journey to the United States (April 15-20, 2008), http://www.cliniclegal.org/resources/statements -pope-benedict-xvi-regarding-immigration.

26. Sacred Congregation for Bishops, *Instruction on the Pastoral Care of People Who Migrate* (August 22, 1969), 7.

27. Pope John Paul II, Apostolic Exhortation, *Ecclesia in America (The Church in America)* 65 (1999).

28. Sacred Congregation for Bishops, *Instruction on the Pastoral Care of People Who Migrate* (August 22, 1969), 7.

29. *Strangers No Longer*, 39.

30. United States Conference of Catholic Bishops/Migration and Refugee Services, Catholic Legal Immigration Network, Inc., Catholic Relief Services, *The Lost Dream: Unaccompanied Migrant Children and Victims of Human Trafficking on the U.S./Mexico Border* (Washington, D.C.: United States Conference of Catholic Bishops, October 2006), http://www.usccb.org/mrs/BorderReport.pdf.

31. Daniel G. Groody, "Jesus and the Undocumented: A Spiritual Geography of a Crucified People," *Theological Studies* 70 (2009).

32. Ibid.

33. The Pew Global Attitudes Project, "World Publics Welcome Global Trade—But Not Immigration" (Washington, D.C.: Pew Research Center, October 4, 2007), http://pewresearch.org/pubs/607/global-trade-immigration.

34. *Universal Declaration*, Art. 13(2).

35. Pope John Paul II, *Message of the Holy Father for the World Day of Migration 2001*, 3.

36. Pope Paul VI, Pastoral Constitution on the Church in the Modern World, *Gaudium et Spes (Joys and Sorrows)* 26 (1965).

37. *PT*, 106.

38. Jill Marie Gerschutz with Lois Ann Lorentzen, "Integration Yesterday and Today—New Challenges for the United States and the Church" (chap. 5).

39. Pope John Paul II, *Message on World Migration Day* 1991, 3 (1991).

40. Pope Paul VI, Dogmatic Constitution on the Church, *Lumen Gentium* (*Light of the World*) 1 (1964).

41. Most Rev. Nicholas DiMarzio, Ph.D., D.D., "John Paul II: Migration Pope Teaches on Unwritten Laws of Migration," *Notre Dame Journal of Law, Ethics & Public Policy* 21, (May 1, 2007) 191, 205.

42. United States Conference of Catholic Bishops, *Welcoming the Stranger Among Us: Unity in Diversity*, 28 (November 2000).

43. Pope John Paul II, *Message for the Celebration of the World Day of Peace 2001*, 13 (January 1, 2001).

44. Pope Benedict XVI, *Deus Caritas Es (God is Love)* 28 (2006).

45. David Hollenbach, S.J., *The Common Good and Christian Ethics* (Cambridge: Cambridge University Press, 2002), 132.

46. *GS*, 26.

47. John Finnis, *Natural Law and Natural Rights* (Oxford: Oxford University Press, 1980), 214.

48. The relationship between rights and the common good can often be seen clearly in the wake of human catastrophes. The failure to invest in the safety and the well-being of the residents of the communities decimated by Hurricane Katrina, for example, violated both core rights and the common good.

49. Pope Benedict XVI, *Address to the United Nations' General Assembly* (Apr. 18, 2008).

50. National Conference of Catholic Bishops, *Economic Justice for All* (1986), 17–18, 79.

51. David Hollenbach, S.J., *The Common Good and Christian Ethics* (Cambridge: Cambridge University Press, 2002), 159.

52. Glendon, *A World Made New*, 227.

53. Pope John Paul II, *Message of the Holy Father for the World Day of Migration 2001*, 3.

54. National Conference of Catholic Bishops, *Economic Justice for All* (Nov. 18, 1986), 91.

55. Daniel G. Groody, "Jesus and the Undocumented: A Spiritual Geography of a Crucified People," *Theological Studies* 70 (2009).

56. National Conference of Catholic Bishops, *Together a New People: Pastoral Statement on Migrants and Refugees* (1986), 10.

57. *Plyler v. Doe*, 457 U.S. (1982), 202, 230.

58. The Border Network of Human Rights in El Paso, Texas kindly collected several immigrant narratives for this project. The narratives are on file with the author.

59. Pontifical Council for Justice and Peace, *Compendium of the Social Doctrine of the Church* (Washington, D.C.: United States Conference of Catholic Bishops, 2005), 164.

60. *PT*, 106 ("[A]s far as the common good, rightly understood permits," states have a duty to accept immigrants and allow them to become members of the community.")

61. Anna Gorman, "Escondido Tries to Rid Itself of Undocumented Immigrants," *Los Angeles Times* (July 13, 2008), http://articles.latimes.com/2008/jul/13/local/me-escondido13.

62. The Catholic Bishops' Conference of England and Wales, *The Common Good and the Catholic Church's Social Teaching* (London: The Catholic Bishops' Conference of England and Wales, 1996), 70.

63. Pope Paul VI, *Populorum Progressio (The Progress of Peoples)* 4 (1967).

64. *GS*, 69.

65. Pope John Paul II, *Centesimus Annus (One Hundred Years)* 31 (1991).

66. Pope John Paul II, *Sollicitudo Rei Socialis (On Social Concern)* 42 (1987).

67. Mathias Risse, "On the Morality of Immigration," *Ethics & International Affairs*, 21, no. 1 (Spring 2008) ("Illegal immigration makes a mockery of those who abide by the rules, so this argument goes. To pardon illegal immigrants would be unfair because it lets them get away with their offense on the basis that they have succeeded thus far. This standpoint, however, presupposes that immigration is a matter for the respective country alone to sort out, and that the 'insiders' are entitled to determine how many and exactly who enters the country. But the argument offered here implies this is not so. If would-be immigrants are being illegitimately excluded, one cannot complain that they are violating due process if they come anyway.")

68. Michael Clemens, Claudio E. Montenegro, and Lant Pritchett, "The Place Premium: Wage Differences for Identical Workers across the U.S. Border" (Washington, D.C.: Center for Global Development, revised December 2008).

69. Mary Ann Glendon, *Rights Talk* (New York: Free Press, 1991), 12, 14.

70. Pope Benedict XVI, *Deus Caritas Est (God is Love)* 15 (2005).

71. *GS*, 26.

72. *The Common Good and the Catholic Church's Social Teaching*, 102.

73. Olivia Ruiz Marrujo, "Immigrants at Risk, Immigrants as Risk: Two Paradigms of Globalization," in *Migration, Religious Experience, and Globalization*, ed. Gioacchino Campese C.S. & Pietro Ciallella C.S. (Staten Island, NY: Center for Migration Studies, 2003), 24.

74. *SRS*, 38.

75. *SRS*, 39.

76. *Universal Declaration*, Art. 28.

77. Susan Gzesh, "America's Human Rights Challenge: International Human Rights Implications of US Immigration Enforcement Actions Post-September 11" (Washington, D.C.: Migration Policy Institute, 2006), 11.

78. Phillip Bobbitt, *The Shield of Achilles* (New York: Alfred A. Knopf, 2002).

79. Daniel G. Groody, *Globalization, Spirituality, and Justice* (Maryknoll, NY: Orbis, 2007), 14.

80. United Nations, Office for the Coordination of Humanitarian Affairs, "No Refuge: The Challenge of Internal Displacement" (New York and Geneva: United Nations, 2003), 36.

81. The International Commission on Intervention and State Sovereignty, *The Responsibility to Protect* (Ottawa, ON: International Development Research Centre, December 2001), 2.24, 2.32, http://www.iciss.ca/pdf/Commission-Report.pdf.

82. Ibid., 2.29.

83. Pope Benedict XVI, *Message of His Holiness Benedict XVI for the 93rd World Day of Migrants and Refugees* (2006); Pope Paul VI, Declaration on Religious Freedom, *Dignitatis Humanae* (*The Dignity of the Human Person*) 3 (1965).

84. *The Responsibility to Protect*, 1.21.

85. *New Catholic Encyclopedia*, Second Edition, Vol. 13. (Thomson Gale, 2003), 372.

86. *DH*, 3.

87. Pope Benedict XVI, *Address to the United Nations' General Assembly* (Apr. 18, 2008).

88. *PT*, 98.

89. John G. Simon, Charles W. Powers, and Jon P. Gunnemann, *The Ethical Investor: Universities and Corporate Responsibility* (New Haven: Yale University Press, 1972), 22–25.

90. *Strangers No Longer*, 39.

91. Amos A. Jordan, William J. Taylor, Jr., and Michael J. Mazarr, *American National Security* (Baltimore, Md.: Johns Hopkins University Press, 5th edn., 1999), 3.

92. Archbishop Celestino Migliore, *Intervention of the Holy See at the Sixth Commission of the General Assembly of the United Nations on Measures to Eliminate International Terrorism* (October 16, 2006).

93. The Judeo-Christian tradition cautions against the ready acceptance of "national security" claims. Following the death of Jacob's son Joseph, for example, the new Pharoh enslaved the exiled people of Israel and afflicted them with "heavy burdens," fearing that they would become "too many and too mighty" (Ex 1:8-22).

94. Center for American Progress, "The Terrorism Index" (April 2006), http://www.americanprogress.org/issues/2006/06/b1763037.html/print.html.

95. Donald Kerwin and Margaret D. Stock, "National Security and Immigration Policy: Reclaiming Terms, Measuring Success, and Setting Priorities," *The Homeland Security Review*, 1, no. 3 (Fall 2007), 131, 202–3.

96. Plato, *The Law*, trans. Trevor Saunders (London: Penguin Books, 1970), 174.

97. *New Catholic Encyclopedia*, Second Edition, Vol. 8. (Thomson-Gale, 2003), 390; Summa theologiae 1a2ae, 90.4.

98. Brian Tamanaha, *On the Rule of Law, History, Politics, Theory* (Cambridge: Cambridge University Press, 2004), 110.

99. American Bar Association, Commission on Immigration, "American Justice Through Immigrants' Eyes" (Chicago: American Bar Association, 2004), 23–52.

100. Jaya Ramji-Nogales, Andrew Schoenholtz, and Phillip G. Schrag, "Refugee Roulette: Disparities in Asylum Adjudication," 60 *Stan. L. Rev.* (2008), 295.

101. Mr. (James) Madison's Report, General Assembly of Virginia (Jan. 7, 1800) (reprinted in The Virginia Commission on Constitutional Government, The Kentucky-Virginia Resolutions and Mr. Madison's Report of 1799 (1960), 36 ("If the banishment of an alien from a country into which he has been invited . . . where he may have formed the most tender of connections, where he may have vested his entire property and acquired property . . . and where he may have nearly completed his probationary title to citizenship . . . if a banishment of this sort be not a punishment, and among the severest of punishments, it will be difficult to imagine a doom to which the norms can be applied.").

102. U.S. Department of Justice, Executive Office for Immigration Review, "FY 2006 Statistical Yearbook" (Falls Church, VA: Executive Office for Immigration Review, February 2007), G1.

103. Donald Kerwin, "Revisiting the Need for Appointed Counsel," *MPI Insight* no. 4 (April 2005), 5–6.

104. Ibid., 5–7.

105. United States Commission for International Religious Freedom, *Report on Asylum Seekers in Expedited Removal, Vol. I: Findings and Recommendations* (February 2005), 41–43.

106. José Luis Rocha, "Why Do They Go?: Theories on the Migration Trend," *Revista Envío* (July 2003), 34, 38.

107. Doris Meissner and Donald Kerwin, "DHS and Immigration: Taking Stock and Correcting Course" (Washington, D.C.: Migration Policy Institute, February 2009), 65, http://www.migrationpolicy.org/pubs/DHS_Feb09.pdf.

108. Randy Capp, Rosa Maria Castaneda, Ajay Chaudry, and Robert Santos, "Paying the Price: The Impact of Immigration Raids on America's Chidren," A Report by The Urban Institute for the National Council of La Raza (Washington, D.C.: National Council of La Raza, 2007), 15–20.

109. Jeffrey Passel and D'Vera Cohn, "A Portrait of Unauthorized Immigrants in the United States" (Washington, D.C.: Pew Hispanic Center, April 2009), 7–8, http://pewhispanic.org/files/reports/107.pdf.

110. U.S. Government Accountability Office, *Illegal Immigration: Border Crossing Deaths Have Doubled Since 1995; Border Patrol's Efforts to Prevent Deaths Have*

Not Been Fully Evaluated, GAO-06-770 (Washington, D.C.: U.S. Government Accountability Office, August 2006), 16.

111. Doris Meissner, Deborah Meyers, Demetrios Papademetriou, and Michael Fix, *Immigration and America's Future* (Washington, D.C.: Migration Policy Institute, September 2006), 19–20.

112. Demetrios G. Papademetriou and Aaron Terrazas, *Immigrants and the Current Economic Crisis: Research Evidence, Policy Challenges, and Implications* (Washington, D.C.: Migration Policy Institute, 2009), 14, 17, http://www.migrationpolicy.org/pubs/lmi_recessionJan09.pdf.

113. Human Rights Watch, *Illegal People: Haitians and Dominico-Haitians in the Dominican Republic* (April 2002), http://www.hrw.org/reports/2002/domrep/domrep 0402-04.htm#TopOfPage.

114. U.S. Conference of Catholic Bishops, *Forming Consciences for Faithful Citizenship* (Washington, D.C.: United States Conference of Catholic Bishops, November 2007), 29.

115. Pontifical Council for Justice and Peace, *Compendium of the Social Doctrine of the Church* (Vatican) http://www.vatican.va/roman_curia/pontifical_councils/justpeace/documents/rc_pc_justpeace_doc_20060526_compendio-dott-soc_en.html, 548.

116. *BBC News,* "Canaries migrant death toll soars" (December 28, 2006), http://news.bbc.co.uk/go/pr/fr/-/2/hi/europe/6213495.stm.

117. J. DeParle, "A Global Trek to Poor Nations, From Poorer Ones," *New York Times,* December 27, 2007.

118. Pope John Paul II, *Undocumented Migrants: Message for World Day of Migration, 1996,* 3, http://www.vatican.va/holy_father/john_paul_ii/messages/migration/documents/hf_jp-ii_mes_25071995_undocumented_migrants_en.html.

Chapter Five

Integration Yesterday and Today: New Challenges for the United States and the Church

Jill Marie Gerschutz with Lois Ann Lorentzen

I want to encourage you and your communities to continue to welcome the immigrants who join your ranks today, to share their hopes and joys, to support them in their sorrows and trials, and to help them flourish in their new home. This, indeed, is what your countrymen have done for generations. From the beginning, they have opened their doors to the tired, the poor, the "huddled masses yearning to breathe free." These are the people whom America has made her own.[1]

In his first visit to the United States, Pope Benedict XVI celebrated the nation's immigrant heritage and called for its continual embrace of immigrants. Migrants have always helped to build and create the nation, whether as diplomats such as Madeleine Albright; scientists such as Albert Einstein; entrepreneurs such as Sergey Brin; athletes such as Roberto Clemente or Dikembe Mutombo or the millions who toil in restaurants, construction, and agriculture. Nearly 38 million immigrants live in the United States today.[2] This is an historically high number, although previous eras in U.S. history experienced higher percentages of immigrants.[3] The foreign-born today account for nearly 13 percent of U.S. residents, and their children account for another 10 percent. The success of these immigrants and their families will "strongly influence the ability of the United States to compete in an increasingly global economy, the health of our democracy, the vitality of civic life, and even the well-being of native born families who have lived in the country for generations."[4] As the Baby Boom generation ages and retires, there will be a growing need for immigrants and their children to replace them in the workforce. However, it is an open question whether America will respond to the Holy Father's call to make its newest members "her own."

Natives and newcomers have struggled to live together ever since Christopher Columbus set foot on American shores. The very presence of newcomers raises the question of what it means to be an American and to whom membership should be extended. The founding fathers set minimum standards for membership; George Washington emphasized good citizenship and allegiance to the country.[5] Since then, cohesion has tended to develop around the common values that most Americans hold: religious faith, hard work, a commitment to family, and patriotism.

When millions of Catholics arrived in the United States in the late nineteenth and early twentieth century, they developed a vast Catholic infrastructure that today includes more than 200 universities, more than 1,000 high schools, and more than 600 hospitals in order to preserve Catholic identity and to promote their socioeconomic mobility. Given this vast infrastructure, the millions of Catholic newcomers, and the millions of well-established Catholics with immigrant roots, the Church is uniquely situated to assume an historic role in the integration of today's newcomers.

This chapter seeks to 1) place Catholic teaching on migrants and newcomers in the context of secular integration theories; 2) illustrate the Catholic Church's pastoral and sociological contributions to integration; and 3) highlight the new integration challenges that it faces. It concludes that the agency of immigrants and their freedom to participate fully in the life of their new communities are key to their successful integration into American society.

The Church's vision for integration is one of a unity in diversity. Its teaching on migration is summarized in *Erga Migrantes Caritas Christi (The Love of Christ Towards Migrants)*:

Migration today . . . imposes new commitments of evangelization and solidarity on Christians and calls them to examine more profoundly those values shared by other religious or lay groups and [that are] indispensable to ensure a harmonious life together. The passage from monocultural to multicultural societies can be a sign of the living presence of God in history and in the community of mankind, for it offers a providential opportunity for the fulfillment of God's plan for a universal communion. This new historical context is characterized by the thousand different faces of humanity and, unlike the past, diversity is becoming commonplace in very many countries. Therefore Christians are called to give witness to and practice not only the spirit of tolerance—itself a great achievement, politically and culturally speaking, not to mention religiously—but also respect for the other's identity. Thus, where it is possible and opportune, they can open a way towards sharing with people of different origins and cultures, also in view of a "respectful proclamation" of their own faith. We are all therefore called to a culture of solidarity, often solicited by the Magisterium, so as to achieve together a real communion of persons. This is the laborious path that the Church invites everyone to follow.[6]

INTEGRATION DEFINED

Terms such as incorporation, assimilation, adaptation, and acculturation all point to the process by which newcomers and their children are accepted into and adapt to a particular society over time. We will use "integration" as a kind of catch-all term in this chapter while describing how the Church views this process.

Conventional wisdom holds that integration into the United States occurs over three generations. Common indicators of "successful" or "complete" integration include linguistic and cultural familiarity, educational achievement, the well-being of the second generation, home ownership, intermarriage, and military service.

Descriptions of integration can be said to lie along a spectrum of maximalist and minimalist expectations regarding the degree to which newcomers adopt the host culture. Assimilation (often depicted by the image of the "melting pot") and multiculturalism (often depicted by the image of the "tossed salad") lie on opposite ends of the integration spectrum. Assimilation describes the unidirectional trajectory from one's home culture to the host culture—usually over generations. Successful assimilation is defined by convergence with the majority population, "becoming more similar over time in norms, values, behaviors, and characteristics."[7] Milton Gordon's "core culture model" in the 1960s posited a white, middle-class, Protestant norm. More recently, Samuel Huntington argued that Anglo-Saxon culture defines U.S. identity. Critics of these models argue that they are coercive and exacerbate the loss of affiliation with migrants' home cultures.

Pluralistic or multicultural models of diversity, as expressed by Diana Eck and Robert Wuthnow, celebrate cultural differences and diversity.[8] The "tossed salad" approach exemplified by Canada calls for mutual accommodation between the host and new cultures. Critics fear this model affords little glue to bind societies. Others believe that multiculturalism implies separateness, which can conjure up images of ghetto-ization of newcomers.

Between the models of multiculturalism and assimilation lie a host of theories that "attempt to nuance the model by emphasizing the multidimensionality and multi-directionality of integration, allowing for biculturalism within different aspects of identity."[9] Some segmented integration theories argue that cultural barriers block some groups—particularly racial or ethnic minorities—from complete integration, even after they have achieved linguistic and cultural assimilation.[10] Other theories hold that migrants choose to conform some aspects of their lives to the dominant culture, while retaining aspects of their native culture: "Immigrants may well succeed in being integrated into

American life in the education system, on the job, socially, and politically . . . while retaining significant elements of their cultural identity at home and in selected venues, bypassing 'cultural assimilation' to one degree or another."[11]

The national parishes of the last century enabled European migrants to retain their cultural traditions of worship and ritual, even in their native languages. National parishes' membership was based upon common language, ethnicity, and national origin, more than on geographic proximity. Under this model, immigrants were expected to integrate into mainstream society, but retain their faith. Peggy Levitt explains: "To be American was to be religious."[12] The Church thus acted as a mediating institution, helping migrants to integrate into the economic and social spheres of society while also enabling them to retain their native customs, cultures, and languages.

Throughout U.S. history, immigrants have both borrowed from and contributed to the dominant culture, helping to create a uniquely American culture. Of course, the openness of the United States to immigrants has been instrumental in their integration. Jeffrey G. Reitz identifies "four dimensions of host societies . . . [that] influence the course of integration: preexisting ethnic or race relations within the host population; differences in labor markets and related institutions; the impact of governmental policies and programs (including immigration policy, integration policies, and policies regulating social institutions); and globalization."[13]

At the root of how and whether new communities integrate into American culture, and the extent to which American communities are open to change lies an important question: what does it mean to be American? Donald Kerwin outlines two predominant theories on the subject: civic nationalism and ethnic or ethno-cultural nationalism. "Civic nationalism does not deny the role of history, tradition and culture in forging ties among citizens, but it views national membership primarily in terms of shared civic values and political institutions."[14] Civic nationalists argue that our country is bound by the ideals of equal opportunity, equality before the law, democracy, and others.[15] "Ethnic nationalism," by contrast, views nations as "distinct peoples connected most deeply by race, religion, and other characteristics that they cannot change or should not have to change. It does not dismiss the importance of shared civic goals and beliefs,"[16] but holds that beliefs are not ultimately decisive in binding people together. A hybrid theory of nationality, with elements of both civic and ethnic nationalism, seeks to perpetuate a core culture that encompasses religion, the English language, European artistic heritage, and Anglo-Protestant values.[17] For the Church, notes Kerwin, "an exclusive view of political membership, particularly one fixed on shared blood and history, is an odd fit with a religion whose mission is to build the human family."[18]

While the Church's teaching on migration would fall most comfortably on the multicultural end of the integration spectrum, it offers a more profound basis for integration: the unity of the human family.

CATHOLIC TEACHING AND PRAXIS ON INTEGRATION

As evidenced by the U.S. Bishops' pastoral letter of 2000, *Welcoming the Stranger Among Us: Unity in Diversity*, Catholic social teaching supports a pluralistic and multicultural approach to migration. It offers a Pentecostal vision, where brothers and sisters in the human family can share their unique gifts. The Most Rev. Nicholas DiMarzio of the Diocese of Brooklyn, who has served on the Pontifical Council for the Pastoral Care of Migrants and Itinerant People and on the United Nations–initiated Global Commission of International Migration, teaches that the "Unity of the Trinity is . . . [the Church's] model for integration of newcomers."[19] The Church expresses that unity in several distinct ways.

Socio-Pastoral Approach

The socio-pastoral approach to integration emphasizes the virtues of welcome and hospitality, especially as carried out by the laity. The pastoral care of migrants means "welcome, respect, protection, promotion and genuine love of every person in his or her religious and cultural expressions."[20] As John Paul II asserted:

> The Church is committed to spare no effort in developing her own pastoral strategy among these immigrant people in order to help them settle in their new land and to foster a welcoming attitude among the local population in the belief that mutual openness will bring enrichment to all.[21]

To welcome immigrants requires acts that "aim at the progressive integration and self-sufficiency of the immigrant."[22] The Church's conception of welcome, like its conception of integration, requires the host community to open itself fully and to offer charity and community.

Hospitality was viewed as a virtue in biblical times. Henri Nouwen offers a definition of hospitality that is particularly appropriate to integration:

> Hospitality . . . means primarily the creation of free space where the stranger can enter and become a friend instead of an enemy. Hospitality is not to change people but to offer them space where change can take place. It is not to bring men and women over to our side, but to offer freedom not disturbed by dividing lines.

It is not to lead our neighbor into a corner where there are no alternatives left, but to open a wide spectrum of options for choice and commitment. . . . To convert hostility into hospitality requires the creation of the friendly empty space where we can reach out to our fellow human beings and invite them to a new relationship.[23] . . . The paradox indeed is that hospitality asks for the creation of an empty space where the guest can find his own soul.[24]

John Paul II called the "sense of open and cordial hospitality" required of a host community: "philoxenia."[25]

The Church's concept of welcome and hospitality highlights the need for a strong relationship between hosts and newcomers. At their best, churches are spiritual homes for new migrants that meet concrete needs by providing social and public services. They serve meals, register people to vote, conduct English classes, shelter migrants in need, encourage inner-city development, provide jobs and job training, mentor migrant youth, visit migrants in detention centers, offer medical and mental health assistance, and more. St. Peter's Catholic Church in San Francisco's Mission District, for example, houses a refugee center, a homeless shelter, legal services for immigrants, and medical and dental services. Nearby, volunteers at Saint Anthony's Church rise at 4:30 AM to cook breakfast for hundreds of day laborers. Table 5.1 illustrates the many Catholic ethnic groups whom the Church serves through formal ethnic ministries.

Table 5.1. Overview of Ethnic Ministries

Ethnic Group	Total # in U.S.	Total # of Catholics
Asian and Pacific Communities	796,700	32,000
Brazilian	800,000	560,000
Czech	50,000	30,000
Ethiopian & Eritrean	250,000	4,000
Filipino	1,850,314	1,536,590
Haitian	1,200,000	800,000
Italian	400,000	360,000
Kmhmu	5,000	3,500
Laotian	300,000	7,000
Maya	200,000	150,000
Portuguese	1,500,000	1,350,000
Samoan	95,000	22,000
Slovak	2,000,000	1,600,000
Tongan	28,000	10,000
Vietnamese	1,500,000	450,000

Source: "Ethnic Apostolate Information 2003," Office of Migration and Refugee Services, U.S. Conference of Catholic Bishops, http://www.usccb.org/mrs/pcmr/stats.shtml.

Although immigrants often integrate in the workplace relatively quickly, their social, civil, political, and cultural integration can be more challenging. Churches often become the face of the host community, fostering social, civic, and political incorporation, while also helping migrants to maintain their own cultural identities and fostering a sense of belonging.

In addition to the aforementioned ministries, the Catholic Church meets the concrete needs of newcomers through institutions like Catholic Charities USA, the Catholic Legal Immigration Network, Inc. (CLINIC), Migration and Refugee Services (MRS), and its vast network of schools and hospitals. More than 9,000 social service organizations fall under the umbrella of Catholic Charities USA, one of the largest charitable networks in the United States, which serves nearly 8 million people of all faiths each year.[26]

The Church's network of educational institutions, including labor schools, elementary and middle schools, and high schools and universities, facilitated the integration of previous Catholic migrants who suffered religious discrimination. High schools and universities created in the late nineteenth and early twentieth centuries, and labor schools such as St. Joseph's in Philadelphia and Xavier in New York City, helped immigrants maintain their Catholic faith tradition while becoming fully "American."

The Catholic Church in the United States now faces a situation similar to the institution-building era of a hundred years ago, when the percentage of the foreign-born was even higher than it is today. Yet Catholic educational institutions have not played the same role in the lives of new migrants today as those of a century ago. Alejandro Portes and Rubén G. Rumbaut write, "Nationwide, about one-quarter of children of Catholic families attend parochial schools today, while children of Latin American (mostly Mexican) families do so at the rate of only four percent."[27]

One bright example of educational incorporation is the Cristo Rey Network of high schools, founded in 2001. The network's mission is to "provide quality, Catholic, college preparatory education to urban young people who live in communities with limited educational options."[28] Though not created to serve migrants per se, 56 percent of Cristo Rey students are Latino, many of them first or second generation migrants. Cristo Rey graduates matriculated into colleges and universities at a rate of more than 99 percent in 2008.[29] Yet the network of schools only begins to scratch the surface of the new immigrant population.

The Church also facilitates civil and political incorporation. CLINIC, for example, supports more than 300 community-based legal agencies. Catholic dioceses run most of these programs, offering immigrants assistance in negotiating the complex processes to secure legal status, work authorization, citizenship, and protection in the United States. CLINIC, MRS,

Catholic Relief Services, Catholic Charities, and various religious orders also advocate with government agencies for improved immigration policies and practices. Faith-based integration services often begin with basic assistance and progress to social, pastoral, and civic orientation for newcomers.

Churches often serve as the first point of entry into active political and civic engagement. In a study of more than 600 immigrant churches in the Washington, D.C. area, Michael W. Foley and Dean R. Hoge identified four ways in which religious organizations could enhance the integration of immigrants into the wider society and polity: (1) the social capital[30] embodied in the worship community itself; (2) their participation in an institution that is itself a participant in civil society; (3) the civic skills fostered within the worship community, as well as opportunities for volunteering and civic involvement; and (4) the ethnic and religious identities through which immigrants and their offspring incorporate into the larger society.[31] In a study of Filipino migrant political participation, Joaquin L. Gonzalez and Claudine del Rosario found that parishes are "the key to continuing struggles against chronic health and other social problems like HIV infection, drug addiction, homelessness, and health insurance, among other social problems."[32]

The U.S. bishops asked Catholics to stand in solidarity with immigrants in *Strangers No Longer: Together on the Journey of Hope*. In 2005, more than 16 Catholic agencies launched the "Justice for Immigrants" (JFI) campaign to educate Catholics on the need for reform of the U.S. immigration system; to bring about reform; and to implement it. Cardinal Roger Mahony of Los Angeles shifted the national immigration debate when he famously asserted in 2006 that he would ask his priests to disobey any law outlawing humanitarian assistance to immigrants. Mahony's stance illustrated the commitment of the Catholic Church to respond to the needs of all people, regardless of their legal status, and it highlighted the importance of moral considerations in public discourse. The U.S. bishops extended the JFI campaign in 2008.

By providing crucial services and helping to organize immigrant communities, religious groups serve as mediating institutions between migrants and what is sometimes seen as a hostile larger society. Robert Putnam posited a "capitalization audit" to argue that social capital formation and civic culture have diminished in American society over the last few decades. He pointed to the decline of bowling leagues to demonstrate his point.[33] However, a study of Filipino migrant Catholics found that a church bowling league in San Jose, California regularly filled 50 lanes. As Gonzalez et al. write, "Filipino migrants to the U.S. are increasing their participation in organized group activities, particularly through their churches. Indeed, their heavy involvement in these social and cultural functions facilitates their own success within American civil society as well as their positive contributions to business and politics."[34] Churches (and bowling alleys!) formerly filled with Irish, German, English, and Italian immigrants, are now spaces for developing the social, political, physical, and intellectual capital of new immigrants.

Because of the safety and familiarity that churches offer, they can serve as incubators for social and political participation. Churches provide immigrants the space to develop new skills and relationships. In this way, immigrant participation in the lives of their faith communities can facilitate their integration into the larger society.

Cultural Approach

The Catholic Church recognizes the importance of culture in seeking to integrate migrants into the economic, social, civil, and political spheres. Culture may be defined as the shared set of values, beliefs, attitudes, and behaviors that characterize a people over a series of generations.[35] Because culture includes the values of a given people, the relationship between faith or religion and culture merits particular attention. Religion plays a key role in forming the values of its followers. Churches provide social belonging, psychological comfort, and religious meaning; migrants enter a space that is familiar, which can feel like "home."

Culture is neither static, nor endlessly malleable. It shifts from one generation to the next, and throughout a lifetime. As the cultures of newcomers begin to influence the culture of a host community, both newcomers and hosts often find themselves in unfamiliar and often uncomfortable positions. Michele R. Pistone and John J. Hoeffner point out:

> As permanence is the illusion of every age, both extremes of the [integration] debate exaggerate the permanence of the contemporary version of their own or other cultures, and their likely importance to distant descendants. Further, as such persons encourage resistance by some to change and highlight resentment at having to change, they likewise exaggerate the ability of certain other people to change.[36]

Catholic teaching recognizes that people must express their faith and values within their particular cultures. Through the process of inculturation, "cultures shed light upon, bring new perspectives to, and make palatable the truths of the Gospel. This ability to find truth in what is other, which occurs only through openness and receptivity, underlies the Catholic tradition."[37]

Welcoming the Stranger Among Us: Unity in Diversity explains:

> The presence of so many people of so many different cultures and religions in so many different parts of the United States has challenged us as a Church to a

profound conversation so that we can become truly a sacrament of unity. We reject the anti-immigrant stance that has become popular in different parts of our country, and the nativisim, ethnocentricity, and racism that continue to reassert themselves in our communities. We are challenged to get beyond ethnic communities living side by side within our own parishes without any connection with each other.

It is important to acknowledge that anti-immigrant sentiment among the host society has accompanied all major migrations to the United States. But Catholic teaching calls us to rise beyond the fear and commodification of newcomers and to treat them with dignity and openness.

Unity in Diversity highlights cultural celebrations and devotions from around the world as "gifts given to the church."[38] Events honoring Salvador del Mundo, Our Lady of Guadalupe, Saint Lorenzo Ruiz, Our Lady of La Vang, and other national or cultural saints occur in most U.S. cities. Across the United States, Latino worshippers carry on their custom of the Day of the Dead on November 1 and 2. A Day of the Dead altar at Misión Católica in suburban Atlanta features photos of Monsignor Oscar Romero, César Chavez, Padre Rutilio Grande and Monsignor Juan Gerardi, creating a pan-Latino spiritual home for migrants.[39] At Visitation of the Blessed Virgin Mary in Philadelphia, a different immigrant community is invited to decorate the altar at Christmas each year according to their tradition, and to explain that tradition to their brothers and sisters in faith. These expressions of welcoming and invitations to share unique gifts manifest the Church's vision of a Pentecostal pluralism. Additionally, the common values of the faith contribute to a shared identity among Catholics across the globe.

Traditions and inculturation enable the Church to facilitate "cultural preservation as well as cultural pluralism," as John Paul II urged.[40] Bishop DiMarzio has written on the way worship communities reinforce culture identities:[41]

> Worship communities . . . carry forward cultural traditions of the immigrant community, bringing together members of an immigrant group around cultural symbols and practices, reinforcing ties among them (including a common language).

"God needs no passport" writes Peggy Levitt, "because faith traditions give their followers symbols, rituals, and stories they use to create alternative sacred landscapes, marked by holy sites, shrines and places of worship."[42] Yet as Foley and Hoge caution, culture can also isolate immigrants.[43] European immigrants at the turn of the last century thrived in national parishes that facilitated the preservation of their native cultures while they joined mainstream society. At the time, classic assimilation models requiring conformity were the vision for integration, and parishes were a cultural oasis for newcomers to return to the familiar.

By emphasizing the gifts of all cultures, the Church today rejects the unidirectional conceptions of classic assimilation theories. Instead, the process of inculturation allows the Church to embrace the gifts of diverse cultures and to thrive in diverse national settings. By calling upon Catholics not only to tolerate, but to fully embrace newcomers and facilitate their integration, Catholic teaching prescribes a deeper integration than secular theories.

Theological Approach

The word "integration" comes from the Latin "integer," meaning whole. The word "integrity" also derives from "integer" and means "undivided, complete." This etymology describes the Church's theological conception of migrant integration: communities that live out the wholeness of the human family. "Being children of one Father, all members of the human race are brothers and sisters with each other and form one single human family."[44] Bishop DiMarzio calls the Trinity the model of integration: "The integrity or wholeness of one God in three persons united in a complete, unimpaired, and virtuous community of love . . . reveals perfect unity in diversity."[45]

In the Golden Rule, Jesus teaches that love toward neighbor derives from a loving relationship between a believer and God. Given this standard of love as a vision for right relationships, how can—and how should—newcomers and natives live together? What are the minimum requirements for a just relationship? Principles of Catholic teaching such as the common good, human dignity, participation, and authentic development establish criteria by which to evaluate just relationships.

According to Catholic teaching, justice between individuals and their society requires that individuals must have access to what they need in order to survive. Vibrant societies provide for the integral and authentic development of everyone within them: that is, they allow individuals to develop socially, politically, and culturally such that each person may become the person God has called him or her to become. As a "privileged agent of the common good,"[46] governments have a duty to promote and protect the basic rights of all people to foster authentic integral development. This may require governments to provide more assistance to the poor and marginalized, including to unauthorized or other vulnerable immigrants. Thus, Catholic teaching argues for policies that facilitate the participation of the poor and marginalized, including noncitizens.

Authentic development requires the protection and promotion of human dignity of all. Among the most basic rights is the right to participate in society: "All people have a right to participate in the economic, political, and cultural life of society. It is a fundamental demand of justice and a requirement for human dignity that all people be assured a minimum level of participation in the community."[47] The marginalization of unauthorized persons and their ineligibility for citizenship restrict their ability to participate in basic decisions affecting them. If they cannot integrate, immigrant communities may become insular. For example, as a result of local measures requiring police to check the legal status of those they stop, even for traffic violations, immigrants avoid public playgrounds, libraries, and other day-to-day activities in public spaces.

Justice requires a commitment by all residents (including immigrants) to contribute to the common good. Paying taxes, public service, and providing for their families are all contributions that immigrants and other residents owe the larger society. Integrated migrants can contribute more to their communities than those forced to remain at society's margins. In 2008, as the result of what was then the largest work-site immigration raid in U.S. history, one in six residents of the small town of Postville, Iowa—nearly 400 people working at a slaughterhouse—was arrested, criminally prosecuted, and placed in deportation proceedings. Not only the immigrant community, but the fabric of the larger Postville community unraveled as a consequence. Schools, businesses, and churches suffered the loss of their friends and community members. One parent explained that the psychological impact of the raid on her U.S. citizen child was devastating, as one-third of the child's friends disappeared overnight.

Family unity merits special attention given its primacy in development and in promoting the common good. The Church teaches that human beings long for communion and unity with others and with God. Families, "a school of deeper humanity,"[48] are the primary and fundamental institution of community. Migrants often forego or delay family unity—leaving children behind in their home countries, for instance—in order to provide for their families. Receiving societies should establish immigration policies that strengthen families. Policies that divide families—whether through raids, visas that preclude accompaniment of family members, or significant caps on family visas—impede integration and undermine the community's most fundamental building block.

As governments promote the integral development of their residents, the Church urges that priority be given to the needs of the poor and to vulnerable families. Rev. David Hollenbach, S.J. provides three "normative ethical standards" to guide consideration of the tensions between newcomers and natives:

1. The needs of the poor take priority over the wants of the rich.
2. The freedom of the dominated takes priority over the liberty of the powerful.
3. The participation of marginalized groups takes priority over the preservation of an order which excludes them.[49]

Church teaching rejects the assumption that tolerance of immigrants is the highest achievable standard of integration. Instead, the Catholic Church invites host communities and newcomers to engage in a deeper relationship as brothers and sisters in the human family. It calls for solidarity, which it defines as a "firm and persevering determination to commit oneself to the common good . . . because we really are all responsible for all."[50] Solidarity opens eyes and hearts to appreciate the gifts newcomers bring to host communities and engenders empathy for migrants in their struggles as outsiders. Solidarity may be lived out with migrants by accompanying them through the integration process. Accompaniment requires a commitment to virtues like compassion, understanding, justice, respect for dignity, and love of neighbor. In moving beyond legal justice into relationships of solidarity and love, communities move one step closer to the Trinitarian unity described by Bishop DiMarzio.

In summary, the Church calls upon host societies to welcome newcomers with hospitality, to appreciate their cultural gifts, and to embrace them as brothers and sisters in the human family.

INTEGRATION IN THE NEW MILLENNIUM: CHALLENGES AND OPPORTUNITIES

Migrants are the face of globalization today. Their vulnerability exemplifies the uncertainty and rapid change experienced globally at the dawn of the third millennium. While immigration is not new, today's migrants present new challenges and opportunities for the Catholic Church and for society as a whole. As record numbers of immigrants enter the United States, the nation may adopt one of three approaches: xenophobia and exclusion; marginalization and discrimination; or solidarity and integration.[51]

Challenges and Opportunities for the Church

How can the Church model unity in diversity? Today's migrants are often met with the same antagonizing stereotypes that previous generations of migrants encountered. Can the Church today—both religious and the laity— live out the Pontifical exhortations to welcome the strangers among us?

One concern is that Catholic institutions may be victims of their own success. These institutions play a critical role in responding to large numbers of persons in a professional manner. However, established institutions also need to adapt to the needs of newcomers and to guard against a business-like approach in their work that feels unwelcoming or uninviting to immigrants. In addition, the work of charities and service providers must be complemented by the more personal support that parishes can provide.

Due to the Church's success at integrating past waves of immigrants, the United States is a "post-immigrant" society, asserts Rev. Bryan Hehir.[52] Catholics are now among the nation's most successful and established groups. And yet significant numbers of Catholic newcomers live on the margins of society. As a "center-edged" institution, the Church is uniquely positioned to respond to the needs of new immigrants. However, these two groups of Catholics are perhaps better described as cousins meeting at the occasional family reunion than as brothers and sisters. In fact, James M. O'Toole suggests that there are two or three different Catholic churches in the United States: the well-off white church; the working class white church; and the poorer people of color church.[53] Because of the successful integration of Catholics into the United States, new immigrants generally do not face the level of discrimination as religious minorities that perhaps united European immigrants in the last century. Still, an initial step toward the full integration of newcomers within society would be their successful integration within the Church itself.

The unique customs and traditions of diverse faith communities can be threatening to communities (whether native or newcomer) accustomed to worshiping in one way. *Erga Migrantes Caritas Christi (The Love of Christ Towards Migrants)* highlights two models for integrated pastoral care: the inter-ethnic model in which many ethnicities celebrate mass together incorporating their diverse traditions, and the ethnic (national) model wherein each ethnicity celebrates through its own tradition.[54] As migrants have increasingly settled beyond the traditional gateway states of California, Florida, Illinois, New Jersey, New York, and Texas since the 1990s, more and more parishes across the United States find themselves confronting this challenge.

Development of inter-ethnic parishes "requires pastors to give ethnic communities space and solid pastoral accompaniment," asserts Rev. Shay Auerbach, S.J., pastor at Sacred Heart parish in Richmond, Virginia. "It requires pastoral agents to be as versed in the Catholic tradition as they can, and to concretely accompany newcomers, respectful of their traditions. The accompanier must also try to become as versed as an outsider possibly can in the cultures of the newcomers." Pastors must reach out to newcomers and draw them into all facets of the community's life. The Day of the Dead celebration is one example of the tradition of popular religion that Latinos bring to the Church. Incorporating popular religion into the more cerebral American Church is sometimes perceived as a threat to the identity of the host community and traditional forms of celebration. But as Rev. Alan Figueroa Deck, S.J. argues, "the effectiveness of ministry with Hispanics depends more upon a positive and respectful understanding of their popular religion than on any other single factor."[55]

Learning to share unique forms and traditions of worship requires new ways of interacting with fellow Catholics of different ethnicities, which can be life-giving and restorative. After the significance of the Day of the Dead altar was explained at St. Raphael's in Raleigh, North Carolina, Anglo-Americans soon filled the altar with more photos than the Hispanics who shared the custom.

Many parishes struggle to implement a successful inter-ethnic model. A study by the U.S. Catholic Bishops in 1999 found that Latino Catholics—immigrants and long-term residents—were twice as likely to worship in "separate and . . . unequal settings," and were often required to "rent" the church to which they belonged.[56] Additionally, John Coleman has identified several tensions in inter-ethnic parish-settings: (1) people prefer to pray in their mother tongue, arguing against multi-lingual prayer; (2) the adornment of the parish provides groups a sense of ownership and belonging, which can be diluted in a multicultural setting; and (3) prematurely merging newcomers with distinct cultural/language needs into a larger congregation can have "a negative effect on the strength of their religious commitments."[57] National parishes, by contrast, have been credited with allowing immigrants to integrate into the larger society from a position of strength. Finally, some argue that even when multiculturalism is achieved, it is a soft-multiculturalism that "regards ethnic Catholicism as culturally interesting and worth preserving for the expressive variety it provides, yet has no profound stake in the spiritual values ethnic cultures bring to Catholicism."[58] If this is the perspective of Latino/a Americans and other minorities in the U.S. Church today, one might hypothesize that this at least partly explains why migrants increasingly defect to other denominations. The situation begs for mutual accommodation and inter-ethnic exchange.

Immigrant youth present another challenge. While youth everywhere struggle to discover the role of faith in their lives, immigrant youth often require special attention. The continuation of home country religious practices and traditions may help parents or immigrant adults feel at home. Yet, immigrant youth often experience tension between their desire to mainstream into host society culture and pressures to preserve their ethnic identities, in both religion and society at large. The Church has begun to emphasize the importance of paying particular attention to the needs of youth.

If the Church lives up to its ideals and promise, it can exemplify intercultural diversity. To do so will require imagination. Simply absorbing new immigrants into institutions developed by Euroamericans may well prove ineffective to building unity in diversity. Small faith-sharing communities, transnational faith movements, leadership development, and incorporation of newcomers' traditions are promising ways to live out these ideals.

Small communities afford an intimate space for deeper cross-fertilization of cultures and trust-building. They can provide a home for people far from home and a space for deeper reflection for host communities. The Church has experienced success with small faith communities that meet regularly. Base ecclesial communities—a common way of sharing faith and building community in Latin America—offer "a process of liberation of persons who in the light of the gospel unite as a community to confront their reality in order to give a creative response."[59] The Church in the United States developed similar small faith-sharing communities in the pastoral program called Renew. Since the program's inception in the 1970s, smaller faith communities have been formed, serving thousands of Catholics.[60] Although small ecclesial communities were adopted in the National Pastoral Plan for Hispanics, Base Ecclesial Communities may not be used as much in parishes as the literature would suggest.[61] Nonetheless, these processes offer great potential for faith sharing across cultural differences, thus engendering unity.

In addition to facilitating the development of spiritually intimate faith communities, the recent formation of international movements facilitates intercultural exchanges and connections to communities of origin. Several of these movements have been approved by the Vatican, including, for example, the San Egidio community, Legionnaries of Christ, and the Focolare Movement. Like many of their secular counterparts, these ecclesial movements are based in local communities but also foster cultural exchanges— often across boundaries—which can help communities experience and comfortably dialogue with other cultures. Given the relative convenience with which migrants today maintain contact with their home communities (through cheaper travel and internet communication) these transnational movements can provide a sense of a transnational Church and faith experience for bi-national/bi-cultural individuals and a sense of community with natives. The ecumenical Focolare Movement in particular aims at facilitating cross-cultural familiarity and could be said to exemplify unity in diversity. The theological underpinning of this movement is that God is love, and that mutual love unites people. This unity transforms differences into mutual enrichment.[62] Ecumenical movements' successes in developing solidarity locally and internationally offer a new way of being Church consonant with the globalizing world.

As with any institution, leadership development proves critical for migrant integration in churches. A common refrain of pastors of migrant parishes is "do with, not for." Immigrant-led groups enable their members to "find their own soul" in their new communities; participation in them helps migrants in their transition from newcomers to partners in their new home. Leaders are the architects and structural engineers of the parish life that respond to migrants' spiritual and sociological needs. Leadership allows migrants to plant a stake in their new communities and nourish those communities as their own. And the mutual interest of developing a flourishing community that nourishes spiritual lives can, in an ideal and open setting, bridge cultural gaps.

Finally, it would be a glaring oversight not to discuss the Hispanicization of the Church in the United States. One-third of all U.S. Catholics are Latinos, many of them foreign born. Rev. Alan Figueroa Deck, S.J. has argued that evangelization of Hispanic-Americans has the potential to evangelize "Catholic American culture."[63] He argues that pastoral approaches that began 20 to 30 years ago were either antagonistic to popular religion or replicated old institutions without helping newcomers to respond to their new culture.[64] In order to respond to the unique experience of Hispanic Americans, more Hispanics must take on leadership roles than the current 4 percent of trained lay ecclesial ministers and 5 percent of priests.[65] Deck argues that a more empowered ministry by Hispanics could re-evangelize the U.S. Catholic community: "Strongly oriented to an affective, symbolic, and ritual search for meaning . . . Latino/a Catholicism offers some fascinating possibilities precisely in the context of a postmodern world characterized by a desperate search for meaning."[66]

New and creative ways to express and live out the faith will serve not only to welcome and integrate migrants into the Church, but they also hold the key for the Church's revitalization. The future of the Church in the United States and the well-being of the nation itself increasingly depend on the leadership and participation of new immigrants. One-third of new priests are migrants. One of four Catholics in San Francisco is of Filipino descent, leading some scholars to claim that Filipino and Latino migrants "save" churches in urban areas. New Latino and Asian immigrants have replenished and rejuvenated declining parishes in cities throughout the United States. The future of the Catholic Church in the United States is inextricably bound with the fate of new immigrants.

Toward an Integration Policy?

An independent panel of policy-makers and researchers has concluded that "[c]lassic indicators such as employment, education, military service, inter-marriage, and home ownership show that today's immigrants are successfully integrating into American society."[67] The ability of immigrants to integrate depends largely on individual, family, and state and local efforts.[68] Given the large number of migrants, many policy-makers are asking whether integration should be left to the status quo: a laissez-faire model. Or should the United States develop a coordinated, comprehensive integration policy and, if so, what would that policy look like?

More and more groups have begun to argue for a larger government role in integration. The Department of Homeland Security–sponsored Task Force on New Americans asserts the need for newcomers to adopt the political principles that comprise American political identity: American democracy, U.S. history, and English language. It leaves cultural integration to the private sphere.[69]

The Independent Task Force on Immigration and America's Future asserts the need for a federal office of immigrant integration as a critical component of an overhauled immigration system to better serve America's needs. It argues that the "skeletal, ad hoc, and largely underfunded"[70] approach of the U.S. government toward integration leaves states and local communities to fund the integration of immigrants, which can be particularly challenging when immigrants enter in large numbers to smaller communities. The Task Force recommends:

> A National Office on Immigrant Integration should be created to provide leadership, visibility, and a focal point at the federal level for integration policy. The office would establish goals for immigrant integration, and measure the degree to which these goals are met. The office would assess and coordinate federal policies and agencies related to integration, and serve as an intermediary with state and local governments. As a principal priority, the office should examine the supply of and demand for English-language instruction among limited English-proficient groups, and provide leadership and expertise for public and private sector initiatives and resources to meet that demand.[71]

The public-private partnership approach favored by the task force implies a significant role for community-based organizations and faith communities. A comprehensive federal policy addressing immigrant integration could help to ensure that new Americans succeed in the United States.

Other groups take the "if it ain't broke, don't fix it" approach. Advocates of the laissez-faire model of integration point to the successful integration of past and current generations as evidence that migrants will naturally integrate and therefore require no further governmental support. They point to the privately funded English as a Second Language (ESL) courses and scholarships

Table 5.2.   Targeted Federal Spending on Immigrants 1999 and 2005, in Millions of 2005 Dollars

	FY 1999 Spending	*FY 2005 Spending*	*% Change 1999 to 2005*
Refugee Resettlement Program	$ 545	$ 470	−13.8%
Migrant Head Start	$ 209	$ 266	27.3%
Migrant Education	$ 421	$ 390	−7.4%
Migrant Education Even Start	$ 5	$ 8	60.0%
Migrant Health	$ 92	$ 144	56.5%
NCLB Language Acquisition State Grants	—	$ 673	—
EIEP (Emergency Immigrant Education Program)	$ 176	—	
Federal Bilingual Education	$ 273	—	—
Adult ESL*	$ 207	$ 277	33.8%
USCIS Office of Citizenship	—	$ 3	—
Emergency Health Care for Unauthorized Immigrants	—	$ 250	—
Total	**$ 1,928**	**$ 2,481**	**28.7%**

* Note: We assume here that expenditures on Adult ESL are proportional to shares that ESL recipients represent of total Adult Basic Education participants in the closest year for which data is available. For FY 1999, we use data from the 1997–1998 school year. Source: Julia Gelatt and Michael Fix, "Federal Spending on Immigrant Families' Integration," *Securing the Future: US Immigrant Integration Policy, A Reader,* ed. Michael Fix (Washington, DC: Migration Policy Institute, 2007), 62.

provided by many larger corporations.[72] Yet as Table 5.2 illustrates, there is a significant dearth of English language programs. Overall, federal funding for integration is limited and ad hoc—aimed primarily at health and education.

A glance across the Atlantic suggests that integration policies and programs are not a panacea. Despite the lack of an integration policy in the United States, new Americans tend to integrate much more successfully than newcomers to Germany, France, or other European nations even though these nations often offer strong integration policies and programs. As Tamar Jacoby puts it, "Europe has the words, but the United States has the music."[73] How can we unravel this paradox?

First, the United States has long embraced the concept of civic nationalism. In Europe, by contrast, the ethnic nationalism model prevailed for centuries. Today, Europeans are not only being asked to change their concept of citizenship from an ethnic nationalism model to one of shared civic values, but also to develop a supranational "European" identity under the aegis of the European Union (E.U.). Second, E.U. integration policy increasingly aims at the supranational level, affording minimal citizen-participation.

Many scholars conclude that the relationship between citizenship and immigration policy at least in part explains the paradox of why the United States enjoys more successful integration than Europe.[74] Eligibility for citizenship has served as an incentive for integration, they assert. Susan Martin of the Institute for the Study of International Migration argues that both the relative ease of attaining citizenship in the United States, as well as the family-based integration system, encourages newcomers to develop roots in the United States.[75] CLINIC points out that citizenship also inspires dedication to and participation in the political system; socioeconomic mobility; and mainstreaming.[76] The U.S. political culture and its economic system demand participation. If immigrants are not politically active, they will not be influential.

The nearly 12 million persons in the United States without legal status can neither fully participate nor therefore fully integrate into U.S. society. Lack of opportunity may also reduce the ambitions of immigrant children and limit their socioeconomic mobility. Moreover, the increase in federal, state, and local enforcement policies between 2006 and 2008, which aimed to force unauthorized immigrants to self-deport, further marginalized them. The impact of deportation-through-attrition policies extends beyond the unauthorized, hurting their families and communities and leading to discrimination against the foreign-born in general. Increasing ethnic tensions threaten to unravel a complex social fabric woven in the United States over generations. If eligibility for citizenship is indeed the key to U.S. success in integration, then current policies need to be reformed.

Do we need an immigrant integration policy today? John Higham points out that the Americanization Movement of the 1910s and 1920s actively sought to "Americanize" immigrants through English-language programs, civics classes, and displays of patriotism, but that this was sometimes forced and therefore often created mistrust and hostility.[77] Thomas R. Jimenez cautions against a coercive approach to integration: "[E]fforts to strip immigrants and their children of their ethnic allegiances altogether can have deleterious academic and psychological outcomes that further inhibit positive integration."[78] Indeed, permitting some cultural preservation enables immigrants to integrate in a way that honors their native culture and welcomes their gifts.

At such an uncertain time in U.S. history, the integration of nearly 38 million immigrants (as well as their children) will strengthen our national fabric and promote our core civic values. An integration program must incorporate lessons from the past. First, it must be developed and carried out in close partnership with civil society. Partnership with locally rooted organizations, especially non-governmental organizations, helps to ensure that integration programs are tailored to particular circumstances. This model reflects the experience of previous eras of large-scale immigration when religious organizations, labor unions, and public education systems made concerted efforts to mainstream newcomers. Moreover, this approach avoids the perception of forced integration by the government. Second, integration policies should aim not to "Americanize" newcomers or to coerce integration, but rather educate them to interact in the civil and political spheres. They must reflect the shift from an assimilation model to one of segmented integration. In "A More Perfect Union: A National Citizenship Plan," CLINIC points to several barriers to citizenship that could be removed to help promote integration: lack of English language proficiency; ignorance of the legal requirements for citizenship; the need for professional assistance in applying; and financial limitations.[79]

Lessons can also be drawn from the U.S. experience in resettling refugees.[80] With cooperation between non-governmental organizations—including the Catholic Church—and the private sector, the U.S. Office of Refugee Resettlement provides funding for job training and placement, English-language classes, social orientation, cash and medical assistance, and aid for victims of torture. Not coincidentally, MRS is the nation's largest refugee resettlement network. Mutual Assistance Associations (MAAs)—non-profit, community-based organizations comprised of settled refugees—are also crucial contributors to the success of refugee resettlement programs. MAAs help to translate U.S. culture to newcomers. Hometown Associations (HTAs) have recently been identified as institutions also capable of sponsoring newcomers. Typically, these diaspora associations come together to develop projects in their native communities. They hold great potential to facilitate integration among ethnic community members. Churches, businesses, and philanthropic organizations would also prove critical partners in a national integration program.

CONCLUSION

The start of the twenty-first century saw immigration in the United States at its greatest peak in history, and more dispersed and diverse than in the past. At the same time, the era is marked by a decline in the strength of religious institutions and labor unions, both of which played lead roles in facilitating immigrant integration in past eras. Nonetheless, religion gives migrants a supranational identity in a complex world where their national identity is in flux. In addition, shared religious values can link newcomers and natives.

Robert Wuthnow contends that the increase in religious tolerance has been accompanied by an internalization of religion in the United States.[81] While tolerance is welcome and facilitates integration, the sense of religion as a purely private enterprise "has severely limited whatever potential American religion may have had for making us a better society." At the same time, however, the growing literature on immigration and religion shows that for many immigrants, the church "is the center of life outside of their jobs."[82] Thus, churches still have an opportunity—even responsibility—to help migrants integrate into American society; in Nouwen's words: to create that "friendly, empty space where the guest can find his own soul." Integration requires that migrants enjoy a space in which they can continue to live out their identities and traditions from their home countries and to develop the skills and relationships that will allow them to navigate life in their new communities. As Bishop DiMarzio asserts, migrants should not be viewed as victims, but as agents of their future.[83] For the dignity of newcomers and the common good of society, U.S. churches must constantly work to model Church teaching on unity in diversity. In doing so, they will provide opportunities for their members—both newcomers and the long-settled—to answer Christ's call: "For I was a stranger, and you welcomed me (Mt 25:35)."

NOTES

1. Pope Benedict XVI, Address to U.S. Bishops (April 16, 2008), 3, http://cnsblog .wordpress.com/2008/04/16/text-of-pope-to-us-bishops/.

2. Marcelo Suarez-Orozco, Keynote Address, National Migration Conference, U.S. Conference of Catholic Bishops, Washington, D.C., July 28, 2008.

3. Ibid.

4. Tomas R. Jimenez, "From Newcomers to Americans: An Integration Policy for a Nation of Immigrants," *Immigration Policy In Focus*, Vol. 5, No. 11 (American Immigration Law Foundation): 5, http://www.ailf.org/ipc/infocus/ipc_infocus_0704 .shtml.

5. Donald Kerwin, "America's Children," *America* 197 no. 8 (New York: America Press, Inc. 2007), 13.

6. Pontifical Council for the Pastoral Care of Migrants and Itinerant People, *Erga Migrantes Caritas Christi (The Love of Christ Towards Migrants)* 9 (2004).

7. Susan K. Brown and Frank D. Bean, "Assimilation Models, Old and New: Explaining a Long-Term Process," Washington, D.C.: Migration Policy Institute, 2006, http://www.migrationinformation.org/feature/display.cfm?id=442.

8. As described in Hien Duc Do and Mimi Khuc, "Immigrant Religious Adaptation: Vietnamese American Buddhists at Chua Viet Nam (Vietnamese Buddhist Temple)" in *Religion at the Corner of Bliss and Nirvana: Politics, Identity, and Faith in New Migrant Communities,* ed. Lois Ann Lorentzen, Joaquin Jay Gonzalez III, Kevin M. Chun, and Hien Duc Do (Durham, NC: Duke University Press, forthcoming), 203–5.

9. Ibid., 205.

10. Brown and Bean.

11. Michael W. Foley and Dean R. Hoge, *Religion and the New Immigrants: How Faith Communities Form Our Newest Citizens* (New York: Oxford University Press, 2007), 6.

12. Peggy Levitt, *God Needs No Passport: Immigrants and the Changing American Religious Landscape* (New York & London: The New Press, 2007), explaining Herberg, 17–18.

13. Jeffrey G. Reitz, "Host Societies and the Reception of Immigrants: Research Themes, Emerging Theories and Methodological Issues," *International Migration Review* 36, no. 4 (2002): 1005–20, as cited in Elzbieta M. Gozdziak and Susan F. Martin, *Beyond the Gateway: Immigrants in a Changing America* (New York: Lexington Books, 2005), 9.

14. Kerwin, *America*.

15. Donald Kerwin, "Catholic Social Teaching and Nationality," paper at National Migration Conference, Washington, D.C., July 29, 2008.

16. Kerwin, *America*, 11.

17. Donald Kerwin, "Catholic Social Teaching and Nationality," paper at National Migration Conference, Washington, D.C., July 29, 2008.

18. Kerwin, National Migration Conference.

19. Bishop Nicolas DiMarzio, "John Paul II: Migrant Pope Teaches on Unwritten Laws of Migration," *Notre Dame Journal of Law, Ethics and Public Policy* XXI, no. 1 (Notre Dame, IN: 2007), 211–12.

20. *EMCC*, 28.

21. John Paul II, *Ecclesia in America (The Church in America)* 65 (1999).

22. *EMCC*, 43.

23. Henri J. M. Nouwen, *The Dance of Life: Weaving Sorrows and Blessings into One Joyful Step,* ed. Michael Ford (Notre Dame, IN: Ave Maria Press, 2005), 79–80.

24. Ibid., 109.

25. Most Rev. Nicholas DiMarzio, Ph.D., D.D., "John Paul II: Migration Pope Teaches on Unwritten Laws of Migration," *Notre Dame Journal of Law, Ethics & Public Policy* 21 (May 1, 2007), 205.

26. "About CCUSA," Catholic Charities USA, http://www.catholiccharitiesusa .org/NetCommunity/Page.aspx?pid=290&srcid=193.

27. Alejandro Portes and Rubén G. Rumbaut, *Immigrant America: A Portrait* (Berkeley & Los Angeles: University of California Press, 2006), 334.

28. Cristo Rey Network, http://www.cristoreynetwork.org/.

29. Ibid.

30. Social capital may be defined as, "the actual and potential resources available to individuals by virtue of their participation in social networks;" (Pierre Bourdieu, in Foley and Hoge, 30).

31. Foley and Hoge, 5.

32. Joaquin L. Gonzalez III and Claudine del Rosario, "Counter-Hegemony Finds Place in a Hegemon: Activism through Filipino-American Churches," in *Religion at the Corner of Bliss and Nirvana: Politics, Identity, and Faith in New Migrant Communities,* ed. Lois Ann Lorentzen, Joaquin Jay Gonzalez III, Kevin M. Chun, and Hien Duc Do (Durham, NC: Duke University Press, forthcoming).

33. Robert D. Putnam, *Bowling Alone: The Collapse and Revival of American Community* (New York: Simon & Schuster, 2000).

34. Joaquin L. Gonzalez III, Andrea Maison, and Dennis Marzan, "We Do Not Bowl Alone: Cultural and Social Capital from Filipino Faiths, Festivals, and Feasts," in *Religion at the Corner of Bliss and Nirvana: Politics, Identity, and Faith in New*

Migrant Communities, ed. Lois Ann Lorentzen, Joaquin Jay Gonzalez III, Kevin M. Chun, and Hien Duc Do (Durham, NC: Duke University Press, forthcoming).

35. Adapted from Webster Dictionary online: www.miriam-webster.com/dictionary/culture.

36. Michele R. Pistone and John J. Hoeffner, "The Acceptance of Immigrants: Lessons from the Past and Questions for the Future," *Mediterranean Journal of Human Rights* 10, no. 1 (2006), 7–53.

37. Alan Figueroa Deck, S.J., "A Latino Practical Theology: Mapping the Road Ahead," *Theological Studies* 65, no. 2, (Milwaukee: Marquette University, 2004), 283.

38. United States Conference of Catholic Bishops, *Welcoming the Stranger Among Us: Unity in Diversity* (2000), http://www.usccb.org/mrs/unity.shtml.

39. Marie Friedmann Marquardt, "Structural and Cultural Hybrids: Religious Congregational Life and Public Participation of Mexicans in the New South," in *Immigrant Faiths: Transforming Religious Life in America*, ed. Karen I. Leonard, Alex Stepick, Manuel A. Vásquez, and Jennifer Holdaway (Lanham, Md.: Rowman & Littlefield Publishing, Inc.), 190.

40. DiMarzio, 203.

41. DiMarzio, 213.

42. Levitt, 13.

43. Foley and Hoge, 10.

44. Pope John Paul II, *Redemptor Hominis (The Redeemer of Man)* 9–10 (1979), as quoted in Archbishop Stephen Fumio Hamao, "The Role of the Receiving Community in the Pastoral Care of Migrants and Refugees," address to the Singapore Archdiocesan Commission for Migrants and Itinerant People, July 7, 2002, http://www.vatican.va/roman_curia/pontifical_councils/migrants/documents/rc_pc_migrants

45. DiMarzio, 193.

46. Thomas Leininger, Ph.D., phone conversation, July 18, 2008.

47. Office of Social Justice St. Paul and Minneapolis, "Principles of Catholic Social Teaching," http://www.osjspm.org/major_themes.aspx.

48. Kristin E. Heyer, "Immigration: A Faithful Approach to Matters of Citizenship," *Journal of Religion and Society* Supplement Series 2 (2008), eds. Dennis Hamm, S.J. and Gail S. Risch, 143, http://moses.creighton.edu/JRS/toc/SS04.html.

49. David Hollenbach, *Claims in Conflict: Retrieving and Renewing the Catholic Human Rights Tradition* (Woodstock Theological Center: Paulist Press, 1979), 204.

50. John Paul II, *Sollicitudo Rei Socialis (On Social Concern)* 38 (1987).

51. Rev. Josep Buades Fuster, S.J., paper at Jesuit Migration Service—South America: Santiago, Chile, May 6, 2007.

52. Rev. J. Brian Hehir, "Catholic Social Teaching and Migration" (U.S. Conference of Catholic Bishops), http://www.usccb.org/mrs/hehir.shtml.

53. James M. O'Toole, *The Faithful: A History of Catholics in America* (Cambridge, Massachusetts: The Belknap Press of Harvard University Press, 2008), 291.

54. *EMCC,* 93.

55. Allan Figueroa Deck, S.J., *The Second Wave: Hispanic Ministry and the Evangelization of Cultures* (New York: Paulist Press, 1989), 6.

56. Lois Ann Lorentzen, "No Longer Strangers," *Sojourners* 32, no. 2 (2003), 28.

57. As cited in Deck, *Theological Studies*, 293.

58. M. Francis Mannion, as cited in Deck, *Theological Studies*, 282, n16.

59. This is the definition used by the National Federation of Priests' Councils, as cited by Deck, 71.

60. Deck, 135.

61. Deck, 72.

62. Focolare Movement, http://www.focolare.com.

63. Deck, *Theological Studies*, 295.

64. Deck, *Theological Studies*, 290.

65. Ken Johnson-Mondragon, *En Marcha!* (Washington DC: Secretariat for Hispanic Affairs of the USCCB, Winter/Spring 2003), 13 as cited in Deck, *Theological Studies*, 278, n8.

66. Deck, *Theological Studies*, 296.

67. Doris Meissner, et al., *Immigration and America's Future: A New Chapter*. Report of the Independent Task Force on Immigration and America's Future (Washington, DC: Migration Policy Institute, 2006), 13.

68. Meissner, et al., 18.

69. U.S. Department of Homeland Security Task Force on New Americans, *Building an Americanization Movement for the Twenty-first Century: A Report to the President of the United States* (Washington, D.C.: 2008).

70. Meissner, et al., 17.

71. Meissner, et al., 18.

72. "U.S. Business and Hispanic Integration: Expanding the Economic Contributions of Immigrants," Council of the Americas (July 23, 2008), http://councilofthe americas.org/article.php?id=1145.

73. Tamar Jacoby, as cited by Gregory Rodriguez, presentation at Transnational Forum on Migration and Integration, Nuremburg, Germany: German Marshall Fund, July 13, 2008.

74. Lauren Gilbert, presentation at Woodstock Forum on Migration: Fairfield, CT, 2007.

75. "New Trends and Processes for the Integration of Immigrants," paper at German Marshall Fund, Berlin, Germany: March 11, 2005, http://www.gmfus.org/event/ detail.cfm?id=22.

76. Jeff Chenoweth and Laura Burdick, "A More Perfect Union: A National Citizenship Plan" (Washington, DC: CLINIC, 2007), vii.

77. As cited in Jimenez, 7.

78. Portes and Rumbaut in Jimenez, 7.

79. Chenoweth and Burdick, vii.

80. Jimenez, 7. I am grateful to Mitzi Schroeder of JRS/USA for her elaboration on this point.

81. Robert Wuthnow, *American Mythos: Why Our Best Efforts as a Nation Fall Short* (Princeton, NJ: Princeton University Press, 2006).

82. Karen Richman, "The Protestant Ethic and the Dis-Spirit of Vodou" in *Immigrant Faiths: Transforming Religious Life in America*, ed. Karen I. Leonard, Alex Stepick, Manuel A. Vásquez and Jennifer Holdaway (Lanham, Md.: Rowman & Littlefield Publishers, Inc., 2005), 169.

83. DiMarzio, 192.

Chapter Six

Christian Hospitality and Solidarity with the Stranger

William O'Neill

Christian hospitality to "strangers and sojourners" (*xenoi kai paroikoi*) shaped the earliest understanding of disciples as "fellow citizens with the saints" in the "household of God" (*oikeioi tou theou*) (Eph. 2:19). Indeed, remembrance—what Walter Benjamin calls "anamnestic solidarity" (a solidarity of remembering) with the stranger—is at the very heart of Christian discipleship.[1] As in Leviticus's "golden rule," love of neighbor bids us respect, not a "generalized other,"[2] but the concrete other in need epitomized by the migrant: "When an alien resides with you in your land, you shall not oppress the alien. The alien who resides with you shall be to you as the citizen among you; you shall love the alien as yourself, for you were aliens in the land of Egypt: I am the Lord your God" (Lev. 19:33f.).

Save for worship of the one God, no command is repeated more often in the Hebrew Bible.[3] In times of prosperity, Israel is summoned to effective remembrance that the land "was a gift not a birthright."[4] In gracious hospitality to the widow, orphan, and stranger—those most vulnerable in kinship societies—Israel realizes her distinctive Covenant identity; to oppress the alien, conversely, is no less than apostasy. Israel, says the Deuteronomist, must ever cherish "the heart of a stranger, for you were strangers in the land of Egypt" (Exod. 23:9).

So too, hospitality (*philoxenia*: love of the stranger) remains a fundamental motif of New Testament discipleship.[5] In Matthew's Gospel, the Holy Family recapitulates the Exodus. In the words of Rev. Donald Senior, C.P., president of Catholic Theological Union, "Jesus begins his earthly journey as a migrant and a displaced person—Jesus who in this same gospel would radically identify with the 'least' and make hospitality to the stranger a criterion of judgment (Mt. 25:35)."[6] And for Luke, "seeing and having compassion" for these least, e.g., the *anāwîm*, the naked, half-dead stranger, marks the "way" of eternal life. Again and again, in the image of the eschatological feast (Amos 9:13–15; Joel 3:18; Isa. 25:6–8), hospitality is offered not to kin and kind, but to those whose only claim is vulnerability and need (Mt. 8:11; 22:1–14; Lk. 14:12–24).

One must, as the Good Samaritan, "pass over to the victim's side." For a "person who loves can *see* in anyone a neighbor in need."[7] "Taking the victim's side"—e.g., *recognizing* the basic rights of migrants—is not only the touchstone of the legitimacy of prevailing institutional arrangements, it is just "what we (disciples) *do*" in "doing likewise." Luke's narrative reveals the boundless, universal scope of love precisely in demanding a moral solidarity with those who suffer—my "neighbor, the masses."[8] For citizens of faith, such recognition is not an occasional glance but a habitual disposition or virtue, which the tradition names hospitality.[9]

In "anamnestic solidarity"[10] with victims of forced migration, those who in their "abstract nakedness"—like the man fallen among thieves, stripped of title, status, and role—are "nothing but human,"[11] disciples "see and have compassion." Compassion (literally, a "suffering with") becomes a way of seeing the stranger "in all her truth." The stranger, that is, is "exactly like me," albeit marked by affliction. The trope, "neighbor," in Luke's parable serves as a metaphorical "bridge" between identity and difference: hospitality enjoins "anamnestic solidarity" where care is offered, not to the alien or stranger, but rather to my neighbor, especially my neighbor, in Simone Weil's words, "stamped with a special mark by affliction."[12]

Just so, biblical hospitality differs from liberal and communitarian uses. In the regnant liberal tradition, hospitality is typically subsumed under the rubrics of benevolence (charity) as a private, supererogative act—a virtuous grace note added to the obbligato of rights. In communitarian treatments, conversely, hospitality may figure as a "local and ethnocentric" virtue, enjoining kinship reciprocity, but for this very reason, remains inimical to universal rhetoric of human rights. Christian hospitality integrates what these traditions rend asunder.[13] The trope, "neighbor," clothes the stranger morally; for dignity is always in local garb, always "attentive" to the stranger in his or her concrete moral truth. Christianly, the Samaritan's hospitality tutors our imagination; the Christian virtue of hospitality, in the words of Jean-Marc Éla, becomes a "pedagogy of seeing" our neighbor's basic human rights.[14] Here, precisely *as* a virtue, hospitality interprets and motivates compliance with the strict precepts of justice.

And yet, there remains a surplus of religious meaning. *Agapē* is never less than just. If the Christian "justices"[15] in her moral deliberations, so justice bears the mark of "loving tenderly, compassionately" (Lk. 10:37). To the lawyer's question in the parable, "Who is my neighbor?"—seeking a precise delimitation of rights and duties—Jesus replies with a question of his own, "Who is it that proved himself neighbor?"[16]

The lawyer's reply, "the Samaritan," is richly ironic, for the Samaritan, a despised schismatic, not only proves himself neighbor, but in exemplifying neighborliness as the fulfillment of the law, is the one whom the lawyer must imitate: "Go and do likewise!" (Lk. 10:37). For the question posed in Jesus' reading of the law is not finally, "Whom shall I love?" but rather "Who shall I become (prove myself to be) in loving?" In Kierkegaard's words, "Christ does not speak about recognizing one's neighbor but about being a neighbor oneself, about proving oneself to be a neighbor, something the Samaritan showed by his compassion."[17] And this makes all the difference.

In salvific irony, Jesus thus answers the lawyer's first question, "What must I do to inherit eternal life?" in reversing the second. For the command to "love the Lord, your God, with all your heart, with all your being, with all your strength, and with all your mind, and your neighbor as yourself" (Lk. 10:27) is fulfilled not in this or that particular deed of love,[18] but in one's "selving as neighbor":[19] if the disciple is to live, she must enter the world of the *anāwîm*, of the half-dead stranger. In Christ, such "anamnestic solidarity" in remembering the Covenant implies not merely taking the victim's side (the "essential" requirement of ethics), but taking the victim's side *as* our own (in Rahner's terms, the formal, existential demand of love).[20]

The distinctively Christian virtue of solidarity with the *anāwîm*—with those "broken and oppressed in spirit"[21]—thus defines discipleship, for "to be a Christian," says Gustavo Gutiérrez, "is to draw near, to make oneself a neighbor, not the one I encounter in my journey but the one in whose journey I place myself."[22] For an ethics of discipleship, "What I must do to *live*" (my *metanoia*) is, then, to "turn" to the world of the poor, of the half-dead stranger—in the martyred Archbishop Romero's words—"becoming incarnate in their world . . . proclaiming the good news to them," even to the point of "sharing their fate."[23]

Compassion, then, not only guides citizens of faith in the fitting application of universal, essential norms, e.g. the rights of migrants, but gives rise to personal and ecclesial imperatives as they walk humbly with Jesus. In "passing over" to the world of the migrant as neighbor, the metaphor is "proven true" by Jesus' disciple. Christian imagery attests to this de-centering of self—this "selving" in utter dependence on God—in imaging disciples themselves *as* "beloved aliens and exiles" (1 Pet. 2:11–12). "Strangers and foreigners on earth," Christians seek "a better homeland," the world-affirming reign of God (Heb. 11:12-15; cf. Rom. 15:7).[24]

For disciples of the *way* (Acts 18:25f.; 19:23; 22:4; 24:14), such displacement becomes the place of revelation. Hebrews recall the revelatory hospitality of Sarah and Abraham at Mamre in Genesis 18: "Do not neglect to show hospitality to strangers, for by doing that some have entertained angels without knowing it" (Heb. 13:2). And in the Synoptic Gospels, the image of a feast "for all peoples" (Isa. 25:6), reveals God "powerfully and eschatologically as Israel's host"[25]—a fundamental motif recalled in the eschatolgial *anamnēsis* of the eucharist.

For Matthew, as for Luke, "doing likewise" becomes the *sine qua non* of salvation: "I was a stranger (*xenos*)" unrecognized, "and you welcomed me" (Mt. 25:35; cf. John 20:11ff; 21:1–14). In hospitality, the Christian, says Gregory Nazianzen, welcomes Christ, who "for your sake was a stranger."[26] For as at Emmaus (Lk. 24:13–35), only in welcoming the stranger on the way is there revelation "in the breaking of the bread"—hospitality lets Easter in.

In the parable of the final judgment (Mt. 25:31–46), the disciple passes over from being "host" to "guest" of Christ at the eschatological banquet: in loving, one comes to see oneself—one *is* revealed—as beloved; the command of love being, finally, love's command. And thus grace "does" what seems to outstrip human possibility; in entering and remaining in the world of the migrant, of the poor, we "pass over" to the One who first "passed over" to us: Christ who, as Augustine wrote, is our Good Samaritan, coming to the aid of our wounded humanity.[27]

In the words of Dorothy Day, founder of the Catholic Worker Movement in December, 1945:

> [The lessons of hospitality] can be proved, if proof is needed, by the doctrines of the Church. We can talk about Christ's Mystical Body, about the vine and the branches, about the Communion of Saints. But Christ Himself has proved it for us, and no one has to go further than that. For he said that a glass of water given to a beggar was given to Him. He made heaven hinge on the way we act toward Him in His disguise of commonplace, frail, ordinary humanity.
>
> Did you give Me food when I was hungry?
> Did you give Me to drink when I was thirsty?
> Did you give me clothes when My own were all rags?
> Did you come to see Me when I was sick, or in prison or in trouble?
>
> And to those who say, aghast, that they never had a chance to do such a thing, that they lived two thousand years too late, He will say again what they had the chance of knowing all their lives, that if these things are done for the very least of His brethren they were done to Him.
>
> For a total Christian, the goad of duty is not needed—always prodding one to perform this or that good deed. It is not a duty to help Christ, it is a privilege. Is

it likely that Martha and Mary sat back and considered that they had done all that was expected of them? [They] did it gladly. . . . If that is the way they gave hospitality to Christ, it is certain that that is the way it should still be given. Not for the sake of humanity. Not because it might be Christ who stays with us, comes to see us, takes up our time. Not because these people remind us of Christ . . . but because they *are* Christ, asking us to find room for Him, exactly as He did at the first Christmas.[28]

NOTES

1. Walter Benjamin, *Illuminations*, ed. H. Arendt (New York, 1969), 253ff.

2. George Herbert Mead, *Mind, Self, and Society from the Standpoint of a Social Behaviorist*, ed. Charles W. Morris (Chicago: University of Chicago Press, 1962), 152–64, 379–89. See Seyla Benhabib, "The Generalized and the Concrete Other: The Kohlberg-Gilligan Controversy and Feminist Theory," in *Feminism as Critique*, ed. Benhabib and Drucilla Cornell (Minneapolis: University of Minnesota Press, 1987), 77–95, at 85.

3. W. Gunther Plaut, "Jewish Ethics and International Migrations," *International Migration Review: Ethics, Migration and Global Stewardship* 30 (Spring 1996), 18–36 at 20–21. Plaut distinguishes the differing legal status accorded temporary or permanent migrants in the Hebrew Bible and Talmud. As Mark Franken observes, "For the Israelites, not only were they commanded to care for the stranger, but they structured the welcome and care of aliens into their gleaning and tithing laws (Lv. 19:9–10; Dt. 14:28–29)," in "The Theology of Migration," paper presented to the board of Directors of the Lutheran Immigration and Refugee Services, Baltimore, Maryland, October 28, 2004, http://usccb.org/mrs/lirspresentation.shtml.

4. Donald Senior, "Beloved Aliens and Exiles," in *A Promised Land, A Perilous Journey: Theological Perspectives on Migration*, ed., Daniel G. Groody and Gioacchino Campese (Notre Dame, Indiana: University of Notre Dame Press, 2009), 20–34, at 21. Walter Brueggemann, *The Land: Place as Gift, Promise, and Challenge in Biblical Faith* (Philadelphia: Fortress, 1977).

5. "The word most often associated with hospitality in the Septuagint and the New Testament (NT) is *xenos*, which literally means foreigner, stranger, or even enemy. In its derived sense, however, the term comes to denote both guest and host alike. Typically, the verb used to describe the extending of hospitality is *xenizein* (Sir. 29:25; 1 Macc. 9:6; Acts 10:23; Heb. 12:2). In the NT, one who receives visitors is said to be *philoxenos*, i.e., "a lover of strangers," or to be "practicing the virtue of *philoxenia*" (1 Tim. 3:2); 1 Pet. 4:9; Rom. 12:13; Heb. 13:2). John Koenig, "Hospitality," in *The Anchor Bible Dictionary*, vol. 3, ed. David Noel Freedman (New York: Doubleday, 1992), 299–301.

6. Senior, "Beloved Aliens and Exiles," 23.

7. Wolfgang Schrage, *The Ethics of the New Testament*, trans. David E. Green (Philadelphia: Fortress, 1988), 74, 76.

8. M. D. Chenu, *"Les masses pauvres,"* in G. Cottier et al., *Eglise et pauvreté* (Paris: Cerf, 1965), 169–76, at 169. Schrage, *The Ethics of the New Testament*, 78, 81.

9. Christine D. Pohl, *Making Room: Recovering Hospitality as a Christian Tradition* (Grand Rapids, Michigan: William B. Eerdmans, 1999).

10. Benjamin, *Illuminations*, 253ff. Cf. Thomas McCarthy, *Ideals and Illusions: On Reconstruction and Deconstruction in Contemporary Critical Theory* (Cambridge, Mass.: MIT Press, 1991), 205–10.

11. Hannah Arendt, "The Perplexities of the Rights of Man," *The Origins of Totalitarianism* (New York: Harcourt, Brace, & World, 1966), 300.

12. Simon Weil, "Reflections on the Right Use of School Studies with a View to the Love of God," *Waiting for God*, trans. Emma Craufurd (New York: G. P. Putnam's Sons, 1951), 115.

13. Pohl, *Making Room*, 61–84. Pohl writes of the original connaturality of rights and virtue, later eclipsed with the domestication of hospitality: The "broad basis for mutual human respect and care allowed concerns about recognition that had been integral to Christian hospitality to provide a significant foundation for early modern political discourse about recognition and human rights" (66).

14. Jean-Marc Éla, "Christianity and Liberation in Africa," in *Paths of African Theology*, 143.

15. Gerard Manley Hopkins, "As Kingfishers Catch Fire," *The Poems of Gerard Manley Hopkins*, 4th ed., ed. W. H. Gardner and H. M. MacKenzie (New York: Oxford University, 1970), 90.

16. John Donahue, "'Who is My Enemy?' The Parable of the Good Samaritan and the Love of Enemies," *The Love of Enemy and Nonretaliation in the New Testament*, ed. Willard M. Swartley (Louisville, Kentucky: Westminster/John Knox Press, 1992), 137–56.

17. Søren Kierkegaard, *Works of Love*, trans. Howard and Edna Hong (New York: Harper and Row, 1962), 38.

18. Karl Rahner, "The 'Commandment' of Love in Relation to the Other 'Commandments,'" *Theological Investigations* 5, trans. Karl H. Kruger (New York: Seabury, 1966), 439–59 at 453; cf. "The Theology of Freedom," *Theological Investigations* 6, trans. Karl and Boniface Kruger (New York: Seabury, 1974), 178–96; and Rahner's observation that "freedom is not simply the capacity to do this or that but (formally) a self-disposing into finality," "Reflections on the Unity of the Love of Neighbour and the Love of God," *Theological Investigations* 6, 231–49 at 240).

19. Hopkins, "As Kingfishers Catch Fire," 90.

20. Karl Rahner, "On the Question of a Formal Existential Ethics," *Theological Investigations* 2, trans. Karl H. Kruger (Baltimore, Maryland: Helicon, 1963), 217–34. Cf. Gustavo Gutiérrez' observation that "[c]ommitment to the poor means entering, and in some cases remaining in that universe with a much clearer awareness." Such solidarity, he writes, "can therefore only follow an asymptotic curve," i.e., an ever richer "seeing and having compassion." *We Drink from Our Own Wells: The Spiritual Journey of a People*, trans. Matthew J. O'Connell (New York: Orbis, 1984), 125–26.

21. As Pohl observes, "Hospitality to needy strangers distinguished the early church from its surrounding environment. Noted as exceptional by Christians and

non-Christians alike, offering care to strangers became one of the distinguishing marks of the authenticity of the Christian gospel and of the Church." *Making Room*, 33.

22. Gustavo Gutiérrez, "Toward a Theology of Liberation" (July 1968), trans. Alfred T. Hennelly, in *Liberation Theology: A Documentary History*, ed. Alfred T. Hennelly (Maryknoll, New York: Orbis Books, 1990), 62–76, at 74.

23. Oscar Romero, "The Political Dimension of the Faith from the Perspective of the Option for the Poor," in *Liberation Theology: A Documentary History*, 292–303, at 298.

24. See Senior, "Beloved Aliens and Exiles," 28.

25. Koenig, "Hospitality," 300.

26. Gregory Nazianzen, "Oration on Holy Baptism," NPNF2, vol. 7, 327. See Pohl, *Making Room*, 33.

27. Augustine, *Quaestiones Evangeliorum* 2.19; cf. also De Natura et Gratia 43, 50.

28. Dorothy Day, *Selected Writings*, ed. Robert Ellsberg (Maryknoll, New York: Orbis Books, 1998), 96–97.

Index

About the Authors

Rev. Daniel G. Groody, C.S.C. earned his Ph.D. from the Graduate Theological Union, Berkeley, and is now assistant professor of theology and director of the Center for Latino Spirituality and Culture at the University of Notre Dame. In 2007 and 2008 he was a visiting research fellow at the Refugee Studies Centre, Oxford University. His recent publications reflect his interest in the intersection of globalization, immigration, and theology: *Border of Death, Valley of Life: An Immigrant Journey of Heart and Spirit* (2002); *Globalization, Spirituality, and Justice: Navigating the Path to Peace* (2007); and the edited collections, *The Option for the Poor in Christian Theology* (2007) and, with Gioacchino Campese, *A Promised Land, A Perilous Journey: Theological Perspectives on Migration* (2008). A theology of migration and refugees and the spirituality of immigrants are in preparation.

Groody's work is supported by the Refugee Studies Centre at Oxford University, the Association of Theological Schools/Lilly Endowment, and the University of Notre Dame's Institute for Latino Studies, the Institute for Scholarship in the Liberal Arts, the Kellogg Institute for International Studies, the Joan B. Kroc Institute for International Peace Studies, and the Nanovic Institute for European Studies.

Mary DeLorey is Catholic Relief Services' strategic issues advisor for Latin America and the Caribbean, based in Baltimore. She is responsible for developing and promoting the agency's public policy positions and advocacy strategies on regional policy priorities, including migration in the Americas and U.S. policy in Colombia. Additionally Ms. DeLorey is responsible for developing CRS's agency-wide strategy and policy positions on the issue of human trafficking. Ms. DeLorey has a B.A. in Mental Health/Human Services and Theology, a Master's in Sociology (Political Economy and International Development) and a Master's in Social Work (Social Administration and Community Organizing) from the University of Maryland.

John Hoeffner is an attorney and former editor of the Catholic Lawyer. He taught appellate advocacy at Georgetown University Law Center, where he was a teaching fellow and received an LL.M. in Advocacy, and practiced law at several leading law firms. He also prosecuted civil rights cases while working at the Department of Justice. His recent publications have appeared in the *Journal of Catholic Social Thought*, *Georgetown Immigration Law Journal*, and the *Mediterranean Journal of Human Rights*. Hoeffner is co-author of a new book, entitled, *Stepping Out of the Brain Drain: Applying Catholic Social Teaching in a New Era of Migration* (2007), which looks at migration of skilled workers from the perspective of Catholic social thought. He maintains a web log on skilled migration and other topics at www.stepoutmigration.com.

Michele R. Pistone is professor of law and director of the Clinical Program at Villanova University School of Law. There she directs and teaches the Clinic for Asylum, Refugee and Emigrant Services (CARES). Students enrolled in CARES represent asylum seekers before the asylum office and immigration court.

Professor Pistone is a national authority on immigration and asylum and refugee issues. She has published a book, book chapters, and articles about immigration and refugee law including: *Stepping Out of the Brain Drain: Applying Catholic Social Teaching in a New Era of Migration* (2007); An Overview of U.S. immigration law, in *Marriage of Undocumented Residents* (Canon Law Society of America, ed.) (2005). Her articles have appeared in *Georgetown Immigration Law Journal* and the *Journal of Catholic Social Thought*, among other journals. She is also the author of an award-winning video designed to train lawyers for asylum cases before the immigration court, entitled "Best Practices in Representing Asylum Seekers: A Video Resource for Pro Bono Attorneys," produced by ALI-ABA.

Before teaching at Villanova, Professor Pistone taught in the asylum clinic at Georgetown University Law Center and served as the Acting Legal Director for Human Rights First. Professor Pistone also serves as a Director of Pennsylvania Immigration Resource Center (PIRC).

Donald Kerwin is vice-president for programs at the Migration Policy Institute (MPI), overseeing MPI's national and international programs. MPI is the nation's pre-eminent think-tank on immigration policy issues. Prior to joining

MPI, Mr. Kerwin worked for more than 16 years at the Catholic Legal Immigration Network, Inc. (CLINIC), serving as that agency's executive director for nearly 15 years. CLINIC is a public interest legal corporation that supports a national network of more than 300 charitable legal programs for immigrants. Upon his arrival at CLINIC in 1992, Mr. Kerwin directed CLINIC's political asylum project for Haitians. During Mr. Kerwin's tenure, CLINIC coordinated the nation's largest political asylum, detainee services, immigration appeals, and naturalization programs. CLINIC also offers the nation's most extensive training and legal support programs for community-based immigrant agencies.

Mr. Kerwin serves as an advisor to the American Bar Association's Commission on Immigration, a member of the Council on Foreign Relations' Immigration Task Force, a member of the board of directors of Jesuit Refugee Services—USA, and an associate fellow at the Woodstock Theological Center. He writes and speaks extensively on immigration issues. Mr. Kerwin is a 1984 graduate of Georgetown University and a 1989 graduate of the University of Michigan Law School.

Jill Marie Gerschutz is migration policy director and outreach coordinator of the Office of Social and International Ministries at the Jesuit Conference, USA. She represents the Society of Jesus in governmental relations regarding immigration policy; as the core member of the Church's *Justice for Immigrants* campaign; and with various other Jesuit migration networks.

Gerschutz's previous positions include work at the International Federation of Red Cross/Red Crescent Societies; Casa Alianza (Covenant House Latin America), and bilingual social work in rural North Carolina. She has authored various journal articles about immigration reform and Catholic teaching and is co-author of "Transforming Visions into Reality: The Convention on the Rights of the Child," with Margaret P. Karns in *Children's Human Rights: Progress and Challenges for Children Worldwide.* She earned an M.A. in International Peace and Conflict Resolution from American University and a B.A. from the University of Dayton.

Lois Ann Lorentzen is professor of social ethics in the Theology and Religious Studies Department at the University of San Francisco (USF), chair of the Theology and Religious Studies Department, co-director of the Center for Latino Studies in the Americas (CELASA), and principal investigator for The Religion and Immigration Project. Professor Lorentzen received her Ph.D. in Social Ethics at the University of Southern California. Prior to USF she taught at Saint Joseph's University in Philadelphia. She has also taught at the Iberoamerican Universities in Mexico City, Puebla, Mexico, and Tijuana,

Mexico, and at the University of Central America in San Salvador, El Salvador.

Professor Lorentzen is the author of *Etica Ambiental* (Environmental Ethics) and *Raising the Bar* and co-editor of *On the Corner of Bliss and Nirvana: The Intersection of Religion, Politics, and Identity in New Migrant Communities* (forthcoming); *Ecofeminism and Globalization: Exploring Culture, Context, and Religion*; *Religion/Globalization: Theories and Cases*; *The Women and War Reader*; *Liberation Theologies, Postmodernity and the Americas*; and *The Gendered New World Order: Militarism, the Environment and Development*. She is Associate Editor for the *Encyclopedia of Religion and Nature* and the *Encyclopedia of Violence, Peace and Conflict*, and has written numerous articles in the fields of women and war, religion and violence, religion and immigration, and gender and the environment.

Rev. William O'Neill, S.J. is professor of social ethics at the Jesuit School of Theology at Berkeley and a visiting professor of ethics at the Jesuit School of Theology, "Hekima" in Nairobi. He has worked with refugees in Tanzania and Malawi and done research on human rights in South Africa and Rwanda.

Rev. O'Neill received a Newcombe Fellowship, a Lilly Theological Research Grant, and held the Jesuit Chair, Georgetown University (2003–2004). He has served on the Editorial Board of *The Journal of the Society of Christian Ethics*, and serves on the Board of the Society of Christian Ethics and of the journal, *Theological Studies*. Recent publications include "What We Owe to Refugees and IDP's: An Inquiry into the Rights of the Forcibly Displaced," chapter in *Refugee Rights*; "Reflections on Evolutionary Theodicy: A Response to 'Shadow Sophia in Christological Perspective'" in *Theology and Science*; "Neither Thick nor Thin: Politics and Polity in the Ethics of Margaret A. Farley," chapter in *A True and Just Love: Feminism at the Frontiers of Theological Ethics: Essays in Honor of Margaret A. Farley*.

O'Neill received his M.Phil and Ph.D. from Yale University; M.A. from the Jesuit School of Theology at Berkeley; and M.Div., S.T.M., S.T.L., and B.A. from St. Louis University.